March 2009

Battle for
Island

Battle for the Baltic Islands 1917

Triumph of the Imperial German Navy

Gary Staff

Pen & Sword
MARITIME

First published in Great Britain in 2008 by
Pen & Sword Maritime
An imprint of
Pen & Sword Books Ltd
47 Church Street
Barnsley
South Yorkshire
S70 2AS

ISBN 978 1 84415 7877

A CIP catalogue record for this book is
available from the British Library

Typeset in 10pt Palatino by Mac Style, Beverley, East Yorkshire
Printed and bound in the UK
By CPI

Pen & Sword Books Ltd incorporates the Imprints of Pen & Sword
Aviation,
Pen & Sword Maritime, Pen & Sword Military, Wharncliffe Local History,
Pen & Sword Select, Pen & Sword Military Classics, Leo Cooper,
Remember When, Seaforth Publishing and Frontline Publishing

For a complete list of Pen & Sword titles please contact
PEN & SWORD BOOKS LIMITED
47 Church Street, Barnsley, South Yorkshire, S70 2AS, England
E-mail: enquiries@pen-and-sword.co.uk
Website: www.pen-and-sword.co.uk

Contents

List of Maps   vii
List of Illustrations   ix
Introduction   xi
Table of German and Russian Ranks   xiii

Chapter 1 Preparations   1

Chapter 2 12 October: The German Landing   15

Chapter 3 13 October: The Germans Trapped at Orrisar   35

Chapter 4 14 October: The Battle on the Kassar Wiek   51

Chapter 5 15 October: The Battle Around Zerel   77

Chapter 6 16 October: The Russians Falter   93

Chapter 7 17 October: The Battle in Moon Sound   107

Chapter 8 18 October: The Capture of Moon Island   127

Chapter 9 19 October: The Landing at Dago Island   135

Chapter 10 20–30 October: Conclusion of the Campaign   143

Appendix I: Sea Forces of the 'The Special Unit'   151
Appendix II: Sea Forces of the Riga Gulf   160
Appendix III:. Ship Comparison   165
Appendix IV: Ship Damage and Losses   167
Appendix V: Russian Batteries on the Baltic Islands   169
Bibliography   170
Index   171

List of Maps

Map 1.   Russian Batteries of the Baltic Islands   7
Map 2.   The Approach Route of the Special Unit   19
Map 3.   The Landing at Tagga Bay on October 12th   26
Map 4.   The Battle at Menust, October 13th   40
Map 5.   The Battle at Uduvere on October 13th   42
Map 6.   Overview, Ösel Island, October 13th 1917   43
Map 7.   The Battle Around Orrisar on October 13th   46
Map 8.   The Battle on the Kassar Wiek, October 14th   54
Map 9.   Situation in Orrisar, 1600hrs October 14th   63
Map 10. Situation on October 14th 1917   68
Map 11. The Situation at Orrisar on October 15th   90
Map 12. Sworbe Peninsula and the Russian Mine Fields in the
         Irben Straits   97
Map 13. The Battle in Moon Sound on October 17th   111
Map 14. Capture of Moon Island (Kassar Wiek and Moon),
         October 15/18th   129
Map 15. Capture of Dagö Island   136

List of Illustrations

1. Vice Admiral Bakhirev's flagship, the armoured cruiser *Bayan*.
2. Vice Admiral M K Bakhirev on the bridge of a battleship earlier in the war.
3. The armoured cruiser *Admiral Makarov*.
4. The battleship *Tsarevitch*, renamed *Graschdanin* after the revolution.
5. *Slava*, the last battleship of the *Borodino* class, seen from astern.
6. The gunboat *Grozyashchi*.
7. The gunboat *Chrabry* at Riga.
8. The Russian destroyer *Grom*.
9. The shallow-draught mine layer *Pripyat*.
10. SMS *Kaiser*.
11. Vizeadmiral Ehrhard Schmidt and his Staff aboard his flagship, *Moltke*.
12. The small cruisers *Frankfurt* and *Augsburg* prior to the operation.
13. A minesweeper of II Minesweeper Flotilla.
14. A German A-type torpedoboat, used by the minesweeper flotillas.
15. Damage caused when the minesweeper M75 struck a mine on 8 October.
16. The *sperrbrecher* (barrier breaker) vessel *Rio Pardo*.
17. The German torpedoboat V100.
18. The German net layer *Eskimo*, originally an English merchant ship.
19. The minelayer *Nautilus* transfers mines to small minesweeper motorboats.
20. The German battleship *Grosser Kurfürst*, just after completion in 1914.
21. The airship SL8 passes over *Grosser Kurfürst*.
22. Damage caused when *Grosser Kurfürst* struck a mine on 12 October.
23. SMS *Bayern* in Tagga Bay after suffering damage from a mine
24. The damage caused to *Bayern* by the mine struck on 12 October.

25. The small cruiser SMS *Emden II* opens fire on a Russian battery.
26. German troops board a transport steamer.
27. Troops transfer from a transport into boats for the landing in Tagga Bay.
28. A close-up of the troops ready to go ashore.
29. German minesweeping motor launch takes troops ashore.
30. The scene at the disembarkation beach in Tagga Bay.
31. German ships in Tagga Bay.
32. The German torpedoboat B98 comes alongside the stricken *Grom.*
33. *König* follows minesweepers through the mine fields of the Irben Straits.
34. The minesweeper A62 towing the Russian barge captured on 16 October.
35. The battle in Moon Sound, 17 October. Russian shells fall near *Kronprinz.*
36. *Kronprinz* fires a salvo.
37. A German shell lands near *Slava.*
38. A Russian salvo falls near German minesweepers in the Moon Sound, 17 October.
39. An aerial view of *Slava* after scuttling.
40. The German torpedoboat S64.
41. S64, scuttled after striking a mine near Kumora Reef on the night of 17 October.
42. The German torpedoboat B111 is towed into Libau after striking a mine.
43. The battleship SMS *Markgraf.*
44. One of the abandoned 12-inch guns at Zerel.
45. The famous lighthouse at Cape Zerel.
46. The grave of a sailor from the German torpedoboat B111.
47. Buried together: German and Russian graves on Ösel.

Introduction

The participation of the High Sea Fleet in the conquest of the Baltic Islands represents one of the many high points in its brief history. The operation was very successful and the cooperation between the Navy and Army was exemplary. The operation also represented a successful example of an 'all arms' affair. The Germans used their air arm for reconnaissance, bombing and torpedo attack; their U-Boats for reconnaissance, laying mines and attacking shipping; their surface fleet to transport and support the Army and to counter the Russian surface and submarine forces; and their army to conduct the amphibious invasion. Their purpose was to capture the Baltic Islands, which were pivotal for the defence of the Finnish Gulf and therefore St. Petersburg, and to finally knock Russia out of the war. With this achieved, vast amounts of men and materials would be freed to support the offensive on the Western Front against the British, French and American forces in 1918. The operation was an unqualified success and contributed in no small way to forcing the Russians to the negotiating table at Brest-Litovsk. It also cleared the way for future operations such as the liberation of Finland and planned occupation of St Petersburg in 1918. Therefore the High Sea Fleet was instrumental in facilitating the political will and objectives of the German Government.

The source material available is remarkable because it was mostly written by those involved, and gives an authoritative and fascinating insight into what was happening and what was being planned and desired. Vice-admiral Michael Bakhirev was in command of the Russian Sea Forces of the Riga Gulf during the campaign and he wrote his report in July 1919. He was a seasoned naval officer, a veteran of the Boxer Rebellion and the Russo-Japanese War. In command he was both courageous and clear thinking, and his writing is not only an accurate narrative but also relates what he was thinking and what his unfulfilled requests to higher command were.

Captain 2nd Rank A M Kosinski was commander of the modern Russian destroyer *Zabiyaka* in 1917. He wrote a comprehensive work on the Moon Sound operations in 1928. His work provides much detail and fascinating quotes from other participants.

Leitenant Nicholai Bartinev was in command of the 30.5cm gun battery at Zerel. His short article captures very well the mood of the garrison on the battery and the general atmosphere in the post-revolution environment. On the other hand, Captain 1st Rank S N Timirev was much less forgiving of the revolutionary element. He was commander of the cruiser *Bayan* during the operation, and he derides the revolutionaries, whom he terms the 'morale element'.

The most extensive work on the Russian Imperial Navy is by Leitenant Harald Graf, who served most of the First World War aboard the destroyer *Novik*. His work covers the entire war and has long been considered the standard work on the Imperial Navy during the conflict.

For the Germans the most detailed work is by Oberst von Tschischwitz, Chief of the General Staff of the Landing Corps. His position allowed him to write with authority and accuracy in his book *Blue Jackets and Field Grey against Ösel* in 1934. The main German source is the official history, *Der Krieg in der Ostsee*.

This was written with reference to all of the log books of the participating ships, so that it was written partly using the observations of the commanders on the spot.

Likewise, the recollections of Leutnant zur See Friedrich Ruge in his autobiography and short publication about his time on the torpedo boat B110. In the late 1970s and early 1980s I was acquainted with Professor Ruge and visited him twice at his home in Tübingen. He related many stories of his time in the navy and was always very encouraging and helpful to a young naval enthusiast. My last visit was just one month before he passed away.

The collected work *Unconquered on the Sea* also provides many valuable eyewitness accounts. Finally Vizeadmiral Albert Hopman's book, *War Diary of a Naval Officer*, completes the eyewitness accounts from the German side.

One of the best books covering this period is *Expendable Glory*, by Commander (Retired) George M Nekrasov. This book is about the career of the Russian battleship *Slava* and the author is well qualified to write about her. Commander Nekrasov was friends with none other than Leitenant Anatoly Vaksmut, who served firstly as navigation officer of *Slava*, and then, during Operation Albion, as commander of the destroyer *Grom*, from which he had to be forcibly removed when she was abandoned. George helped me greatly with questions about the Russian Imperial Navy and *Slava*. I owe him my gratitude and am greatly thankful for his help.

In writing this book I did not seek to make any great analysis of the fighting, but rather wanted to present a balanced and accurate narrative that gives the reader a genuine feel for the time, experienced in part through the eyes of those who participated. I wanted to present the story from both sides in a fair and unbiased way. I hope I have achieved this.

Gary Staff,
January 2008.

Russian, German and Equivalent Naval Ranks in the First World War

Russia	Germany	Royal Navy
——	Grosseadmiral	Admiral of the Fleet
Admiral	Admiral	Admiral
Vice Admiral	Vizeadmiral	Vice Admiral
Kontre Admiral	Kontreadmiral	Rear Admiral
——	Kommodore	Commodore
Capitan 1st Rank	Kapitän zur See	Captain
Capitan 2nd Rank	Fregattenkapitän	Commander
Starchi Leitenant	Korvettenkapitän	Lieutenant Commander
Leitenant	Kapitänleutnant	Lieutenant
	Oberleutnant zur See	
Michman	Leutnant zur See	Sublieutenant
	Fähnrich zur See	Midshipman
Praporshchik		Ensign

CHAPTER ONE

Preparations

The campaign and battles on and around the Baltic Islands in October 1917 constituted the largest naval operation to take place in the Baltic during the course of the First World War. The Baltic Islands formed the central axis and pivotal point of naval warfare in the Baltic theatre. The German Commander-in-Chief of the Baltic Theatre (Oberost or ObHdO), Grossadmiral Prinz Heinrich, had long stated the importance and significance of the Baltic Islands, which dominated the entrance to the Riga Gulf and the Finnish Gulf. Ever since the abortive break-in to the Riga Gulf in August 1915, the Baltic Command had consistently restated the importance of capturing these islands as a prerequisite to any further operations into the Riga Gulf. When it became apparent that there were insufficient German forces available for this task, Grossadmiral Prinz Heinrich had reluctantly agreed to the massive and widespread minelaying campaigns of 1916 and 1917.

In the meantime the revolution had occurred in Russia. There was much turmoil in the Imperial Russian Navy and many officers had been murdered and others had been replaced, in a Navy which was already short of trained and experienced officers. Nevertheless, after the chaos of the revolution there was no weakening of resolve on the Russian side, even after the halting of the Kerensky (or so-called 2nd Brusilov) Offensive, and then the German capture of the city of Riga. The Russians were as determined as ever to continue the struggle.

The Moon Sound Archipelago received its name from the passage which in turn took its name from Moon Island. The Moon Sound separates the archipelago from the coast of Estonia. On the continental side is the island of Worms and other low-lying islands. The length of the sound is 35 miles, from Worms in the north, to Moon Island in the south. Moon Sound varies in width from 6 miles in the north to 3.5 miles in the south, and varies in depth from around 105 metres in the north, to about 5 metres near Moon. Between the islands of Dagö and Ösel lies the Kassar Wiek, a shallow stretch of water separated from Moon Sound by the Kumora reef. Along the coast of Moon runs a narrow, natural channel known as the *Strumpf*, or 'stocking', which allows shallow-draught vessels to pass into the Kassar Wiek. The Strumpf was first charted by Colonel MacDonald in 1888, but it was not until twenty-seven years later, in 1915, that the first dredging work was undertaken to increase the depth of Moon Sound. A group of up to seventy dredgers began work to increase the depth to 8.5 metres and then 9 metres, to allow battleships and cruisers to transfer from the Gulf of Finland to the Riga Gulf.

The largest islands of the archipelago are Ösel and Dagö. The Soelo Sound runs between them with a width of about 3 miles, but there are many shoals and small islets, and the water depth seldom exceeds 2 to 3 metres. The island of Ösel is relatively flat, rising to 59 metres elevation in the north and falling away steeply at the coast. It is covered with scattered woods, pastures, marshes, small villages and farms. Many fields are delineated by juniper hedges. There are seven large depressions on Ösel, the largest of which is Lake Kaami. These were formed by meteorites. The south part of Ösel is formed by the Sworbe Peninsula, which has Cape Zerel as its southernmost tip. From Zerel to the Kurland coast is a distance of 16 miles and the Zerel Reef extends out from the cape. There was a large lighthouse at Cape Zerel, which provided an excellent lookout station and was strategically and morally very important. A fresh water spring lay next to the lighthouse.

There were several channels through the passage between the Sworbe Peninsular and Cape Domesnas on the Kurland coast, known as the Irben Straits. The water channels were to the south, but there was also a passage over the Zerel Reef that was known only to the Russians. The deep water passage led directly to Arensburg Bay and Arensburg, the capital city of Ösel.

Arensburg was once a powerful fortress, where the German Bishop Osnabriuksky was based in 1341. For centuries the inhabitants of Ösel Island were known as pirates, but during the Northern War of 1708–1711, and after a plague and famine, the fortress of Arensburg fell to the Russians on 26 September 1710. Emperor Peter I made Arensburg an advanced position in the Baltic, but he was not the only one to appreciate the importance of Moon Sound. During the Swedish-Russian War in 1809 the English supporting Sweden used the northern part of Moon Sound as an anchorage. During the two campaigns of the Crimean War in 1854–55 the English fleet used the Moon Sound archipelago as an anchorage, where they were poised as a threat to St Petersburg. Throughout the First World War the islands of Dagö and Ösel held great significance. With the islands remaining as Russian possessions, the Russian Imperial Navy could still outflank the Germans in the Riga Gulf and had the option of staging a landing on the Kurland coast behind the German lines, or of bombarding the German shore positions more or less at will, which they had done since 1915. From their support bases in the Riga Gulf and Moon Sound the Russian destroyers and Russian and English submarines could penetrate into the middle and western Baltic, striking at German trade routes with Sweden. The Baltic Islands and the Riga Gulf were again pivotal for naval warfare in the Baltic. With the islands in German hands the Riga Gulf, and therefore the German Army rear, would be secure, and the facilities at Riga could be utilized as a supply base to further the German offensive. The Russian 'Forward Position', the outer defences of the Finnish Gulf, would be under threat. The continued German offensive and the perceived threat to St Petersburg would increase pressure on the Russian government to conclude peace, and with the conclusion of a negotiated peace vast resources of German men and equipment would be freed to join the battle in the west against America, France and the British Empire.

With all due consideration, orders for the attack on the Baltic Islands were issued on 18 September 1917, and read:

> For the domination of the Riga Gulf and the security of the flank of the East Army, a combined attack by the land and sea forces is to take the Islands of Ösel and Moon, and the use of the Greater Moon Sound is to be denied to the enemy sea forces.

The operation was code named 'Albion' and the following day the troops entrained for the port of Libau. The Army forces consisted of the reinforced 42nd Division, commanded by General von Estorff, and the 2nd Infantry Cyclist Brigade, together with artillery, pioneers, a wireless section and transport column. In total the Landing Corps consisted of around 23,000 men, 5,000 horses, 1,400 vehicles, 150 machine-guns, 54 guns, 12 mortars and munitions and provisions for thirty days. To convey the Landing Corps to their assault beaches in Tagga Bay, on the northwest coast of Ösel, a transport fleet of nineteen steamers was assembled. It was to be the largest combined operation undertaken by the Germans so far during the war. To support the operation the most modern units of the High Sea Fleet were detached and were formed into the Special Unit of the Baltic. The composition of the Special Unit was as follows:

Chief of Special Unit : Vizeadmiral Schmidt
Chief of Staff: Kapitän zur See Levetzow
Flagship: *Moltke*.

III Battle Squadron
Commander:Vizeadmiral Behncke
König, Bayern, Grosser Kurfürst, Kronprinz, Markgraf

IV Battle Squadron
Commander: Vizeadmiral Souchon
Friedrich der Grosse, König Albert, Kaiserin, Prinzregent Luitpold, Kaiser

II Reconnaissance Group (II AG)
Commander: Kontreadmiral Reuter
Königsberg, Karlsruhe, Nürnberg, Frankfurt, Danzig

VI Reconnaissance Group (VI AG)
Commander: Kontreadmiral Hopman
Kolberg, Strassburg, Augsburg, Blitz, Nautilus

Torpedoboats
I FdT (Führer dur Torpedoboote or Leader of Torpedoboats):
    Kommodore Heinrich
Flagship: *Emden*
II Torpedoboat Flotilla (10 boats)
VI Torpedoboat Flotilla (11 boats)
VIII Torpedoboat Flotilla (11 boats)
X Torpedoboat Flotilla (11 boats)
7th Torpedoboat Half Flotilla (7 boats)

U-Flotilla Kurland
6 U-boats.

Sperrbrechergruppe (literally Barrier-breaker Group)
Rio Pardo, Lothar, Schwaben, Glatz

II Minesweeper Flotilla
3rd Minesweeper Half Flotilla
4th Minesweeper Half Flotilla
8th Minesweeper Half Flotilla
3rd S-Half Flotilla (S- denotes a 'picket' or anti-submarine unit)

S-Flotilla of the Baltic

Netbarrier Unit of the Baltic

Fleet Train.

Appointed to lead the Special Unit was the hitherto commander of the I Battle Squadron, Vizeadmiral Ehrhard Schmidt. He was an excellent choice. Vizeadmiral Schmidt had begun the war as commander of the IV

Battle Squadron, stationed in the Baltic. This led to him being appointed commander of the first attack on the Riga Gulf in August 1915. The campaign lasted from 8 to 21 August. The first attempt to break in to the gulf failed because of the insurmountable mine barriers. A continuation of the attack led to a German force entering the gulf for a short period on 19 August. Prinz Heinrich came to the conclusion that a recurrence of the break-in attempt

> Would only make sense when we could remain in the Gulf. For this purpose it is necessary for the Army to occupy Riga and the mouth of the Dvina. Then the possession of the Gulf can be facilitated, but nevertheless would require considerable naval forces. Only the capture of Ösel and Dagö will simplify the operation and provide an anchorage for the large ships, and also provide opportunities for us to approach the fortified points of the Finnish Gulf.

Riga fell in September 1917 and the situation now allowed the Germans to prosecute their attack plans.

The Russians had long perceived the threat to the Baltic Islands and as early as August 1914 the Fleet Commander, Admiral H O Essen, had said:

> Today the 1st Torpedoboat Division was sent to Moon Sound and Riga Gulf, and work began on installing batteries for the protection of Moon Sound. I attach great value to the maintenance of communications with the islands of Ösel and Dagö. The occupation of the latter by the enemy would deprive us of advanced observation posts and aviation stations and would entail the loss of Moon Sound.

Theoretically the Riga Gulf and islands were reasonably well protected. Ösel was defended by three infantry regiments, the 425th, 426th and 472nd, who together with the coastal batteries had a strength of around 24,000 men. Tagga Bay was protected by Battery No 45 with four 15.2cm guns at Cape Hundsort and Battery No 46, likewise with four 15.2cm guns, at Cape Ninnast. Work on these batteries had been started on 10 December 1916 and they were completed in April 1917. On Dagö, Battery No 34 was constructed at Serro, a little west of the village of Emmast. It comprised four 120mm guns taken from Amur class monitors and had been completed in early 1916. Dagö was defended by a further two batteries at Cape Tachkona. Battery No 38, of four 15.2cm guns, was mounted at Cape Simpernes and Battery No 39, at Cape Tachkona, consisted of four 12 inch guns. Battery No 37 at Cape Dirhamn consisted of four 15.2cm guns, which, like those of Battery No 38, were also taken from Amur class gunboats. The southern entrance to the Moon Sound was also well protected with batteries. Five 254mm pieces that were originally intended for Nargon Island on the 'Central Position' were sent to Moon Island and were installed as Battery No 36 near Woi. However, only two guns could be mounted on concrete bases and the remaining three were mounted on wooden bases. This battery was ready on 5 July 1915. Battery No 32, between the villages of Woi and Resse, consisted of four 15.2cm pieces and was ready on 13 September 1915. A battery on the mainland side, on the island of Werder, completed the southern Moon Sound entrance defences. This battery, No 33, comprised four 15.2cm guns.

The main battery of the island defences was Battery No 43 placed at Cape Zerel. This battery was constructed under extremely difficult conditions. The 12 inch gun barrels weighed 50.7 tonnes each and everything had to be brought to Zerel by barge. In addition to the mountings, power plants, barracks and magazines had to be constructed. When first test fired in April 1917, the four 12 inch guns had the portentous range of 152 cable lengths (one cable equalling 200 yards or approximately 183 metres) and not only covered the entire Irben Straits, but also the shore of the Kurland coast. However, advantage of this reach could not always be taken because of frequent fog and mist, especially in autumn, when visibility did not exceed 90 to 100 cables. Nevertheless, this extremely important battery had a couple of drawbacks. The installations were in the open, without protection, and the magazines were constructed of timber and earthworks with oak doors. This would later have tragic consequences.

There were two other batteries on the Zerel Peninsula. Battery No 40, of four 120mm cannons, was built near Karust and Battery No 41, of four 130mm guns, was positioned between Mento and Lebera. Most of the aforementioned batteries were well protected by numerous 75mm anti-aircraft gun batteries.

The second part of the defences of the Irben Straits were the extensive minefields laid over a long period. Since the beginning of the war the Russians alone had laid over 10,000 mines in the Irben Straits, and the Germans had laid thousands more along the Kurland coast as part of their so-called 'mine shield'. However, from the Russian point of view, there were no guarantees the mine position could be supported. The southern coastline of Kurland lay in German hands and they were thus able to conduct minesweeping operations close under the coast, without the support of their fleet units. These minesweepers, however, frequently came under attack from Russian destroyers and gunboats operating in a swept area under the Sworbe Peninsula, the so-called 'manoeuvre basin', and also from the newly-commissioned Zerel battery. The struggle between laying and sweeping mines continued over 1915, 1916 and 1917 and was referred to as the 'static war', or a maritime version of trench warfare. The

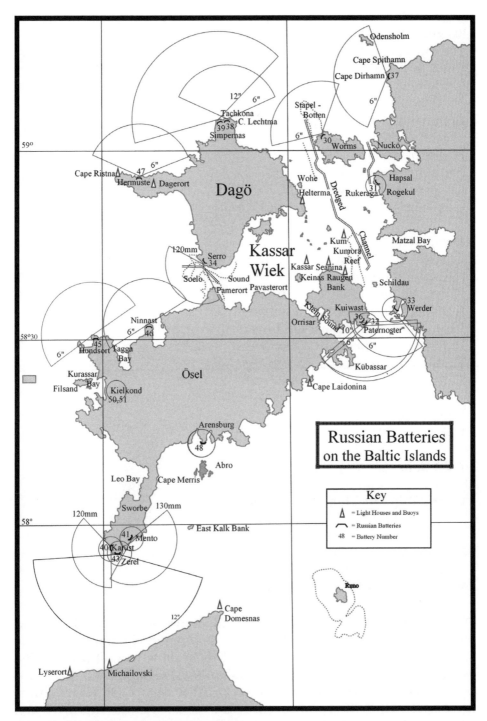

Map 1: Russian Batteries on the Baltic Islands.

southern Moon Sound was protected by two large minefields of around 1300 mines.

The third part of the Russian defence were the naval units, which were known as the Naval Forces of the Riga Gulf, or MSRZ. This force was considerable and consisted of the following:

Commander: Vice Admiral Bakhirev.
Chief of Staff: Captain 2nd Rank Muromtsev.
Flagship: *Bayan*
Battleships: *Slava, Graschdanin*
Cruisers: *Admiral Makarov, Diana*
Gunboats: *Chrabry, Grozyashchi, Chivinetz*

Destroyers
Commander: Rear Admiral Stark.
Flagship: *Novik*.
I Division Torpedoboat-Destroyers
II Division Torpedoboat-Destroyers
III Division Torpedoboat-Destroyers
IV Division Torpedoboat-Destroyers
V Division Torpedoboat-Destroyers
VI Division Torpedoboat-Destroyers

Submarines
C26, C27, C32.

Fleet train

Guard Ship Division of the Baltic

VIII Torpedoboat Division
XI Torpedoboat Division
Minelayers: *Pripyat, Amur, Wolga*
Five Divisions of Minesweepers.

The air stations at Lebara, Kielkond and Arensburg could field around fifty seaplanes and flying boats and ten land-based Nieuport types. The Russian forces were well balanced and their ships had all had combat experience and had proved themselves tough adversaries.

The main base for the Naval Forces of the Riga Gulf was Kuiwast Roadstead, which was convenient and safe, as was the destroyer and submarine base at Rogekul, but they were removed from the Irben Straits. There were auxiliary bases at Arensburg and Piya Bay for the light forces but they were not secure against U-boats. The Moon Sound channel was the main arterial link for reinforcements but even with its dredged depth it was considered impassable for the battleships *Andrei Pervozvannyi* and *Respublika* (formerly *Imperator Pavel I*).

The leader of the Naval Forces of the Riga Gulf was Vice Admiral Michael Koronatovich Bakhirev, known to his colleagues as 'Crown'. Rear Admiral K K Pilkin wrote of him: 'He was a clever, simple and kind person. He was trusted, listened to the opinions of those older, more experienced in naval traditions, and was very popular in the Fleet'. Vice Admiral Bakhirev was born on 17 June 1868. He served with distinction in the Russo-Japanese War and was much decorated. He began the First World War as commander of *Rurik*, the fleet flagship. In December 1914 he was promoted Rear Admiral and was given command of the 1st Cruiser Brigade. He led this unit in the Battle of Ostergarn on 2 July 1915. In December 1915 he was appointed commander of the 1st Battleship Brigade, the dreadnought squadron. He survived the murderous ravages of the revolution and was already a Vice Admiral and Commander of the Mine Defences of the Baltic when in summer 1917 the Commander of the Fleet, Vice Admiral Verderski requested him to familiarize himself with the state of affairs in the Riga Gulf. On 2 August the new Fleet commander, Rear Admiral Razvozov, gave him the following order: 'In the case of the beginning of an operation by the German fleet in the Riga Gulf, I charge you, honorable Vice Admiral, to take up the overall command of the Naval Forces of the Riga Gulf and Moon Sound Position and to conduct actions as previously discussed'. Vice Admiral Bakhirev was frequently in the Gulf after that and collected the staffs aboard the transport *Libau*, on Kuiwast Roadstead, which was connected to shore by telephone. M K Bakhirev was later murdered by a Bolshevik court on 9 January 1920, after refusing to flee to Finland.

The morale of the Russian crews and garrison was also an imponderable circumstance. During the revolution many officers had been murdered or replaced and new commanders were sometimes elected by the crews. Each ship had an elected committee with which the officers had to consult. In 1919 Vice Admiral Bakhirev wrote a report about the actions of the Naval Forces of the Riga Gulf and he described the situation thus:

The ships committees wished to interfere with everything, not only military matters, and even demanded their presence be allowed to read and analyze operational telegrams....The cheap politics was easily spread: there were nearly daily gatherings of the ships delegates and eternally messages were passed by semaphore and signal lamp....The failing discipline of the crews was expressed in many apparent trifles, but these had tremendous value to life aboard the ships. Leave was given freely and there were unaccountable political and economic business trips given freely to essential crew.

Despite this I was still sure of the crews of those ships that had been in the Riga Gulf since the early spring, and sincerely believed they would be able to repulse the enemy and successfully defend the Gulf from being mastered by the enemy.

Nevertheless, a period of bad weather intervened towards the end of September as autumn storms raged and the German operation had to be postponed. The Germans had planned preparatory air attacks but many of these could not be carried out. There were some successes however. As the Russian torpedoboat destroyer *Okhotnik* carried out picket duty in the manoeuvre basin near buoy number 4 on 26 September, she struck a German mine. This mine had been laid by a German aircraft and *Okhotnik* carried the dubious distinction of being the first warship sunk by an aerial mine. Neither the commander nor officers wished to abandon ship. Harald Graf described the situation as follows:

Soon all the boats were overflowing with sailors and nobody thought to offer the officers a place. They considered it improper to ask for a place and remained aboard the torpedoboat, silently observing the leaving of the boats. The torpedoboat sank, and soon water flooded over the deck on which the officers stood….With *Okhotnik* two more officers were lost, the commander Senior Leitenant V A Fok, and Leitenant V K Panferov.

At the beginning of October the German air offensive was stepped up and during the nights of 1, 5, 9 and 10 October a total of 5,900 kilograms of bombs were dropped on Zerel, Hainasch and Pernau. During the night of 30 September/1 October a bombing raid was conducted against the 12-inch gun battery at Zerel. The results were devastating. The following is from a copy of the telephone conversation between Captain 1st Rank Knüpfer (formerly commander of the torpedoboat *Voiskovoi* and now the commander of the Zerel Battery) and Captain 2nd Rank Muromtsev, the one and only Staff Officer of Vice Admiral Bakhirev.

Captain Knüpfer asks Captain Muromtsev to come to the telephone. 'Captain Muromtsev on the telephone'.

Knüpfer speaks: 'I request to report to the Admiral on the following. I have ordered Leitenant Stepanov to make inquiries to find the reason for the explosion of the magazine and he has already started and given the following picture: the bomb has fallen before the door of the magazine and a splinter has punched a hole, the powder was ignited and a fire started inside the magazine; cases of powder were thrown out by the explosion and set fire to a shed and a mill.

Captain 2nd Rank Loman, Leitenants Timofeev, Maksutin, Ensign Voskresensky, Sub-Leitenants Polikarpov, Grigorev, Manikhin, Leitenant Bartinev, Ensigns Volsky and Razdenov and most of the crew of Battery No 43 and the other batteries tried in every way possible to extinguish the fire inside the magazine, smothering it with earth and turf and pouring water through the ventilation pipes. A moment after there were no more flames visible, there was an explosion of one shell and after that 44 shells all at once. The forward wall of the magazine was taken out and the roof was wrecked. Logs and splinters rose to a very significant height and, for example, the body of Captain Loman was found two hundred *sazhen* [426 yards] from the place where he faced the magazine. Besides Loman, Timofeev and Maksutin, whose body has not yet been found, were also killed. Sub-Leitenant Manikhin, Leitenant Bartinev, Sub-Leitenant V B Polikarpov and Ensign Voskresensky are wounded and contused. I have replaced most of the sailors from separate Guards Regiments, but it is extremely desirable to promptly replace the experts and officers.'

Captain Knüpfer went on request a work crew of 300 men to complete concreting of the magazines. Captain Muromtsev continued: 'I ask him to explain: firstly whether it is established the bomb was incendiary or ordinary; and secondly whether the fire detonated the charges or the shells.

'The bomb was not incendiary, but ordinary, with few suffocating gases, and fell outside the door of the magazine. The fire burned for almost 30 minutes and I almost had time to reach the battery before the explosion. It was possible to extinguish the fire so that it could hardly be seen, and I think that an intermediate wall has burnt through, a shell was heated, which then resulted in the first explosion. Instantly after this there was a very big explosion which meant that the other 43 shells detonated, and this is quite possible according to the experiences of the scientific technical laboratory in Petrograd.'

The loss of the experienced officers could not be made good and replacements had not been found by the time the Germans attacked. The morale of the crew was also badly affected.

A further bombing raid on Zerel during the night of 8/9 October caused little additional damage, but three bombs badly damaged the steamer *General Zimmerman*, which was lying off Mento.

On 8 October German aerial reconnaissance reported two steamers lying off Zerel, which were thought to be minelayers. The first, of approximately

800 gross register tonnage (GRT) , lay off Zerel, whilst the other, of around 1500 GRT, lay off Mento. The I Torpedo Flugzeug Staffel at Windau were ordered to attack with their five torpedo-carrying aircraft. Each torpedo plane would be escorted by a single-seat fighter seaplane, whilst other seaplanes would fly at high altitude overhead to attempt to distract the anticipated heavy anti-aircraft fire. The targets lay about 1,000 metres from shore, in a water depth of 5 metres, but with a firing range of 1,500 to 2,000 metres the aircraft would be launching their torpedoes in a depth of approximately 10 to 11 metres, according to the charts; Torpedo Trial Kommand stated that although a greater depth was desirable, torpedoes could be launched normally in this depth of water. At this critical phase of preparations for Operation Albion, the destruction of two minelayers had great military importance, and Kapitänleutnant Mans, commander of the Windau Airstation, did not hesitate to order the attack, even though it would expend half the *staffel*'s available supply of ten aerial torpedoes.

Towards 1330hrs the five Gotha WD 11 torpedo-bombers lumbered into the air, led by Leutnant zur See Stinsky in aircraft 1378. Following close behind were aircraft 1372, 1374, 1376 and 1377. Although visibility was good, there was a strong wind and swell, and the weather threatened to turn bad. The port squad, comprising aircraft 1372 and 1374, took course NNW towards the lighthouse at Zerel, initially at an altitude of 600 feet but later reducing to 300 feet. The smaller steamer lay on a north-northwest heading and therefore the *staffel* took up an attack course of northeast, further reducing altitude to avoid anti-aircraft gun fire from the battery near Zerel. About 1427hrs Leutnant zur See Tornau, in aircraft 1372, launched his torpedo at a range of 1,700 metres. It broke surface twice and then appeared to run normally. Shortly after, Leutnant der Reserve (Marine Artillerie) Esser launched his torpedo but the track of this torpedo could not be seen. The aircraft flying high above the scene observed one torpedo pass behind the stern of the steamer, whilst the track of the other was not sighted.

Meanwhile, Leutnant zur See Stinsky led the other aircraft in the attack on the larger steamer off Mento. This vessel lay on an east-southeast heading. The torpedo-bombers reduced their altitude to just 30 to 60 feet, flying *en echelon* to starboard, and began their attack run. At about 1430hrs the lead aircraft launched her torpedo at a range of 1,700 metres. The torpedo went straight to the bottom. Next Leutnant zur See der Reserve Schurer in aircraft 1377 launched his torpedo. After breaking surface several times it ran normally, but after traveling just 800 metres it suddenly veered off to port. At around 1432hrs Leutnant zur See der Reserve Rowehl, flying the last aircraft, dropped his torpedo. According to observation aircraft this missile passed 10 metres behind the stern of the steamer and later detonated on the bottom. After launching their torpedoes and whilst flying away the *staffel* were subjected to a violent anti-aircraft fire by guns ranging from 15cm artillery to machine guns, but without success. By 1530hrs all aircraft had safely landed in Windau.

The attack had failed completely, due mainly to the erratic performance of the torpedoes, which was thought to be due to the unfavourable water depth. Half the available aerial torpedoes had been expended without result. This poor outcome caused Vizeadmiral Schmidt, Chief of the Special Unit, to order that the I Torpedo Staffel be used primarily for bombing attacks and to conduct torpedo attacks only on especially rewarding targets and under favourable conditions.

After the failure of the torpedo-bombers it was decided to dispatch a hydroglider, under the command of Oberleutnant zur See Peytsch, to attack one of the steamers. The hydroglider was a small light craft, weighing just a few tonnes with a crew of three, and powered by 2 or 3 aero engines driving aero propellers. It was armed with a single torpedo. On 24 August Peytsch had sunk the transport *Penelope* with a torpedo in almost the same position. On 10 October at 1500hrs, the hydroglider put to sea from Windau and took course northeast along the coast, intending to conduct the attack in the evening twilight. The boat steered to Michaelsturm and from there took course through the mined area toward the roadstead off Mento. About 1718hrs the battery at Michaelsturm observed the boat traveling on a northeast course, but just a few moments later, at 1727hrs, the battery at Gross Irben observed a heavy detonation and bright flash, where just previously the hydroglider had been. The boat did not return and was probably destroyed by either a shallow positioned mine or an internal explosion.

The German airships were also active during the preparations for operation Albion. In addition to reconnaissance missions they also conducted bombing raids. During the night of 24/25 September at about 0245hrs, LZ120 (commanded by Kapitänleutnant von Lossnitzer) dropped 3,700kg of bombs on the Zerel battery and was followed up by LZ113 (Kapitänleunant Zaeschmar) with 2,000kg of bombs. The bombs were reported to have been dropped accurately. On the evening of 1 October, L30 (Oberleutnant zur See Vermehren) , L37 (Kapitänleutnant Paul Gartner) and LZ120 attacked Salis, Salismunde and the surrounding areas, dropping a total of 8,000kg of bombs. This area was poorly defended and L30 bombed from just 4,000 feet. The results of the attack remain unknown.

CHAPTER TWO

October 12th: The German Landing

The German operational plans for Albion called for a surprise landing by pioneer troops inside Tagga Bay on the northwest coast of Ösel, and simultaneously near Pamerort, a little further to the east. A breakthrough in the Irben Straits, to mount a landing somewhere inside the Riga Gulf, was not considered because the mine defences and battery No 43 at Zerel were simply too strong. Nevertheless, minesweeping work would be undertaken in the Straits in preparation for the later phases of the operation. Tagga Bay was not so well protected by mine barriers, although the approach route would have to be swept. It offered a secure, protected shelter, inside which troops could be landed and which could be sealed off with net barriers to protect the transport fleet from submarines. The first wave ashore, the pioneers, would be landed by torpedoboats and small steamers, which would provide supporting gunfire. After the beaches were secure, more troops and heavier equipment would be landed from the larger ships and transports.

The forces to be landed in Tagga Bay were the 131st Infantry Regiment (131 Regt) under Oberstleutnant Fischer, the 255th Reserve Infantry Regiment (255R Regt) under Oberst Berring, and the 65th Infantry Brigade commanded by Oberst Matthiass, which consisted of the 138th Infantry Regiment (138 Regt) and 17th Infantry Regiment (17 Regt). The four regiments were to be landed on the first operational day and spread out to the east and south; their bold objective was to capture the entire Russian garrison. After initially acting in support, 131 Regt was to strike south and capture the Sworbe Peninsula, including the Zerel Battery, and therefore facilitate the forcing of the Irben Straits by the naval forces. The 255R Regt were to strike SE towards Arensburg and capture the town. The 65th Brigade would move to the south and east and try to cut off any Russians retreating towards the east and Moon Island, and prevent any reinforcements coming westward. In consideration of this it was clear that the Island of Moon and its connection to Ösel by a 4 to 5 metre-wide, 3.5 kilometre-long stone dam were of vital importance, particularly to the Russian defenders of Ösel. Reinforcements could come across the dam from Moon and the mainland, and the garrison would also have a secure line of retreat. With this in mind the Russians had constructed bridgeheads at both ends of the stone dam. On Ösel a 6 to 7 km bow stretched from Masik to Saika to Neuenhof. It consisted of field fortifications and barbed wire. The stone dam was also important to the Germans, as to possess it not only prevented reinforcements and precluded the defenders from retreating, it would also isolate them. The earthwork defences were not permanently occupied by the Russians so the German leadership determined on a plan to land some mobile forces, cyclists, on the northern tip of Ösel near Pamerort; they would immediately race across the north of Ösel through Orrisar to the stone dam, in an effort to take the Russians by surprise and occupy the defences first. The Russian line of communication would then be severed. The forces allocated for this task were the I and II Cyclist Battalions and the *sturmkompanie* (assault company) of Hauptmann von Winterfeld, together with a half battery of guns. The Germans hoped that they would be able to hold the stone dam, or at least delay the Russians.

The German preparations for Operation Albion did not go unnoticed by the Russian forces. The Russian Intelligence Service (SNIS) was still operating with a good deal of efficiency. Vice Admiral Bakhirev wrote:

> On September 24th I received news about the arrival in the Baltic of large enemy units in the near future. I let Captain 1st Rank Knüpfer know about this.
>
> On October 3rd the XII Army communicated to me that a night attack and landing on Ösel was expected. I notified the Moon Sound chief in Arensburg about this, and again notified Captain 1st Rank Knüpfer.
>
> On October 10th the Chief of the Operations Department of the Fleet Commander notified me that on the 11th a German fleet operation unknown to us would begin in the Baltic. I communicated the contents of the telegram to Rear Admiral Sveshnikov and ordered Captain 1st Rank Knüpfer to maintain a state of increased readiness.
>
> With the disturbing news about the German fleet I detained some units in the Riga Gulf that were previously detached for leave.

It is clear, therefore, that the Russian fleet commander knew of the commencement date of the German operation. Vice Admiral Bakhirev also passed on this news to the commander of the land forces on Ösel, Kontre Admiral Sveshnikov. Yet when the German sea forces arrived off the Ösel coast it appeared as if their appearance came as a surprise to the defenders.

Before the German operation could be mounted, preparatory minesweeping would have to be undertaken. Nevertheless, a storm which lasted almost two weeks at the end of September had caused a postponement of the operation and only when the westerly blew out in early October could II Minesweeper Flotilla, under Kapitänleutnant Max Doflein, finally begin work in the Irben Straits. This work did not proceed without loss. On 6 October, the minesweeper T54 struck a mine NNW of Lyserort and sank with the loss of seven lives. The following day M31, of the 8th Minesweeper Half Flottille (8 MSHF), struck a mine southwest of Lyserort and sank with the loss of one life. The following day, October 8th, was a particularly bad one, with three minesweepers, M75, T85 and the auxiliary minesweeper *Cladow* all being damaged, but luckily all were towed safely in. Kapitänleutnant Doflein later wrote:

> Sleep only came after coal was replenished and weapons for the coming day were repaired and made serviceable. House high water spouts and explosive clouds, bound with the thunderous crash of the exploding mines, gave news of the progress of the work. Four of my *Bootes* were blown up in the course of the pioneer work and many brave *Offiziers*, *Deckoffiziers* and men perished with them.

Finally, after a delay of around two weeks, the weather improved enough to allow the commencement of the operation. On the evening of 10 October the III and IV Battle Squadrons departed Putzig Wiek and took course northwards. At 0715hrs the following morning they rendezvoused with the unit from Libau and Vizeadmiral Schmidt, General der Infanterie von Kathen and their staffs boarded *SMS Moltke*. Later in the day the forces from Windau joined the unit so that by early afternoon the invasion fleet was complete and traveling north in four sections at a speed of 9 knots. The first section consisted of light forces: trawlers and torpedoboats of the S-Flotillas fitted for minesweeping and anti-submarine work.

Then came the second section comprised of II Minesweeper Flotilla, II Torpedoboat Flotilla with II Pioneers aboard, three small steamers with III Pioneers aboard, and then the tender *Ammon* with II Minesweeper Division. The third section was III Battle Squadron with I Pioneers aboard, *Moltke*, *Emden* and IV Battle Squadron. Finally came the fourth section, consisting of the transports and fleet train, escorted by II Reconnaissance Group (II AG). The entire force was screened against submarines by the torpedoboat Flotillas, whilst overhead it was covered by seaplanes from the Libau air station. The English submarine E1 was stationed off Libau in an ambush and observation position and observed some of the units from Libau putting to sea, but neither carried out an attack nor realized the significance of what she had observed, and therefore made no report. On 12 October E1 set course back to Hango.

During the afternoon of 11 October the Special Unit progressed slowly northward. Ahead was the first section, preceded by the trawlers of the S-Flotilla of the Baltic with broken out minesweeper gear, then came the second section preceded by the II Minesweeper Flotilla, likewise with sweeper gear set. So far no mines had been encountered. Towards late afternoon the S-Flotilla of the Baltic handed over the minesweeping duties to the other trawlers and Fregattenkapitän Rosenberg hurried ahead to lay out the light vessels along the foreseen route at the nominated points: S, Epsilon, Alpha, Beta, Gamma, Delta and White; some of which were already indicated by U-boats.

Meanwhile, the minesweeping trawlers continued their difficult work. Due to the increasing swell and clinkering of their fires, however, their speed reduced to 5½ knots and then 4 knots. They began to fall behind schedule. At point Gamma there was a ninety degree course alteration to almost due east and in the darkness the 1½ mile-wide sweeper formation fell into complete disarray. A further delay of two hours was incurred before the confusion was unravelled and the trawlers could continue their advance. Fregattenkapitän von Rosenberg realized something was amiss and therefore he made the following wireless signal to the trawlers: 'Clear the fleet area by 0200hrs'. Nevertheless, towards midnight the II Minesweeper Flotilla caught up with the trawlers and eventually had to bypass them before resuming their minesweeping work. Soon the heavy ships would be approaching from the south.

The third and forth sections of the Special Unit advanced according to schedule. At about 1934hrs the main body passed point S and steered towards Epsilon. At around 2100hrs the 1st Division of the IV Battle Squadron detached to take up their allotted bombardment positions off the Sworbe Peninsula. Towards midnight SMS *König* arrived at point Gamma but then had to reduce speed as the II Minesweeper Flotilla now lay close ahead. The entire German formation was now beginning to bunch up. If the element of surprise was not to be lost, the pioneers needed to be at the anchorage by 0300hrs at the latest, but this was quickly becoming an impossibility. The Chief of the Special Unit was now faced with a difficult decision - either renounce the minesweeping, or else lose the effect of surprise. Without hesitation, Vizeadmiral Schmidt determined to forgo further minesweeping and gave the order to the minesweepers: 'Immediately give room for the Fleet. Take on gear'.

Ahead of III Battle Squadron were the countless stern lanterns of the minesweeper Units and due to those and the dense clouds of funnel smoke it was difficult to discern the lights of the navigation marks. Nevertheless,

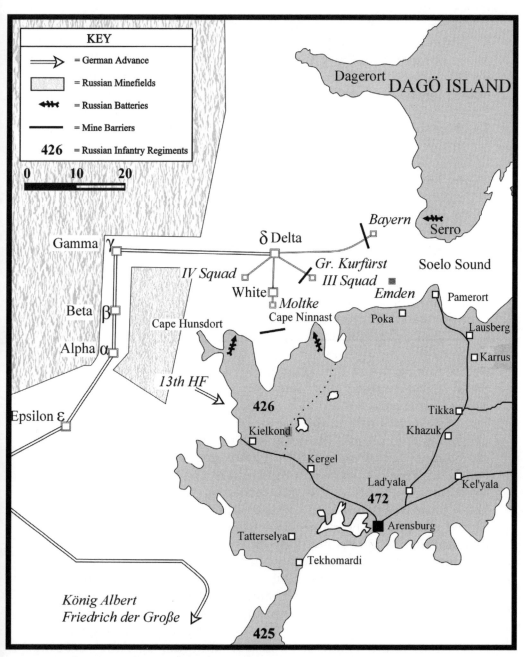

Map 2: The Approach Route of the Special Unit.

because of Vizeadmiral Schmidt's courageous decision to forgo further minesweeping, the battleships were able to anchor at their allotted positions at 0300hrs. By 0340hrs the pioneers aboard the battleships of the III Battle Squadron had disembarked and were on their way towards Tagga Bay. Ahead of them were the torpedoboats of the II Torpedoboat Flotilla and the steamers *Blitz, Equity* and *Corsica*, which were carrying the main body of the pioneers. *Moltke* followed this unit as support. After disembarking their troops the battleships steamed towards their bombardment positions. The three ships of IV Battle Squadron, under the command of Kommodore Meurer, would take battery No 45 at Cape Hundsort under fire, whilst the III Battle Squadron would fire on Battery No 46 at Ninnast. To cover the nearby landing at Pamerort, SMS *Bayern* would bombard Battery No 34 at Cape Toffri and *Emden* would fire on the supposed battery at Pamerort. All the ships were to remain within areas swept for mines by the S-Flotilla. However, due to a navigational error, the light vessel at point Delta was displaced 3 nautical miles from its intended position, and as the S-Flotilla had used the light vessel as a navigational fix, this meant that the areas swept for the intended bombardment positions were likewise displaced. It later transpired that all the battleships were actually operating in unswept waters during their bombardments. Therefore, it was only due to providence that there were no serious losses during the landing.

Meanwhile, the progress of the motor launches laden with pioneers was beginning to fall behind schedule, with the result that the chief of the II Torpedoboat Flotilla ordered the torpedoboats to advance and the steamers and launches to follow as quickly as possible. *Moltke* followed just 1,500 metres behind the last steamer, *Corsica*. Suddenly at 0535hrs *Corsica* ran onto a mine. The detonation was to starboard aft, beneath the engine room, which quickly filled with water. *Moltke* came forward and two of her torpedoboat escorts were sent to *Corsica* to take off the troops, the II Battalion, 138 Regt. This was carried out expeditiously and without loss. *Corsica* was towed to Cape Merris and beached, where repairs were carried out before she returned to Libau. Evidently there was a small Russian mine barrier running eastwards across the entrance to Tagga Bay and this was subsequently swept by the II Minesweeper Flotilla.

Just prior to this, at about 0520hrs, the sound of cannon thunder was heard to port. It could only be coming from *Bayern*, despite the fact that fire was only to be opened on receipt of orders from the flagship. The pioneers had already pushed forward into Tagga Bay and were poised to land. Vizeadmiral Schmidt, therefore, gave the order 'open fire' at 0527hrs. At 0544hrs the ships of the IV Battle Squadron, *Kaiser, Prinzregent Luitpold* and *Kaiserin*, opened fire on the guns at Hundsort, which were clearly visible. At the same time the Russian battery replied with a salvo, which, however, was aimed at *Moltke*. The Russian firing was accurate, the first salvo fell just 100 metres short of *Moltke*, the second was over and the third was 50 metres off the bow. *Moltke* joined in the firing and she and the IV Battle Squadron continued for some time: by 0617hrs the battleships lay just 8 kilometres from Hundsort. The command and communication post at Cape Hundsort was taken under bombardment but all twenty-five men of the 5th Company of the 426th Povenets Regiment remained resolutely at their posts. The firing continued while the landing took place but by 0745hrs the IV Battle Squadron had anchored.

Meanwhile, the III Battle Squadron, under Vizeadmiral Behncke, took up their positions to bombard Battery No 46 at Ninnast. At 0440hrs *Bayern* had been detached for her task of silencing Battery No 34 at Toffri. When the order to open fire arrived at 0527hrs, the III Battle Squadron were still unable to make out their allotted target and initially mistook Cape Pank for Cape Ninnast. It was only at 0545hrs that the Russian battery was sighted and taken under fire with the medium calibre guns at a range of 4,600 metres. Vizeadmiral Behncke had decided to conserve the barrels of his heavy artillery. The Russian battery did not reply so that after nine minutes fire was ceased, only to be reopened shortly after 0600hrs when lively activity around the battery was observed. With that the Russian gunners finally abandoned their battery and towards 0752hrs the III Battle Squadron dropped anchor to conserve coal.

Earlier, whilst still en route to their bombardment position, the battleship *Grosser Kurfürst* had run onto a mine at about 0509hrs. The mine struck to starboard forward and the wing passage, protective and outer bunkers all filled with water, although a total of only 280 tonnes entered the ship. *Grosser Kurfürst*'s draught increased by a third of a metre but she held her place in line and completed the bombardment. Later in the afternoon she, together with the other ships of the III Battle Squadron, was detached to Putzig Wiek, and from there to Wilhelmshaven, which she reached on October 18th. She was repaired in the Imperial Dockyard and was returned to the Fleet on 1 December.

The landing at Pamerort and the eventual breakthrough into the Soelo Sound were under the direction of the I FdT, Kommodore Heinrich, aboard the cruiser SMS *Emden*. The battleship *Bayern*, mounting eight 38cm guns, was to silence Battery Toffri and support the landing, and, as mentioned previously, had detached from the III Battle Squadron at 0440hrs. A short time later, at 0507hrs, a detonation occurred to port forward and a grey-black water column of comparatively small diameter was thrown up 8 to 10 metres. A watch-engineer aboard *Bayern*, Oberleutnant (I) der Reserve Lorenz, described the situation which followed:

The siren of the engine telegraph howled as the three black indicators hastily jumped into the red part of the scale: 'Utmost power astern

– stop!' The ship sank perceptibly deeper by the bow to a new trim position. On the bridge they had seen a grey-black water and smoke column….Announced by shrill whistles, many speaking tubes delivered their reports: 'Bow torpedo room and forward torpedo broadside room full of water, approximately 1,000 tonnes of water in the ship, the leak is secure!' Quietly and orderly, just as in battle practice, further reports and confirmations arrived: four large compartments were flooded, their crews, (seven men), gave no answer….

From the damage control centre the First Offizier and Stabsingenieur Laebell undertook the first measures for the security of the ship. The bulkhead door to the flooded compartment, in the large transverse bulkhead near frame 117½, just forward of turret 'Alsen', was quickly shored up by carpenters and damage control personnel. However, water was penetrating the rivet and seam joints and the *pumpenmeister* personnel worked nimbly at their electric leak pump stations to master the flooding.

Meanwhile, on the orders of the Commander, the FT (Wireless) Offizier, Leutnant zur See Lindemann, sent a report about our misfortune to the Chief of the 'Special Unit'.[1] The propellers renewed their revolutions and slowly the ship steamed with a southerly course, down along the side of the mine barrier, to take up its position for the bombardment off Cape Toffri.

At about 0524hrs, a submarine alarm to port was given. The *Bayern* turned away to starboard onto a southerly course. Before endangering the element of surprise of the entire operation, the commander, Kapitän zur See Rohardt, asked for confirmation of the submarine attack. The 3rd and 4th Artillerie Offiziers irreproachably confirmed that they had seen a periscope and torpedo track. Under these circumstances *Bayern* was forced to open fire, the firing observed by *Moltke*. Of course there were no allied submarines present.

Nevertheless, *Bayern* was able to continue her allotted task. By around 0600hrs Battery Toffri could be made out clearly and at 0602hrs the heavy calibre guns opened fire, followed briefly by the medium calibre guns. At ranges varying from 10,200 to 9,300 meters the battleship fired twenty-four 38cm shells and seventy 15cm shells. After the third salvo from *Bayern* the Russian battery replied; however, they took the boats of the S-Flotilla as their targets. As observed from *Emden*, the battleship's fire was landing over the battery, but soon a warehouse and barracks were hit and caught fire, burning for several hours. *Emden* opened fire at 0608hrs at a range of 8,000m, but her first and second salvoes fell short and landed in the water and on the beach. Meanwhile the boats of the S-Flotilla under F K von

Rosenberg, with men of the cyclist and *sturm* (assault) companies embarked, manoeuvred in Poka Bay, searching for a favourable landing site. The Russian battery took these vessels under fire and quickly obtained a direct hit aft on the torpedoboot A28 at a range of 25 cables, but the shell failed to detonate. The *Emden*'s third salvo then landed amongst Battery No34 and destroyed the telephone wires and speaking tubes, and after this the battery could only continue with independent fire. One cannon remained serviceable. The fight continued for ten minutes and the battery fired up to twenty-five shells. When the battery commander, Warrant Officer Lesgaft, gave orders to retire there no longer remained any crews by the cannon. At around 0700hrs the German Landing Corps began going ashore and landed unopposed. There was no Russian battery at Pamerort as had been supposed. Once ashore the cyclist and assault companies immediately began to advance towards the stone dam at Orrisar.

In the meantime, in accordance with the operational plan, a diversion was being conducted to the east of the Sworbe Peninsula. The object was to deceive the Russians into thinking that a landing was imminent on Sworbe. At about 2100hrs the previous evening Vizeadmiral Souchon had led 1st Division of the IV Battle Squadron, *Friedrich der Grosse* and *König Albert* , away from the main body to the southeast, where they anchored out of sight of land. Towards 0400hrs on the morning of October 12th the unit weighed anchor and steered towards the coast, screened against submarines and mines by the boats of the 15th Torpedoboat Half Flotilla (15 TBHF). The torpedoboats were inexperienced in minesweeping and slipped their gear on the bottom twice, delaying the advance sufficiently that the coast was still out of range when the timetable called for them to open fire. Nevertheless, fire was inaugurated and the first salvoes fell short of the beach, although subsequently the shore was taken under fire. The Russian heavy battery No 43 at Zerel did not return the fire even though they were within effective range. By 0835hrs the German unit had begun the journey to Tagga Bay, preceded by the 15 TBHF.

Another special purpose for the German forces was the bombardment of the airstation at Papensholm. At 0200hrs Kapitänleutnant Zander, with the boats V82, S64 and V74, was detached from the 13th Torpedoboot Half Flotilla (13 TBHF) to fulfill this task. Towards 0500hrs they arrived in Papensholm Bay, south of Hundsort. Towards 0600hrs fire was opened on the air station and wireless station at Papensholm. At first the fire was inaccurate, but corrections given by the floatplane spotters quickly enabled the fire to become effective. Initially the fire lay far from the buildings and hangers, being 200 *sazhen* (425 metres) from the airstation, but then the shells began falling around the hangers.[2] One of the torpedoboats, V82, approached to within 3,600m of Papensholm and took deliberate fire on the air station. The German fire was answered by the fire of I and II

Air Station Field Battery, but their shells lay far and wide and over, and in general the fire was poor. The batteries soon ceased fire because of a shortage of ammunition.

The airstation suffered great damage, and in part the roofs of buildings were blown off, pipes were dislodged, the walls of hangers and other buildings were holed and telephone lines were torn down. Towards midday part of the German 131 Regt reached Papensholm and took the Russians completely by surprise. The station commander, Leitenant Vavilov, ordered the base to be evacuated and then began demolishing the station. Attempts to set the buildings on fire, and blow up the stores of bombs, gasoline and launches failed because of the unexpected appearance of German pioneers. The demolition party fled across the bay and into the forest under the fire of the German troops. The gallant Leitenant Vavilov remained behind and it was thought that the last explosions at the air station during the evening were the work of his hand.

Late in the morning the senior pilot, Leitenant Safonov, reported to Vice Admiral Bakhirev that the air station was under fire and that all thirteen serviceable aircraft had been transferred to Arensburg, from where they would undertake reconnaissance. During the evening Michman Severski undertook reconnaissance in the Papensholm area.[3] He was attacked by four German aircraft and having insufficient altitude to manoeuvre he alighted in one of the bays, dismounted his machine gun and then went ashore. He fought off the Germans from behind a stone fence and escaped.

The Germans made the air station operational the following day. After the infantry arrived, a wireless signal from the Special Unit ordered Kapitänleutnant Zander and his boats to hurry to Pamerort and place themselves at the disposal of the I FdT aboard *Emden*.

Whilst these events were occurring, the main landing was being launched in Tagga Bay. As the torpedoboats of II Flotilla entered the bay towards 0500hrs, Korvettenkapitän Heinecke dispatched the 4th Torpedoboat Half Flotilla (4 TBHF) to the eastern side of the bay whilst the lead boat, B98, took 3rd Torpedoboat Half Flotilla (3 TBHF) towards the western side. Initially there was no response from ashore and it appeared as if the surprise was complete. The landing of the assault troops and pioneers from aboard the torpedoboats progressed quickly with the men being put ashore by the torpedoboat cutters. The troops from aboard *Blitz* and *Equity* were taken ashore by the motorboats of II Minesweeper Division. After the troops had landed, a Russian field battery, hidden behind some woods on the eastern side of the bay, opened fire. Their targets included the beachhead on the shore, the torpedoboats, and *Blitz* and *Equity*. However, there were no losses or damage. The German torpedoboats returned the fire, but at the express wishes of the brigade commander, Oberst Matthiass, who was aboard B98, fire was ceased as he thought it endangered 138 Regt, who were landed on the eastern shore of the bay. However, under the direction of 131 Regt, some targets were taken under indirect fire, including Kielkond before it was captured. After the first wave was ashore the second wave, the motor launches of the III Battle Squadron with the troops of the I Pioneers aboard, began landing.

Meanwhile V100 penetrated further into Tagga Bay and took course towards Terwassa, on the eastern lower half of Hundsort. Here half a *sturmkompanie* was landed and once ashore they directed the supporting fire of V100. With this support they quickly captured six guns of the II Light Field Artillery Battery of the 107th Division. On interrogation the commanding officer revealed that the Russians knew of the planned landing, and of the probable landing positions and had adjusted their troop dispositions to suit. Under these circumstances the Germans were amazed that the landing achieved surprise. After capturing Terwassa the assault troops turned on the battery at Hundsort, which was taken at 0830hrs.

On the eastern side of the bay the landing was also successful. The boats B109, B110, B111, B97 and B112 landed their *sturmtruppen* south of Cape Merris without reaction from ashore. After the assault troops were landed, 138 Regt began disembarking. Now the Half-Flotilla came under fire from a battery of field guns located behind a wood, which could not be observed. Leutnant zur See Friedrich Ruge takes up the story:

> Then a white cloud appeared over the ship, and the Army Artillerist dived behind the linen bridge screen, to seek protection from the Russian shrapnel. Muzzle flashes and dense smoke behind a coppice showed the approximate area of the battery....Our stereoscopic gear could measure the range to the smoke and the guns received direction with the help of a high tree....we moved slowly to the south, at first followed by the white smoke clouds, then they stopped.

Towards 0700hrs the six gun field battery was captured by the I Battalion, 138 Regt. B112 landed assault troops of the 10 Assault Section on Cape Merris, however this landing came under heavy machinegun fire from ashore. Nonetheless, the men were thrown ashore, under the covering fire from the torpedoboats, and by 1000hrs Battery No 46 at Cape Ninnast had fallen and the Russians had retreated. The troops were able to report that the fire of the III Battle Squadron's medium artillery had been well laid and effective. Of the four 15cm guns, one had suffered a direct hit and had been put out of action, the crew being killed, and the others had all been struck by splinters; another hit had destroyed the command position.

The landing appeared to be progressing well with the pioneers meeting only light resistance and making good progress. By around 0800hrs all

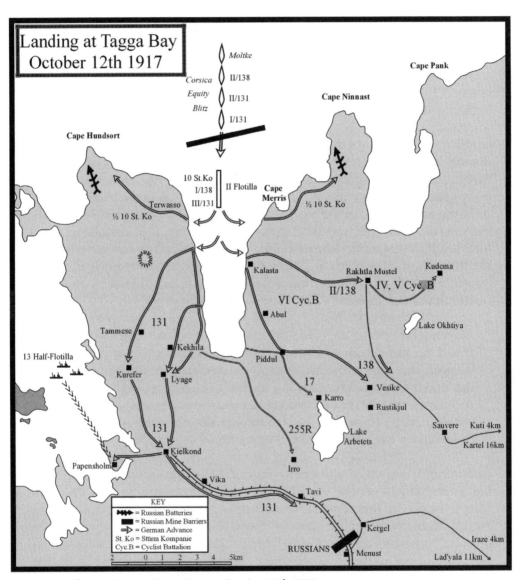

Map 3: The Landing at Tagga Bay on October 12th 1917.

the pioneers were ashore and they had secured the bridgehead. Earlier Vizeadmiral Schmidt had ordered Kontreadmiral Reuter, who lay between point Delta and point White, to quickly bring the transport fleet into Tagga Bay so that disembarking of the main body could commence. The transport fleet was preceded by the II Minesweeper Flotilla and the Sperrbrechergruppe and by 0815hrs SMS *Königsberg* and the I Transport Section stood off Tagga Bay. Within half an hour the first transport, *Bahia Castillo*, anchored and the first troops were put ashore. At 1050hrs *Nürnberg* and the II Transport Section arrived. The landing now proceeded swiftly; not only were the infantry disembarking but also the horses, guns and vehicles. It took just three and an half hours to land the main body of infantry. The landing and unloading work continued after darkness fell, using the searchlights from the two cruisers for illumination, so that by 2000hrs the entire infantry, their wagons and machineguns were ashore and in addition so were 530 horses and 100 vehicles.

With the initial bombardments over and the arrival of the transport fleet it became necessary to secure Tagga Bay as quickly as possible. During the course of the morning it had become clearly evident that there were Russian mine barriers in areas hitherto thought safe, and therefore the chief of the II Minesweeper Flotilla was ordered to immediately begin sweeping work. Before noon the 8th Minesweeper Half Flotilla (8 MSHF) initiated a search-sweep of Tagga Bay and simultaneously began work to sweep the barrier where *Corsica* had been damaged. This barrier consisted of small, cylindrical, very rusty mines with three lead horns each. Next the area between Cape Ninnast and Cape Pank was swept. The 3rd Minesweeper Half Flotilla collected the III Battle Squadron and then the IV Battle Squadron and delivered them to Tagga Bay, whilst 4 MSHF collected *Bayern*. By 1700hrs all the heavy ships were safely anchored in Tagga Bay.

The security of Tagga Bay against submarines was the responsibility of the Net Barrier Unit of the Baltic, under the command of Korvettenkapitän Kaulhaussen. It was the first occasion that the nets were being used offensively on the enemy coast. It was planned to lay a double net square across the mouth of the bay from Cape Ninnast to Cape Hundsort, with a total length of 12 kilometers. Two gaps, which would be closed at night, would allow ships to enter and exit the bay. By 0930hrs on 12 October the net layer *Rossal* began laying the western part of the net, whilst an hour later *Eskimo* began the eastern wing. By 1550hrs *Rossal* had concluded her work whilst *Eskimo* finished her sequence at around 1900hrs. For further security against submarines a 'listening line' was established between Hundsort and Dagerort. This consisted of a series of trawlers fitted with hydrophones laid out at intervals.

Meanwhile the 2nd Gruppe of the 1st S-Half Flotilla were working to secure a route into Soelo Sound, which separated Dago from Ösel. Control of the Soelo sound was particularly important because the Russians could use this passage to mount a destroyer attack on the German flank. Therefore, possession of the sound was a prime consideration for the Germans, both to prevent Russian destroyer attacks and also to provide support for troops ashore, particularly those who were to take the stone dam which ran from Ösel to Moon Island. Already before dawn the A28 and her drifters had pressed forward, sweeping for mines and taking soundings as they went. When *Bayern* and *Emden* opened fire on Battery No 34 at Serro, the Russians responded by taking A28 and her boats under fire. Seven salvoes landed amongst the S-Flotilla and A28 was hit, as previously mentioned; however, after that fire was ceased. The small torpedoboat and drifters resumed their advance and succeeded in locating the narrow, buoyed channel. Whilst conducting this work, at 0812hhrs, the battery at Serro reopened fire for a short time, but was again brought to silence by *Bayern*. With that the I FdT dispatched S61 and S63 to silence the battery permanently, which they did during the course of the morning by landing a commando of men who removed the locks from the cannon.

After the channel through Soelo Sound had been located, the lead boat of the 2nd S-Half-Flotilla, T130, and three sweeper boats pushed forward into the Kassar Wiek, to bombard the wireless station at Pawasterort. The passage through the Soelo Sound was particularly treacherous, with many uncharted rocks and strong, difficult currents. However, even the largest Russian destroyers had utilized this passage previously for operations. Now the small German unit penetrated into the Kassar Wiek, which aerial reconnaissance had reported clear of Russian ships. Ominously, a smoke cloud soon became conspicuous to the east.

With the receipt of the first news of the appearance of enemy forces off Tagga Bay, the commander of the Naval Forces of the Riga Gulf, Vice Admiral Bakhirev, ordered all units to be at a state of half hour readiness and to refill their stocks of coal and oil. The greater part of the torpedoboats had participated in the production of defensive mine barriers off Pernau the previous day. The duty torpedoboats which were waiting in readiness, *General Kondratenko* and *Pogranitschnik*, under the command of the chief of the IV Division Torpedoboat-Destroyers, Captain 1st Rank Postelnikov, were ordered to conduct reconnaissance on the Kassar Wiek. The gunboat *Grozyashchi* was in Rogekul for minor maintenance and Vice Admiral Bakhirev ordered her to go to the Kassar Wiek and place herself at the disposal of the IV Division chief.

At 0930hrs Captain 1st Rank Postelnikov reported the German torpedoboats in Soelo Sound. *General Kondratenko* opened fire and forced the German unit to retire back into the Soelo Sound. The two Russian destroyers followed but were taken under fire by *Emden* at a range of 15,800 metres, and subsequently moved off to the east, out of range.

Meanwhile, ashore, the Germans were making rapid progress. The cyclist company under Hauptmann von Winterfeld was nearing Orrisar by noon and support for them from inside the Kassar Wiek was assuming greater importance. For the time being the I FdT only had Fregattenkapitän von Rosenberg's T144 and six A-Boats available to support the infantry, and Winterfeld thereby determined to postpone any advances until after Kapitänleutnant Zander arrived with the remainder of 13th Torpedoboat Half Flotilla. When he arrived at 1330hrs, Kapitänleutnant Zander was immediately ordered to push the Russian destroyers to the east to allow von Rosenberg to push through the southern Kassar Wiek towards Keinast, the westerly part of Moon.

As the Russian destroyers moved east they were joined by the large torpedoboat-destroyer *Desna*, with the chief of the torpedoboat divisions, Rear Admiral Stark, aboard. He had been en route to Rogekul to find the state of readiness of the destroyers there when he received the wireless message from the commander of the IV Division Torpedoboat-Destroyers (IV Div TBD) about the appearance of the enemy. Rear Admiral Stark was given material recovered from a crashed German reconnaissance floatplane, which included maps and other material. Then, since the Germans no longer seemed to threaten, and the gunboat *Grozyashchi* had meanwhile approached, *Desna* made off to the east. At around 1400hrs, IV Div TBD was four nautical miles east of Serro as *Grozyashchi* approached and thereon the division chief ordered her to open fire on the German vessels with her long-range cannon. Shortly afterwards, at 1430hrs, the five torpedoboats of the 13 TBHF passed into Soelo Sound. The commander of *Grozyashchi*, Captain 2nd Rank Ordovski-Tanaevski, decided to utilize the disadvantageous situation of the Germans, manoeuvring in the narrow and fractious sea channel, to best advantage and he took course west and opened fire at 1426hrs at a range of 70 cable-lengths, or 12,800 metres. The fourth and fifth salvos straddled the Germans who immediately developed a smoke screen. Shortly afterwards the five torpedoboats of 13 TBHF emerged from the smoke at high speed. However, the Russian gunboat was not supported by the destroyers and at 1440hrs the division chief ordered *Grozyashchi* to return to the destroyers, which she did whilst continuing to fire from her stern guns. This allowed the German torpedoboats to negotiate Soelo Sound and deploy into the Kassar Wiek. To get to within effective range, 13 TBHF made a sudden dash forward at high speed and then deployed onto a course for a firing position and opened fire. This manoeuvre was repeated four times.

Later in the course of the battle, the Russian IV Div TBD was joined by *Razyashchi*, which Admiral Bakhirev had dispatched forward to recover the package from the German floatplane. *Razyashchi* travelled a little ahead and to port of *Grozyashchi* and the Germans initially fired on all the Russian vessels before shifting to the gunboat and concentrating on her. *Grozyashchi* was now straddled. The range opened and the German torpedoboats repeated their dash forward, then again deployed on the broadside. Captain 2nd Rank Kosinski, commander of the destroyer *Zabiyaka* during the campaign, described the German firing as follows: 'The range alternated from 40–45 cables to 60–65 cables. They shot with three gun salvoes and the shots fell in very small groups, which were wonderfully corrected for aim'.

Nevertheless, *Grozyashchi* remained untouched for a time, but then at 1717hrs, as the Germans performed their manoeuvre for the third time, she received her first hit. The German shell struck the port side below the upper deck level and started a fire among wooden panelling, but caused little other damage. The fire was extinguished by the deck division. Almost immediately afterwards a second hit struck beneath the bridge, below the waterline. The entire ship was vibrated heavily as the armoured belt was hit and later a small amount of water was found inboard, coming from a slight leak. A third shell cut through the boom and exploded on the starboard locker. Splinters penetrated part of the funnel casing and a fan, and brought down the gaffe and wireless antenna. The motor launch was damaged and the head of the shell holed the upper deck and outer hull above the waterline. Two men on the upper deck were killed, five were wounded, and two were dazed. At the conclusion of the action, at 1720hrs, the steering on *Grozyashchi* failed in the steering compartment and it was necessary to steer using the engines. This damage was quickly rectified. Admiral Bakhirev wrote: 'In his report Captain 2nd Rank Ordovski-Tanaevski remarks on the extremely creditable behavior of the officers and crew and the excellence of individuals performing their duties'.

In the meantime, the chief of the torpedoboat divisions, Rear Admiral Stark, heard the cannon thunder from the Kassar Wiek and at 1625hrs received a wireless message from Captain 1st Rank Postelnikov that his unit was being pursued by German torpedoboats. Admiral Stark, who was near Schildau Buoy on his way to report, turned about and *Desna* took high speed towards the Kassar Wiek. Admiral Bakhirev also received this wireless message and therewith ordered the Chief of III Division Torpedoboat-Destroyers, Captain 1st Rank K V Shevelev, to take all the available boats on Kuiwast Roads, *Izyaslav, Novik, Zabiyaka* and *Grom*, and go to assist IV Division.

As *Desna* neared Seanina Buoy she met the retreating Russian unit and manoeuvred to open fire on the German 13 TBHF. The first salvo, ranged at 64 cable lengths, fell accurately and with this Kapitänleutnant Zander's unit developed a smoke screen and turned to the west. *Desna* continued to fire until extreme range and in all fired fifty-seven high-explosive shells. Shortly after, the group from Kuiwast approached, but the approach of darkness meant that both sides were calling it a day. From the German point of view, Hauptmann von Winterfeld at Orrisar did not require immediate support and the I FdT had ordered that the German boats should return to the west with nightfall. Therefore, towards 1605hrs Fregattenkapitän von Rosenberg ordered his boats to return to Soelo Sound, whilst 13 TBHF followed just behind. The Germans safely negotiated the narrow channel and by nightfall were lying safely at anchor in Poka Bay, not far from *Emden*. The I FdT knew that the Russians would return in strength the following day and requested reinforcements in the form of the large boats of 4th Torpedoboat Half Flotilla. Rear Admiral Stark took the Russian units back to Kuiwast Roads and left the two destroyers *Zabiyaka* and *Grom* to patrol along the meridian of Raugen Buoy.

The troop landing in Tagga Bay had progressed quickly. An assault section had disembarked half on each side of the bay, at Terwassa and Cape Merris, to quickly neutralize the batteries at Cape Hundsort and Cape Ninnast. The 131st Infantry Regiment landed on the western shore and quickly advanced to the southwest. By noon they had occupied Kielkond and Papensholm and had forced the Russians to retire. They then continued to the southeast along the road towards Menust and Arensburg. The 255th Reserve Infantry Regiment also landed on the western shore and advanced to the southeast, reaching Irro by nightfall. The 17th and 138th Infantry Regiments were landed on the eastern shore and likewise advanced to the south and east. By nightfall the bridgehead had been extended and was secure.

Meanwhile the landing southwest of Pamerort had begun. The first report to be sent back to the flotilla was: 'The inhabitants take us for Englishmen!' Troops hurried to Cape Pamerort to take the supposed battery there, but to their surprise nothing was found. The cyclists of I Battalion mounted their bikes and set off in three directions: south towards Arensburg, southeast towards Tikka and towards Konnau (Kenno). Their baggage train followed. They met several cavalry units on outpost duty but these were quickly dealt with. Towards evening they encountered stronger opposition as they reached the main road running from Arensburg to Moon.

The II Cyclist Battalion was only disembarked towards 1000hrs and the companies immediately set off along the north coast towards the stone dam: towards dusk they had reached the area of Orrisar and the Kleinen Sound. The Russians only occupied single farm houses and were taken completely by surprise, so that between fifty and eighty men were taken captive. A small bridgehead was occupied at the entrance to the stone dam and patrols were dispatched over the dam towards Moon. They were forced to retreat under a lively fire.

Around midnight Hauptmann von Winterfeld arrived at Orrisar with his *sturmkompanie* (assault company) and took command of the cyclists.

The troops were distributed as follows: three cyclist companies formed the line Saikla (1st Company) – Lewwal (3rd Company) – Neuenhof (2nd Company). The *sturmkompanie* was behind them as a reserve at Thomel and IV Company formed a bridgehead at the stone dam.

As day gave way to dusk on 12 October the following situation revealed itself: the surprise landings at Tagga Bay and Pamerort had been successful at comparatively low cost; the coastal batteries at Hundsort, Ninnast and Serro had been neutralized or captured; the transport fleet had entered Tagga Bay without loss and was engaged in disembarkation, whilst the anchorage was secure against submarines. The Soelo Sound had been reconnoitred and marked with buoys and good progress was being made with minesweeping in the Irben Straits. The air station at Papensholm had been captured intact. The 131st Infantry Regiment, reinforced by 17 Regt and 255R Regt, had captured the northwest corner of Ösel with a bridgehead that was deep enough to protect Tagga Bay against attack. Of the cyclist battalions that had been landed at Poka, I Battalion had advanced towards Arensburg and Tikka, whilst II Cyclist Battalion, together with Section Winterfeld and part of Sturmkompanie 18 had pushed eastwards along the coast and had only been halted in the Orrisar-Thomel area. Overall the Russian resistance had not been strong, except for that being encountered by Section Winterfeld, whose situation was becoming dangerous. It was very important for them to hold out as they had cut the Russian line of communication with Moon, but assistance for them would have to come from the sea. Therefore, the control of the Kassar Wiek was becoming increasingly important.

Earlier that afternoon Vizeadmiral Schmidt received a message from the Intelligence Department in Libau stating that a deciphered Russian wireless message indicated four submarines had departed Hango at about 1300hrs. With that the battleships not required in Tagga Bay were immediately detached to supplement their fuel stocks. At 1630hrs III Battle Squadron, with the exception of *Markgraf*, were detached to Putzig Wiek from where *Grosser Kurfürst* and *Bayern* would be dispatched to Kiel for repairs. The 15th Torpedoboat Half Flotilla would escort them. The *Markgraf* would remain with the Special Unit and anchored in Tagga Bay. The IV Battle Squadron were likewise to remain in Tagga Bay and towards 1930hrs passed through the net barrier and anchored. Meanwhile, the III Battle Squadron began their journey at around 1700hrs but proceeded at slow speed to allow *Bayern* to catch up. Towards 1820hrs she joined her squadron at a speed of 11 knots, but soon had to reduce speed as her bulkheads were beginning to suffer. Further speed reductions followed and finally at 2000hrs she had to stop near Point Gamma for an hour while her collapsing bulkheads were shored up with timber. *Bayern*'s situation was becoming serious and Vizeadmiral Behncke decided to detach her back to the Tagga Bay. This message was passed by searchlight and *Kronprinz* and three torpedoboats were dispatched as escorts. Towards 2230hrs Vizeadmiral Schmidt sent a recovery group consisting of 3rd Torpedoboat Half Flotilla to Point Gamma to assist. By 2100hrs *Bayern* was making just 4 knots and only at 0130hrs on 13 October did she reach Point White. Now *Bayern* was again forced to stop and only recommenced her journey at 0530hrs. The whole time torpedoboats circled her as an anti-submarine screen. Finally the stricken battleship entered Tagga Bay and at 0930hrs dropped anchor, whereupon the difficult and time-consuming temporary repair work was begun. On 17 October, minesweepers found the Russian mine barrier onto which *Bayern* had run. It consisted of spherical, lead-capped mines with an explosive charge of 100 to 120 kilograms. In consideration of this charge and the resulting damage it seemed likely that the compressed air accumulators in cell 12, which were used to launch torpedoes, had exploded with the detonation of the mine, and added to its destructive effect.

After the appearance of the German invasion fleet the Russian command had been quick to react. Already at 1025hrs Vice Admiral Bakhirev received the following telegram from the Commander of the Fleet, Rear Admiral Razvozov:

> A copy for your attention. I confirm the commitment to hold Sworbe and Zerel as I think they are entirely necessary for the conduct of resolute, active operations against the enemy's armies landed on Ösel. For this purpose I have requested the Commander in Chief for reinforcement of the Ösel group of armies. I myself have dispatched the 'Death Battalion' and in addition the 173rd Regiment.

Command of the 'Death Battalion', a special unit created by the provisional government of Russia for use in special actions, was given to the hitherto commander of *Gavriil*, Captain 2nd Rank P O Shishko, who had previously successfully led the landings at Domesnas in October 1915. Further troops were to be assembled in Hapsal. However, not all of the Russian commanders were of a like mind about resolute defence. When he received reports about the landing, the commander ashore, Rear Admiral Sveshnikov, immediately planned to leave Arensburg for Hapsal on the mainland, to lead the defence from there. Vice Admiral Bakhirev believed it was necessary for him and his staff to remain on Moon Island to maintain communications with the Army. Nevertheless, Rear Admiral Sveshnikov boarded the gunboat *Chrabry*, which was transferring to Kuiwast together with the gunboat *Chivinetz*, and arrived in Kuiwast at 0600hrs on October 13th. Later that same day, during the evening, and after discussions over the telegraph with the fleet commander, Rear Admiral Sveshnikov departed for Hapsal of his own volition.

During the evening of 12 October, Vice Admiral Bakhirev requested Rear Admiral Stark to assemble the division chiefs to determine, in detail, the condition of the forces and to develop plans to expel the Germans from the Kassar Wiek, which as Vice Admiral Bakhirev said, 'had a tremendous importance to the safety of Moon Sound'.

At the conference it was learned that the condition of the torpedoboat-destroyers had been found to be satisfactory in general. It was also decided to try to clear the Kassar Wiek of German torpedoboats the following morning; the modern destroyers of the *Novik* type were designated for this task, with the support of the heavy and long- ranged guns of the gunboats *Chrabry* and *Chivinetz* from Arensburg. By far the most important part of the plan was the operation that was to blockade the Soelo Sound. This would be accomplished by sinking the steamer *Latvia* in the channel and laying a mine barrier there. An order was sent to Rogekul to prepare *Latvia* for this purpose and for the shallow-draught minelayer *Pripyat* to take aboard sixty mines and go to the Moon Sound. Admiral Bakhirev entrusted execution of this operation to Rear Admiral Stark.

A further event occurred during the night. A train carrying mines was wrecked in Rogekul and the mines detonated. Red hot glowing splinters started spontaneous fires on the breakwater and flames threatened to burn *Pripyat*. The minelayer was compelled to cast off. There was general panic but Leitenant Shternberg and some sailors and workers successfully extinguished the flames and prevented potentially enormous destruction at the base. Admiral Bakhirev believed the wrecking of the train was the work of German agents.

Vice Admiral Bakhirev's final action for the night was to organize a landing party of eighty-six men from the big ships, under command of Michman Klesti, to bolster defences at the stone dam.

Notes

1. Leutnant zur See Lindemann was later commander of the battleship *Bismarck* .
2. 1 sazhen is 2.13 metres.
3. Severski was later the founder of the Republic Aircraft Corporation in the United States.

CHAPTER THREE

13 October: The Germans Trapped at Orrisar

The quiet, foggy weather which had dominated the first day of the operation was replaced on the morning of 13 October by a fresh wind from the south-southwest at strength 6 to 7, and although Tagga bay was sheltered, this increased the difficulty of the unloading work. In addition there were periods of rain.

At dawn the destroyers *Avtroil* and *Leitenant Il'in* were dispatched to Domesnas for reconnaissance. Near Rüno they were overflown by two German aircraft which were taken under fire. They did not find any German units and subsequently returned to Kuiwast.

In accordance with the plans developed at the conference the previous evening, at dawn, around 0500hrs, Rear Admiral Stark departed Kuiwast Roads for the Kassar Wiek with the torpedoboat-destroyers *Novik*, *Izyaslav*, *Samson*, *Pobeditel* and *Razyashchi*. The torpedoboat-destroyer *Konstantin* did not depart until later because of engine defects. At Raugen Buoy they were joined by *Zabiyaka* and *Grom*. To provide support Vice Admiral Bakhirev ordered *Graschdanin* to proceed to Schildau so that she could fire into Kassar Wiek and the Kleinen Sound. A little later *Chivinetz* was dispatched to Rear Admiral Stark to assist with her long-range artillery, whilst *Chrabry* had to replenish her coal stocks on Kuiwast Roads. As mentioned, these two gunboats had departed Arensburg at midnight, and had arrived at Kuiwast at 0600hrs.

The destroyers were to be split into the following pairs: *Novik* and *Grom*, *Izyaslav* and *Konstantin*, *Pobeditel* and *Zabiyaka* and *Desna* and *Samson*. However, as *Konstantin* was delayed, and *Desna* had wound a steel cable around a propeller whilst moving away from an oiler, *Samson* was paired with *Izyaslav*. *Razyashchi* was attached to *Novik* for communications.

At 0731hrs a German aircraft reported the approach of eight Russian destroyers in the Kassar Wiek, steering towards Soelo Sound. Around this time Fregattenkapitän von Rosenberg's S-Flotilla were manoeuvring in the western entrance of the Soelo Sound. To support the S-Flotilla, towards

0745hrs *Emden* weighed anchor and moved northwards into shallow water, bringing herself closer to the picket flotilla. *Novik* and *Grom*, followed by *Razyashchi*, took course on the eastern entrance to Soelo Sound and at 0950hrs, as the range reached 55 cables (10,050 metres), they opened a concentrated fire on the nearest of the German boats. The Russian group manoeuvred to the north at slow speed and then stopped engines. As the area behind Cape Pamerort was revealed to them a German cruiser, *Emden*, came into view. At 0756hrs *Emden* opened fire on the Russians at a range of 13,800 metres and quickly obtained straddling salvoes. The Russian boats increased speed to 15 knots and moved off to the east, whilst the S-Flotilla moved off to the west. During the exchange of fire *Grom* lost her wireless antenna and both boats were showered in splinters, but there were no casualties.

The German boats took further soundings and *Emden* shifted her anchorage to the shallows south of Serro, a further 2,000 metres closer to the Russians. Meanwhile Rear Admiral Stark took all his torpedoboat-destroyers to the meridian of Cape Pavasterort, where they anchored in readiness.

In the meantime the torpedoboat-destroyer *Konstantin* had approached and together with *Izyaslav* was ordered to guard the eastern exit of Soelo Sound, outside the range of the cruiser.

At 0930hrs *Izyaslav* and *Konstantin* entered into an exchange of fire with *Emden* and then moved off. By this time the weather had changed for the worse. There was light rain and wind and the view of the horizon had considerably deteriorated. Nevertheless, a German signal station, established on Pamerort the previous day, assisted *Emden* with observations and directing fire.

At 1000hrs, B98 and the 4th Torpedoboat Half Flotilla arrived to reinforce the I FdT, Kommodore Heinrich, aboard *Emden*; a conference was then held between Kommodore Heinrich, Fregattenkapitän von Rosenberg, Korvettenkapitän Faulborn and Kapitänleutnant Zander. They were in agreement that an advance into the Kassar Wiek by their forces was still premature without heavy support to help force the Russians back. Therefore the presence of a battleship was requested for the following morning. The intervening period would allow further soundings to be taken in the treacherous channel and the 13 TBHF to replenish their depleted ammunition stocks, much of which had been expended in the preliminary bombardment at Papensholm. For the time being Vice Admiral Bakhirev and the Russian destroyers had gained sea mastery in the Kassar Wiek.

In the meantime further Russian forces arrived on the Kassar Wiek. At 1220hrs, when the weather had become clearer, Rear Admiral Stark ordered the newly-arrived gunboat *Chivinetz* to go to *Izyaslav* and *Konstantin* and use her long-range guns to drive *Emden* away, whilst staying out of range herself. *Chivinetz'* guns were ranged to 93 cable-lengths, or 17,000 metres, and Admiral Stark thought that *Emden's* 15cm pieces were limited to 85 cable-lengths. However, *Emden* had a slight advantage with a range of 17,600 metres.

Chivinetz approached Soelo Sound at about 1300hrs and turned to port onto a southerly course. *Emden* opened fire when the Russian gunboat came within range and straddled with the second salvo. After completing the turn the gunboat opened fire with single, deliberate shots. These fell some 80 to 300 metres short of *Emden*, but from the gunboat observation was almost impossible in the haze. The gunboat suffered from the disadvantage that observation to the east was better than to the west. However, although straddled, *Chivinetz* remained unhit. Under these conditions the Russian gunboat moved away to the east.

At around 1200hrs *Pobeditel*, with the chief of I Division Torpedoboat-Destroyers aboard, was sent along with *Zabiyaka* to replace *Izyaslav* and *Konstantin* guarding the eastern entrance of Soelo Sound.

The afternoon then passed quietly in Soelo Sound and the Kassar Wiek and later the I FdT directed *Emden* and the torpedoboats to take up new anchorages close under the shore near Poka. In assuming these positions V82, the *leaderboot* of the 13 TBHF, ran onto a shoal and damaged her starboard propeller so badly that she had to be dispatched to Libau for repairs. Kapitänleutnant Zander shifted his pennant to S61 and the 13 TBHF now had only four combat-ready boats.

Towards 1500hrs, Rear Admiral Stark sent *Chivinetz* and the torpedoboat-destroyers to anchor near Seanina Buoy.

At about 1100hrs, in accordance with Vice Admiral Bakhirev's orders, the tug *Black Sea Nr 2* appeared from Rogekul towing the steamer *Latvia*, which was designated as the blockship for Soelo Sound. The tow unit was escorted by the torpedoboat-destroyer *Amurets*. The wind was a fresh southerly. As the unit passed Rukeraga the tow parted and as *Latvia* did not have steam up she drifted onto a shoal of the island. The ship could not be got off the shoal in time to make Soelo Sound that night and therefore Rear Admiral Stark decided to confine his effort to the production of a mine barrier by *Pripyat*.

The shallow-draught minelayer *Pripyat*, under the command of Leitenant S I Medvedev, arrived on the Kassar Wiek at 1500hrs. Admiral Stark gave Leitenant Medvedev his assignment to lay mines in the eastern entrance of Soelo Sound. The torpedoboat *Razyashchi* was assigned to escort *Pripyat* to the mine barrier position, and then return with her to Kassar Wiek Buoy, where *Novik* and *Samson* would be waiting.

Whilst waiting for darkness to arrive, *Pripyat* and *Razyashchi* remained on the meridian of Cape Pavasterort. Whilst in this position the sailors of *Pripyat* categorically refused to conduct the minelaying mission. Their reasons were the difficulty of preparing the mines to be laid in the rain, the nearness of the enemy, and the fact that the torpedoboats had moved off to the east. Two sailors said to Leitenant Medvedev that they had laid mines in the Irben Straits and to the east of Zerel in these conditions, and that it was dangerous and difficult, and therefore they should return to Admiral Stark at Kassar Buoy. Vice Admiral Bakhirev wrote:

> Neither the requests of the commander, nor his indication of the extreme importance of the operation, or the exceptionally favourable circumstances, nor the persuasion of two or three senior sailors who maintained their honour – nothing could influence the men to perform their military duty, and *Pripyat* joined the group of shamed.

The significance of the failure of *Pripyat* to carry out this assigned mission was immense. The addition of a mine barrier would greatly increase the difficulty of negotiating the narrow, fractious sea lane and it would be easier for the Russian units to prevent a breakthrough. Protecting the waters of Moon Sound was essential for the Russians. If the Kassar Wiek was secure, the torpedoboats and gunboats used in its defense could be redeployed to the Riga Gulf and the Irben Straits, where they were urgently required.

On the late evening of 12 October, at 2355hrs, the German Army staff issued orders for the following day. The advance would be made in two columns: 255R Regt would march on Lad'yala, 7km NNE of Arensburg, and 65th Infantry Brigade (17 Regt and 138 Regt) would march on Khazik, 20km NE of Arensburg. The 131st Infantry Regt, which had been in support, was ordered to concentrate at Menust. There they were reinforced by 77th Company and were ordered to immediately advance on the Sworbe Peninsula.

At 0530hrs on the morning of 13 October, 255R Regt, which had lodged for the night at Irro, moved off through Tavi, where they encountered 131 Regt, which had advanced as far as Pajekül. A report from an aircraft confirmed the reports of 131 Regt; the Russians had occupied positions at Menust and Kergel and were firing from heavy and light artillery. It was quickly established that the Russian northern flank rested on the church at Kergel. The regimental commander, Oberst Berring, ordered an attack for 1100hrs by 5th Company against the Russian right flank. The attack was successful and the company captured 150 men and 5 machine guns.

After winning this fight at Kergel, 78th Company, 255R Regt, continued advancing towards Karmis. The regiment's 80th Company was ordered to pursue the enemy in the direction of Arensburg and to clear any Russian positions encountered.

At 1530hrs the regiment reached Iraze (Irrasse), 10km north of Arensburg, in a very tired condition and settled down to rest. They had reached their appointed position for this day. Hardly had the regiment entered the village and settled down than the sound of horse hooves was heard from the rear. Von Tschischwitz quoted the following: 'What the?! We don't have any cavalry with us. Blast! It is the Russians'. He continued:

> Already the squadron was clattering past down the village street, at it's head was the Regimental Commander. The isolated Russian unit was moving away from the Landing Corps to the east. But instead of waiting for darkness and reducing the risk, the Russian Colonel was now leading his Regiment to certain death. Badly hit he plunged to the ground, and his and the following squadron were either shot or taken captive. The innumerable horse cadavers delayed the advance until the following morning.

At midday it was already clear 131 Regt were no longer required to assist in the east and therefore they were ordered to begin the advance to Sworbe. At 1340hrs the regiment set off to the south, but was repeatedly delayed by groups of Russians. Therefore I and II Battalions were ordered to Tatterselya and the advanced guard to Tekhmardi (Tehomardi), at the northern end of the Sworbe Peninsula. The highway between Arensburg and Sworbe was now cut and the garrison at Sworbe was cut off. Almost the entire Russian 425th Infantry Regiment was now isolated. During the evening the regimental train had joined 131 Regt, together with 5th Battery of the 8th Field Artillery.

At around 0930hrs that morning, the second column of the German advance, 65th Brigade, concentrated at Sauvere. The 17th Infantry Regiment arrived from Karro and 138 Regt arrived from Vesike. Unlike the 255R Regt a few kilometers to the south, the brigade met little resistance and the advanced guard, 1st and 3rd Company of 138 Regt along with 6th Battery, 8th Field Artillery, under the command of Major Falck, reached Karmezap, where they settled down to rest.

Meanwhile reports were received that 1st Company of I Battalion, and 4th and 5th Companies at Kelyala, were engaged in combat with superior Russian forces which were attempting to break out in a northerly direction along the road towards Orrisar. It was reported that Medel was occupied by Russians in great strength.

The III Battalion of 138 Regt advanced on Karmel-east and came under heavy rifle and machine-gun fire from north of Uduvere. The 6th Company suffered mounting losses as they approached within 800 metres of the Russian position and were under constant enemy fire. A frontal assault would obviously fail and suffer great losses, so I Battalion dispatched two companies to the north of Karmel and one to the south. In support, 6th

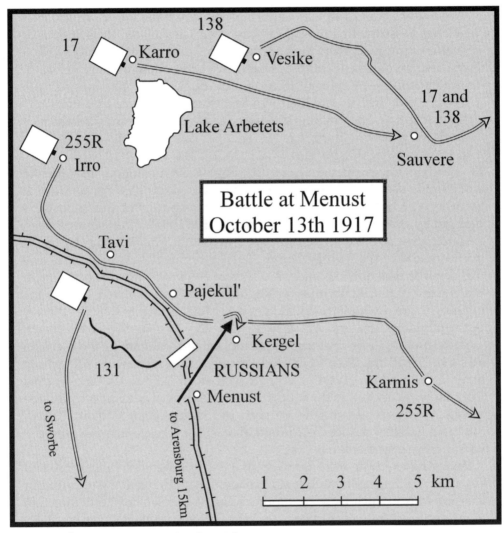

Map 4: The Battle at Menust, October 13th.

Battery, 8th Field Artillery, went into action. The battle in the wood lasted until darkness and was vicious, with 138 Regt mounting a hand-grenade attack at one stage. When darkness arrived, a large part of the Russian force, 1000 men of the 426th Regiment, had been taken into captivity, along with light guns and numerous machine guns. The remainder of the 426th Regiment departed in an easterly direction.

The 138 Regt commander, Oberst Matthiass, then swung his column north along the road, to deny this route to Orrisar to the Russians, to restore communication with the division, which he presumed was at Tikka, and to obtain his allotted objective of Khazik. However, the battle had delayed the Germans so that Khazik could not be reached, and only between 2200hrs and 2300hrs did the brigade pitch camp, 138 Regt at Putla and 17 Regt at Mustla. Parts of the brigade were still without their train and machine guns, although some local supplies had been requisitioned and these proved sufficient.

As mentioned previously, I Cyclist Battalion had landed near Pamerort and then set off in three directions along roads to the south. The 2nd Company of this battalion had some skirmishes with the enemy south of Karmel. About midday they came in contact with 138 Regt who were also facing Karmel.

The 1st Company of the I Cyclist Battalion was repeatedly attacked by superior Russian forces supported by field artillery, near Uduvere, so that the Germans were compelled to retreat a little to the north.

The 4th and 5th Companies of the I Cyclist Battalion had advanced in a southwards direction and had either captured or repulsed any Russians they encountered. By 1300hrs they had reached Kel'yala on the southern highway between Arensburg and Orrisar, and captured a Russian battery which was enroute to Orrisar. Subsequently, however, the two German companies were forced to retreat 2km to the north under considerable pressure from Russian forces. Further to the north, 6th Company, I Cyclist Battalion, under Major Sluyter, advanced as far as Khazik, and 3rd Company advanced to Tikka.

The windy and rainy weather on 13 October caused many difficulties for the troops; in particular the muddy roads, with mud up to 10 to 20cm deep, caused great difficulties for the cyclists. Even so, I Cyclist Battalion ranged over a wide front and prevented the Russian forces utilizing the northern road from Arensburg to Orrisar, through Tikka and Tagafer. The action by some cyclists and the 138 Regt at Uduvere had stopped a Russian attempt to retreat.

During the night of 12/13 October, the II Cyclist Battalion and Section Winterfeld occupied Orrisar and the surrounding area. Their left flank lay on the Kleinen Sound, their right on a marsh. There was open ground to the north and south. From the east and west it was only possible to

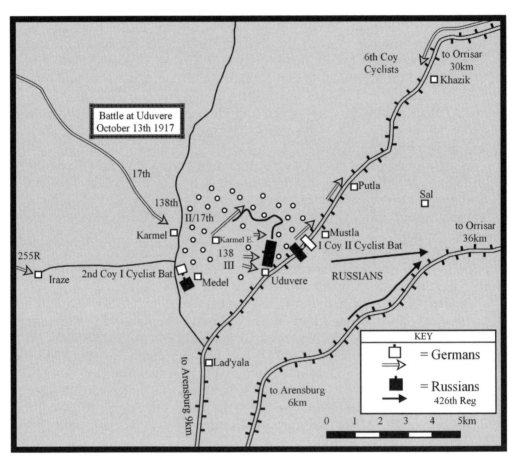

Map 5: The Battle at Uduvere on October 13th.

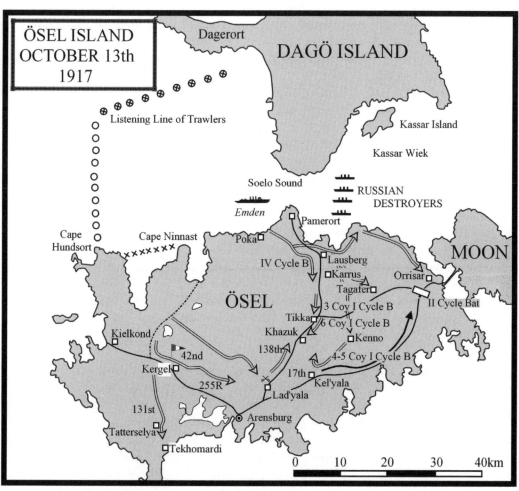

Map 6: Overview Ösel Island October 13th 1917.

approach this position in columns, from the east across the stone dam over the Kleinen Sound, and from the west along the highway from Tagafer to Orrisar, running through the marsh.

During the evening of 12 October the commander of the Russian 107th Division, General Ivanov, ordered the troops at Arensburg to fall back towards Moon, a general retreat. It was the Russian intention to occupy the prepared positions around Orrisar and await reinforcements to come from the mainland, via Moon and the stone dam. The Russian leadership had no idea that these positions had already been occupied by Section Winterfeld and the cyclists.

The first units to be dispatched to the rear were the support units. Convoys of vehicles, the baggage train, and a field hospital retreated towards the stone dam. As the front vehicles, loaded with officers, roared into Lewwal, they clashed with the 3rd Cyclist Company. The Russians were taken under fire and were forced to ground. The unsuspecting military field hospital ended up in the same position after being taken under fire by German machine guns. Their escort could manage only a few shots. The numerous ensuing baggage trains met a similar fate. A long convoy of 130 vehicles was bringing the officers' baggage to safety, together with women and friends of the officers, and they also fell victim to the German troops. The escorting troops gave battle for a quarter of an hour before they too surrendered into captivity. A desolate scene remained of wrecked vehicles, horse cadavers and dead and wounded Russians. Still others retreated.

A member of the staff of the 2nd Aerial Division, Yakov Popov, gave this description of the retreat from Arensburg:

Along the highway from Arensburg was an almost continuous crowd of soldiers with and without rifles and in places were drawn up long strings of vehicles which we left behind. A mass of carts and horses was being dragged along the road. To their sides wandered others, exhausted to the last degree, with hung heads as they retreated. In one place a heap of boxes had been thrown out which contained books and papers - like some clerical office. Elsewhere we passed a burning lorry. This was a sad and oppressing sight, and was painful and offensive, and would bring you to tears. We arrived eight *verst* [8½ kilometers] from Orrisar, always passing the remains of chattels. Ahead of us there turned out to be Germans, and one must say the highway was jammed with several rows of conveyances, complete with soldiers, and beside the highway a thick crowd had already gathered, mostly without rifles. Up ahead climbed the sound of desultory rifle fire...the soldiers pushed to the sides and back in a wave, the carts began to turn back and there was then unimaginable trouble on the highway. Subsequently everything calmed down and again moved forward, and again the same story was repeated. An officer on horseback came along the road and prevailed on them for any men with rifles to go ahead in order to blast the way along the highway, but no-one came out. I only saw a group of sailors, about fifteen to twenty men, with rifles, by-pass the mess in a field and then scatter.... We travelled back and forth along the road until evening, and I came to the conclusion that something must be done. At this time the members of the Brigade Committee who had seized an automobile from a village came along the road from Arensburg. It turned out that the automobile met the Germans, and the people were in part killed and partly taken into captivity. Then only motorbikes and bicycles came along.

Nevertheless, the battle to the southwest of the stone dam was increasing in intensity. Russian troops advanced and appeared before the 1st, 2nd and 3rd Cyclist Companies. These three companies were spread over a 7km long front. Towards 1100hrs a strong Russian force attacked the 3rd Company, but they could not affect a breakthrough. About 100 Russians were taken prisoner. By 1400hrs this number had risen to 500, but this only served to weaken the number of German troops at the front.

Towards midday the 5th and 6th Cyclist Companies arrived near Thomel from Tagafer. They were positioned as a welcome reserve.

The 2nd Company occupied the earthworks to the south of Neuenhof. They were attacked constantly during the day by groups of Russians numbering between thirty and fifty men. Their advanced position was exposed on the flanks, particularly when the Russian troops turned off the road south of Thomel and advanced to the east, towards the stone dam. The 2nd Company was in danger of being surrounded and cut off. At 1600hrs the company was attacked at Neuenhof by a considerably superior Russian force, supported by machine guns and artillery, and the 2nd Company could no longer hold their position. After a vicious fight, the German cyclist company retreated through Saltak Manor towards the stone dam.

The Russian landing corps under the command of Michman (Sublieutenant) Klesti, also attacked across the Moon Island stone dam. Klesti and his detachment stayed on the stone dam until 15 October, when the Death Battalion arrived from Reval for the defense of the dam. It was reported that the 'defense of the dam lay exclusively with the sailors of the landing corps, because those from the company of the Dankov Regiment retreated away, abandoning all when the first enemy shots were heard'.

The 4th Cyclist Company were holding this area and found themselves being attacked from the south and from the stone dam. They were also under fire from Battery No 36 on Moon. The company was under

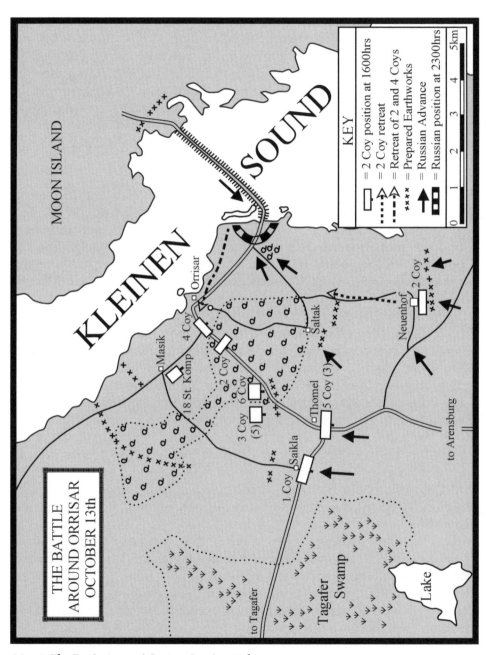

Map 7: The Battle Around Orrisar October 13th.

considerable pressure and requested Hauptmann von Winterfeld to allow them to retreat. Hauptmann von Winterfeld wanted to see the situation for himself and at 1500hrs went from Thomel to Orrisar. At 1700hrs he dispatched Sturmkompanie 18 to replace the 4th Company, which was sent to Orrisar as a reserve.

At around 1900hrs, just as the exchange was being completed, some elements of 2nd Company from Neuenhof arrived. The situation was becoming very serious – to have the Russians dug in at Saltak Manor would mean that the German forces at Thomel were outflanked and that the Russians were no longer cut off. Hauptmann von Winterfeld realized the gravity off the situation and immediately ordered the 2nd Company back to Saltak manor and to dig themselves in there. As the company departed, heavy machine-gun fire and gunfire was heard from the direction of Orrisar and the surrounding coppices. Hauptmann von Winterfeld committed his reserve, the 4th Company, there.

Thus a critical night battle began and continued for some hours. The Russians maintained a dogged advance towards the stone dam. The German forces resisted stubbornly. The assault company was hard pressed as the Russian landing party, under Michman Klesti, again attacked across the stone dam from Moon into their rear. The savage fight was continued at such close quarters that hand grenades were thrown as ammunition began to run low. The Germans retreated towards Orrisar and were in danger of being cut off.

At 2230hrs, with ammunition running low, Hauptmann von Winterfeld was compelled to make the difficult decision to clear his position, and the Germans began a general retreat. The 4th Company remained on the road from Orrisar to Thomel. The 2nd Company was dispatched 500 metres along the road towards Thomel to maintain communications with the other units of II Cyclist Battalion. Sturmkompanie 18 went towards Masik as a reserve.

Hauptmann von Winterfeld's position had indeed become very serious. He was 60km from Tagga Bay and running low on ammunition. The Russian forces were in command of the stone dam and their troops were pushing forward from the south. Oberst von Tschishwitz was quite correct when he later referred to the German force as 'Winterfeld's Small Spartan Band'. However, he could not know that the Russians themselves were under considerable pressure and were in considerable disarray.

Ensign Ver, the Adjutant of the 3rd Independent Battalion of Artillery of the Sea Front, Moon Sound, wrote:

We were together again and two *verst* (2.1 kilometers) from Thomel, where we had information that the enemy resided. Here also was the crew of Battery No 46 and some of the 107th Infantry Division, two batteries of field artillery, together with one hundred Frontier Guards. Individual shots were heard. After a conference, part of the carts, several automobiles and people became fearful and set off, going back to Arensburg. Another group, including some support troops and part of the crew of Battery 46, also feared to go further, and remained at that place, whilst the greater part decided to break through and went further ahead. The artillery went forward, and the cavalry went to the sides, and altogether the others occupied a line of more than two *verst*. Around an estate at Thomel the machine-gun crew caught up, and moved to the west, and here there was an initial exchange of fire. The field artillery opened fire on a building, occupied by the enemy, at a mill on the estate near Thomel…. Initially there was a brisk exchange of rifle and machine-gun fire. The fight continued for half an hour and was accompanied by an attack by the enemy, which was beaten off and the highway was cleared to the right of Thomel. During this fight several sailors, formerly of the Intelligence Service, were killed. At the beginning of the fight many soldiers had shown the desire to unharness the horses and make off to Arensburg, and they had to be urged forwards with pistols in hands. In the darkness [and rain] it was possible to drive some of the carts around the enemy and the forwardmost cart finally stopped near the dam which led to the island of Moon. Here, again, the scouts discovered the enemy, with a machine gun. The enemy launched a rocket which illuminated the string of transport vehicles, and set fire to a hay barn beside the dam, so that all the transport was brightly illuminated, and then opened fire on the transport column with machine-gun fire.

At this time heavy gunfire began, which fortunately flew over the transports, and candescent shells exploded. [Subsequently it turned out that this fire came from Battery No 36 at Woi.]

All along the dam was illuminated by searchlight. When the artillery and first part of the transport drove out onto the dam, the heavy machine-gun fire of the enemy split the transport into two parts. Besides twenty horses and several people being killed, there were many wounded. It became necessary for the second part of the transport, with whom I was, to spend the night in the forest beside the stone dam. During the night, Ensign Doronin, with weapon in hand, took some more of the transport across the dam, and, just as the first part, they safely reached Moon and Kuiwast. The third part of the transport, with whom I found myself, rested on Ösel and some wished to surrender into captivity (already three white flags had been hung out) and at the cost of considerable effort 20 armed men were found and attacked the Germans, who sat beside the stone dam and whom were twenty in number. By this time some Germans, being about one hundred in number, approached from Thomel, and took us in the rear, opening fire with machine-guns, and the Germans by the dam also fired on us. But the losses were not in vain. At that time an armoured car from Moon drove half way across the dam to meet us. Only then was the transport column successfully convinced to move again, and as nobody wanted to be first, I set a cart in motion. On the dam, among the heaps of slaughtered people and horses, we took onto our cart about ten boxes of machine gun ribbons, thanks to the exceptional energy of one soldier, and we found among the horses one gun. When we went out onto the dam several of the enemy men fired at us from the small island to the right of the dam, but no harm occurred. On Moon a German floatplane whirled all around us and brought great panic.

The general retreat from Arensburg came as an unpleasant surprise for Vice Admiral Bakhirev. In addition to the retreat of the 107th Division and the flight of Rear Admiral Sveshnikov, the other Russian naval forces also fled the capital. Admiral Bakhirev wrote:

> Despite my order to remain in Arensburg and maintain a patrol and provide artillery support for the ground forces, the chief of the 5th Torpedoboat-Destroyer Division, Captain 1st Rank Zelenov, autocratically and without warning, removed the communications post in Arensburg and at about 1700hrs arrived in Kuiwast Roads with *Vsadnik* and *Zabaikalets*... The chief of the 5th Division accepted many soldiers aboard the torpedoboats, who had retreated from other parts. Afterwards they were found to be deserters.

These men later congregated on Kuiwast pier and sought to be transported across to the mainland. Admiral Bakhirev had them formed into units to help with the defence of Moon Island.

When the garrison at Zerel heard that the troops at Arensburg had retreated to Moon, the men of batteries No 43 and No 44 organized general meetings to discuss events. Delegates were sent to the isthmus to clarify the situation and they found the 4th Company, Guard Regiment, who were determined to keep the Germans from Zerel, and keep the batteries intact. The batteries carried the resolution 'to resist until the last shell'. However, the committee sent a message to Rear Admiral Stark demanding that torpedoboats and transports be sent immediately, so that when the last shell was spent they could be evacuated. Admiral Bakhirev sent an encouraging reply, and promised he would go to Sworbe the following day with *Bayan*.

In addition the capable Army Commander, General Henrikhson, had been assigned to take over the defense of Ösel. He immediately ordered a counterattack, but apparently he did not know that Arensburg had already been abandoned and Orrisar was occupied by German forces.

Despite the poor weather on 13 October, the Commander-in-Chief of Reconnaissance Forces of the Baltic (BdAdO), Kontreadmiral Hopman, reported good progress with minesweeping in the Irben Straits, so that on the evening of that day he was ordered to breakthrough with his forces to Arensburg as soon as possible. The II Minesweeper Flotilla and Sperrbrechergruppe would begin work immediately. The battleships *König* and *Kronprinz*, escorted by the 15th Torpedoboat Half Flotilla, would arrive in the Irben Straits on 15 October, after returning from fuel replenishment in the Putziger Wiek.

CHAPTER FOUR

14 October: The Battle on the Kassar Wiek

At daybreak on 14 October Rear Admiral Stark dispatched the Chief of I Division Torpedoboat-Destroyers, Captain 2nd Rank Pilsudski, to the Kassar Wiek with the destroyers *Pobeditel*, *Zabiyaka*, *Grom* and *Konstantin*, to reconnoitre the situation in the Soelo Sound. The gunboat *Chivinetz*, which was anchored near Moon Sound buoy, was also placed at his disposal. The remainder of the torpedoboat-destroyers would stay on Kuiwast Roads. After replenishing her coal stocks on Kuiwast Roads, the gunboat *Chrabry*, known to the Germans as 'Chablis', would also go to the Kassar Wiek, whilst the battleship *Graschdanin* would remain to the west of Schildau in support. At 0600hrs the gunboat *Grozyashchi* went to Rogekul for repair work. The shield of the stern gun, which had split, was removed and a diver examined the underwater damage, a crack in the hull, and began blocking up the hole.

The destroyers *Ukraina* and *Voiskovoi* were dispatched to Zerel for reconnaissance and to support the beleaguered battery and troops, especially if the Germans went on the offensive. No German forces were discovered, so the chief of the III Division Torpedoboat-Destroyers was dispatched for reconnaissance near Cape Domesnas with the destroyers *Izyaslav*, *Avtroil* and *Gavriil*. The English submarine C32 was also dispatched to the Domesnas position number 2.

It can be seen that the German two-pronged attack, through the Irben Straits and Soelo Sound, was causing a division of the valuable Russian torpedoboat-destroyers, even though they still had sea mastery on the Kassar Wiek and the German minesweeping operations in the Irben Straits were progressing only slowly. The failure of *Pripyat* to produce a mine barrier in the exit of Soelo Sound was being revealed as a failure with escalating consequences, and the shortage, because of unserviceabilities, of shallow-draught minelayers and light forces in the Irben Straits was also very serious. Further reinforcements would have been welcome. Vice Admiral Bakhirev wrote:

Owing to the assumption that the enemy had a swept channel along the southern shoreline of the Irben Straits, and could possibly break into the Riga Gulf with his torpedoboats and cruisers, I stressed the necessity of having the long-range artillery of the cruisers *Bogatyr* and *Oleg* present, and as the cruisers had previously served under me for more than a year and had participated in several campaigns against the German coast I knew their capabilities. Their transfer to me was refused.

Vice Admiral Bakhirev had also intended to take the flagship, *Bayan*, to the Irben Straits during the morning, but the arrival of the Fleet Commander, Kontreadmiral Razvozov, and Major-General Henrikhson, forced him to postpone this operation. They arrived on Kuiwast Roads at 1000hrs after the torpedoboat *Finn* collected them from Rogekul. A report of the previous day's events was made, and plans and assumptions concerning future actions were given. Vice Admiral Bakhirev was given guidelines for operations by the fleet commander and then at 1030hrs he raised his flag on *Bayan* and departed for the Irben Straits, together with the torpedoboat-destroyers *Desna*, *Leitenant Il'in*, *General Kondratenko*, *Pogranitschnik* and *Zabaikalets*. At the exit of Kuiwast Roadstead *General Kondratenko* suffered engine damage and was forced to return to Kuiwast.

Near Cape Domesnas the *Bayan* group encountered the returning III Div TBD, whose chief reported by semaphore that nothing had been observed near Domesnas. Because of the lateness of the hour and anxious about the situation on the Kassar Wiek, where Rear Admiral Stark had been left in command and had requested reinforcements, Admiral Bakhirev turned back towards Kuiwast at 1217hrs. Captain 1st Rank Shevelev, commanding III Div TBD, went to 25 knots speed to return to Kuiwast as swiftly as possible. Southeast of Abro the detachment was attacked by a German U-boat. The torpedo passed behind *Bayan* and under the stern of *Pogranitschnik*, which was traveling to port, astern of the flagship. According to German reports the Russian unit was sighted by the U-boats UC57 and UC78. Whilst UC57 did not get an opportunity to attack, the UC78 was able to dive under the escorting destroyer screen and at around 1307hrs approached unseen to within 300 metres of *Bayan*. However, owing to an unfortunate accident the torpedo jammed fast in its tube when firing was attempted, but the bubbles from the launch attempt were seen from the cruiser and she stood away to the east at high speed. When the detachment entered Kuiwast at about 1730hrs (1930hrs Russian time) it was already dark.

The German plan to obtain sea mastery in the Kassar Wiek on 14 October called for the battleship *Kaiser* and the cruiser *Emden* to occupy positions at the entrance to Soelo Sound to provide fire support for the torpedoboat flotillas, which were to break through the Soelo Sound and then divide into four groups to comb the Kassar Wiek as far as the western entrance to the Moon Sound. T144 and six A-boats would follow the larger T-boats into the Kassar Wiek and then break off for the Kleinen Sound, where they would support the embattled Section Winterfeld near Orrisar. Accordingly, at 0600hrs, *Emden* weighed anchor and moved to the new position. Soon after, *Kaiser*, escorted by V46 and S50, arrived and dropped anchor near Cape Pank. After *Kaiser*'s foreseen anchorage had been swept for mines and sounded for shoals the battleship finally took up her station southwest of the entrance to Soelo Sound at 1145hrs.

The weather was clear and the visibility was good. The wind was a weak southerly. The Russian destroyers *Pobeditel*, *Zabiyaka*, *Grom* and *Konstantin* observed *Emden* at 0730hrs and advanced at slow speed. They anchored northwest of Cape Pavasterort, outside the range of the cruiser's guns, with short chains and ready to move quickly.

At 1000hrs the gunboat *Chrabry* approached I Div TBD. The division chief, Captain 2nd Rank Pilsudski, ordered her to reconnoitre the entrance to the Kleinen Sound, and to bombard the cape on her return journey. A demonstration of sea supremacy by the Russian forces would have been demoralizing for the German troops at Orrisar, who had requested German fire support. When the gunboat returned to the destroyer detachment they would separate into two groups and open fire on the German cruiser and torpedoboats with the aim of forcing them to move away, so that the proposed sortie of *Pripyat* that night – to lay her mine barrier in the exit of Soelo Sound – would proceed undetected.

At 1150hrs *Chrabry* weighed anchor and got underway, and almost at the same time *Kaiser* opened fire on the Russian destroyers with her heavy guns at a range of 19,200 meters. The shooting was exceptionally good and the second salvo landed squarely amongst the destroyers. The Russian division immediately got underway and began to withdraw. Whilst they were turning, at 1155hrs, a projectile from the third salvo struck the destroyer *Grom* in the starboard engine room. However, the shell did not detonate and passed through the ship. *Grom* immediately began to list, decreased speed on both engines and pulled out of formation. The Russian boats soon passed out of range so that at 1208hrs *Kaiser* ceased fire. The gunboat *Chrabry* had not proceeded far and turned back towards *Grom*. Captain Pilsudski confirmed *Chrabry*'s action with the order to take *Grom* in tow and take her to the east. The commander of *Chrabry*, Starchi Leitenant Rennenkampf, relayed his orders to *Grom* by loud hailer, but he received the answer that *Grom* hoped to proceed independently. The division chief turned the other destroyers towards Soelo Sound and as *Pobeditel* passed under the stern of *Grom* she laid a smoke screen, which, however, was quickly dissipated on the wind.

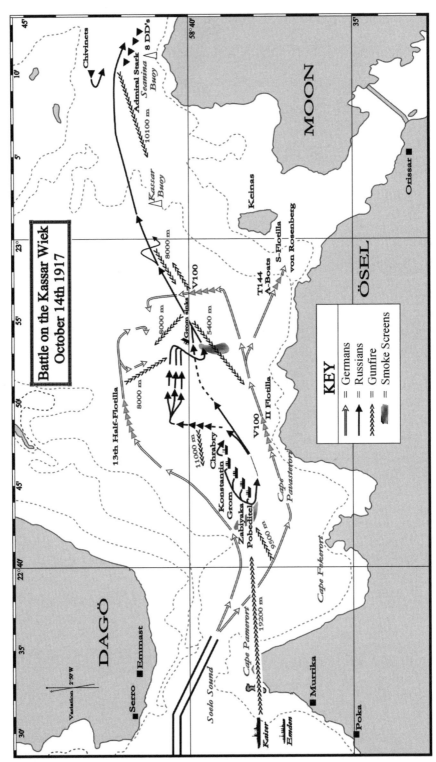

Map 8: The Battle on the Kassar Wiek, October 14th 1917.

As the Russian destroyers quickly withdrew out of range *Kaiser* had ceased fire at 1208hrs. However, as the Russian boats briefly turned towards Cape Pamerort *Kaiser* reopened fire, but only for a short time. Then *Konstantin* passed behind *Grom* and *Chrabry* and laid another smoke screen. The I Div TBD then took course to the north-northeast at slow speed, and on account of the shallow water depth their maximum speed was reduced to 15 knots.

Meanwhile, under the covering fire of *Kaiser*, the German torpedoboats had entered the Soelo Sound. The minesweepers T55 and T62 traveled at the head with sweeper gear set, but under these conditions the speed of the unit was comparatively slow. This exaggerated the effects of the strong cross current and at 1250hrs G101, the second boat in the line, went aground. An A-boat and V46 towed her off but she had to be dispatched to the rear, so that the I FdT, Kommodore Heinrich, who was leading the advance, now had only thirteen boats remaining, as S50 had previously fallen out due to engine damage. With the abeam wind and fast current the danger remained that further boats would run aground, and therefore the I FdT decided to forgo further sweeping and issued the order '*Durchhalten - Grossfahrt*', meaning 'hold course regardless - maximum speed'. The torpedoboats now quickly left the minesweepers behind and by 1320hrs had cleared the channel. Knowing these facts now reveals the refusal of *Pripyat* to lay the mine barrier as a decisive mistake. If the mines had been laid close to the exit from Soelo Sound, the Germans would not have gained sea mastery of the Kassar Wiek, and the troops at Orrisar would have been denied critical fire support and resupply.

Once inside the Kassar Wiek, the German torpedoboats divided into four groups and set course to the east-northeast and southeast at 17 knots. The shallow water depth precluded a higher speed. Captain 2nd Rank Pilsudski ordered his Russian I Div TBD to prepare for battle and deployed into a line running north-south, approximately two nautical miles east of the damaged *Grom*, which had been taken in tow by *Chrabry*, proceeding at a speed of 3 knots. The drag of *Grom* was affecting the helm of *Chrabry*, so that she could proceed with only the power of one engine. At 1321hrs the Russian destroyers opened fire on the German boats at the great range of 10,000 to 11,000 meters, outside the range of the German guns, which could not reply. The German boats quickly formed into battle formation. The Russians then turned onto course 050°, presenting a stern target to one of the German groups, and increased speed to 15 knots. The Russians were caught in a cross fire. A running battle now developed at a range of 9,500 metres.

The Russian leader boat, *Pobeditel*, fired on the southern German group, that is the boats of the II Torpedoboat Flotilla. The other Russian destroyers joined in, and *Chrabry* and *Grom* fired from their stern cannon. Their salvoes were accurate and G103 was damaged from a near miss astern. The German fire was also accurate and *Zabiyaka* was hit. A shell struck the deck and damaged the third gun, killing five men and wounding four others. The Russian division now lay under continuous straddling salvoes and Captain 2nd Rank Pilsudski ordered course to be taken to the east.

At 1345hrs, somewhat to the southwest of Annerakhu Buoy, the towline between *Chrabry* and *Grom* parted as the destroyers of the division passed to the left. Vice Admiral Bakhirev blamed the parting of the line on the fact that *Pobeditel* passed too close to the tow unit at high speed, causing a great wash, a manoeuvre she had been guilty of on several previous occasions. Now much of the German fire was concentrated on the gunboat and *Grom* and panic broke out aboard the crippled destroyer. Up to fifteen crewmen jumped into the water, but there was no time to fish them out, so the crew of *Chrabry* threw them life belts as the gunboat approached to make a renewed towing attempt. The commander of *Chrabry*, Starchi Leitenant Rennenkampf, approached the stern of *Grom* with his bow and attempted to fasten his anchor chains to the destroyer and continue the tow. The attempt failed, however, so the remaining crew were then taken aboard the gunboat. The commander of *Grom*, Leitenant Anatoly P Vaksmut, refused to abandon his ship and had to be forcibly removed from the destroyer. Now a shell from V100 struck *Grom* on the stern deck and started a fire, occasioning much smoke.

Once on deck aboard *Chrabry*, panic again broke out amongst the rescued crew of *Grom* and they would not follow orders to go below, instead hindering the gunboat crew in performance of their duty. Starchi Leitenant Rennenkampf ordered his bugler to play assembly, then he announced that for success in this matter he demanded complete calm, and immediate and precise performance of orders, and he forbid the crew of *Grom* from demonstrating on deck. The brief, but calm and firm speech by Leitenant Rennenkampf revived the will of *Grom*'s crew and they passed below. Soon afterwards *Chrabry* was able to engage the German torpedoboats at a range of 8,000 metres.

The author H K Graf also wrote about this incident, and he had spoken to Leitenant Vaksmut. He wrote:

> Having arrived in Kuiwast and boarded the transport Libau we learned from the commander of *Grom*, Leitenant A P Vaksmut, how he had fallen victim. The destruction of *Grom* had taken place under the following circumstances. When the enemy torpedoboats had broken into the Kassar Wiek reach, our torpedoboats set off at great speed and in great excitement and the wash from the boats had broken the towline. *Chrabry* had then returned to *Grom* to reattach the towline but by this time the other units had already departed. The enemy, having observed

the helpless condition of *Grom*, concentrated their fire on him and some shells hit. The crew was seized by panic. When *Chrabry* approached the sailors rushed aboard her as if mad, instead of resecuring the towline. Only the officers remained aboard. When the commander was requested to abandon the ship he refused and had to be removed by force. When the last of the crew of *Grom* departed the ship burned fiercely. The fire raged, especially in the wardroom, from whence nothing was saved.

A German shell had struck *Grom* on the poop and initiated a fire which emitted much smoke.

Meanwhile, the chief of I Division could see the difficult situation and ordered *Pobeditel* to turn back towards *Grom* and *Chrabry*. Yet another smoke screen was laid, but the division chief could now see that the position was hopeless and he again turned the destroyers to the east, escorting the gunboat. Now *Pobeditel* and *Zabiyaka* came under effective fire and were straddled. *Pobeditel* was hit under the stern so that an aft compartment leaked. *Konstantin* laid a smoke screen and the German torpedoboats ceased fire for a time.

The gunboat *Chrabry* followed the destroyers, firing from her stern cannon. In order that *Grom* should not fall into German hands, Starchi Leitenant Rennenkampf ordered the destroyer to be fired on as well and *Chrabry* fired several shells into the waterline of the stricken destroyer. During the battle one shell tore off *Chrabry*'s wireless antenna, whilst another projectile struck the superstructure on the upper deck and exploded over a hatch to the accommodation deck, holing a stokehold compartment. Six men of the crew of *Chrabry* were wounded, and from *Grom* four were killed and seven were wounded.

The destroyer now lay with a heavy list to port and burning. The II Torpedoboat Flotilla quickly approached and the boats G103 and G104 laid a smoke screen to the east, whilst B98 went alongside and put a boarding party aboard *Grom*. It is reported that five Russians were taken captive, and it must be assumed that they were those who had leapt overboard. A mine chart and a log book were also taken. B98 then took the Russian destroyer in tow. It was a curious sight: two vessels, almost identical, one Russian, the other German. The German torpedoboat design had been based on the Russian design. However, the situation aboard *Grom* deteriorated and at about 1510hrs *Grom* capsized and sank whilst still under tow. The wreck lay conspicuously out of the water.

Meanwhile, at 1440hrs, the I FdT, Kommodore Heinrich, assembled his remaining boats and pushed eastwards through the smoke screen towards Moon Sound. The Russian destroyers could be seen to the east but they remained outside German gun range. The Germans continued their advance.

The Russian gunboat *Chivinetz* did not support the destroyers, but remained anchored near Moon Island Buoy. Her long-ranged artillery could have been of great assistance but her commander, Leitenant Afanasev, did not exhibit any initiative when he heard the gunfire to the west of him: because he had not received any orders from the chief of I Division Torpedoboat-Destroyers, he remained calmly at anchor. In stark contrast to this was the behavior of the commander of *Grozyashchi*, Captain 2nd Rank Orlovski-Tanaevski. His gunboat was lying in Rogekul effecting repairs to the damage received during the previous day's battle, yet when he heard about the battle in the Kassar Wiek he did not await orders, but immediately got under way from his mooring. Unfortunately, however, he was too late to join the battle.

Earlier the chief of the I Div TBD had wirelessed to the chief of the torpedoboat divisions, Rear Admiral Stark, reporting 'nine enemy torpedoboats on the Kassar Wiek, I am in extended battle, require assistance'. When Admiral Stark received this message on Kuiwast Roads he ordered *Chivinetz* to place herself at the disposal of Captain 2nd Rank Pilsudski, whilst he himself immediately weighed anchor with *Novik*, *Samson*, VI Div TBD consisting of *Stregushchi* and *Zabaikalets*, V Div TBD consisting of *Vsadnik*, *Moskvityanin* and also *Amurets*, the latter being near Schildau escorting the transport conveying the Death Battalion to Moon Island. This group immediately got under way for the Kassar Wiek and were accompanied by the fleet commander, Rear Admiral Razvozov, aboard the destroyer *Finn*.

Towards 1520hrs, as Admiral Stark's group approached Seanin Buoy, he encountered I Div TBD and *Chrabry*. *Chivinetz* lay stopped near the buoy. To the west the German torpedoboats could be seen. The flotilla navigation officer, Leitenant Stankevich, expressed the opinion to Rear Admiral Stark that the general attack signal should be given. The admiral was unconvinced however, giving the reason for his reluctance as there being only two *Novik* types available as reinforcements.

Failing to muster the resolve to attack, Rear Admiral Stark deployed along the meridian of Seanin Buoy and opened fire on the Germans. The chief of VI Division TBD, Captain 1st Rank Ekimov, continued to the west and north and also opened fire. Towards 1535hrs Kommodore Heinrich's boats again came under an accurate fire. The heavier shells of the gunboats were mistaken by the Germans to be from a cruiser. Towards 1545hrs the Russians ceased fire as visibility decreased and darkness approached. During the battle *Samson* fired 24 shells, *Pobeditel* 400 shells, *Zabiyaka* 80 shells and *Konstantin* 120 shells.

Captain 2nd Rank Pilsudski and his destroyers were detached to Rogekul to repair their damage, surrender their dead and wounded and to accept oil. The VI Div TBD was sent to Kuiwast. The V Div TBD was ordered to Kassar Wiek Buoy with *Vsadnik* and *Moskvityanin* to await the arrival of

Pripyat and the other minelayers, which would conduct their operation during the night. Then they would retire to Moon Sound. However, only *Vsadnik* could locate the minelayers; *Moskvityanin* and *Amurets* spent the night near Rauten Buoy. During the evening the fleet commander returned to Rogekul aboard *Finn*.

Whilst the battle was taking place on the Kassar Wiek, the chief of the S-Flotilla aboard T144, Fregattenkapitän von Rosenberg, had entered the Kleinen Sound with his six A-boats. A liaison officer was dispatched ashore to make contact with Section Winterfeld but this proved difficult and it was not until 1630hrs that communications were established. Hauptmann von Winterfeld requested a bombardment of the stone dam and both ends of it, and in addition requested ammunition replenishment and provisions, but it was already too dark for the bombardment.

With the conclusion of the action the I FdT determined to spend the night in the western Kassar Wiek, so, shortly after darkness fell, the II Torpedoboat Flotilla and 13 TBHF anchored off Cape Fekkerort. T144 and the A-boats lay to the west of there. During the course of the day G101 had rejoined the Flotilla but one of her propeller shafts was damaged and causing severe vibration. It was decided to detach her to Libau and to send G103, which had suffered considerable leakage due to a near miss, with her. After these two boats transferred their remaining ammunition to the other boats, who had expended about half their outfits during the day, they departed for Libau dockyard.

During the course of the day the orders to lay a mine barrier in the Kassar Wiek were reiterated. Because of the rainy weather the night was exceptionally dark and visibility was reduced to a minimum. Towards midnight, *Pripyat* approached alongside *Vsadnik*, which was anchored between 1 and 2 cable-lengths (200 to 400 metres) from the Kassar Wiek buoy. In view of the fact that some of the crew of *Pripyat* were unsteady, and had expressed protestations about their assignment, they were removed and replaced with steady men from the torpedoboat. Kosinski wrote: 'With the agreement of the commander of the torpedoboat-destroyer *Vsadnik* - six men were appointed to the minelayer, whom by their behavior quickly raised the spirits of the crew'. Shortly after midnight *Pripyat* and three minelayer boats of the MT type departed to lay the mine barrier, despite the proximity of the German torpedoboats. During the night they laid 135 mines north of Cape Pavasterort, without being disrupted.

The day, 14 October, was one of great progress with minesweeping in the Irben Straits. This was an important part of the plan of the German command to simultaneously infiltrate the Moon Sound from the flank, on the Kassar Wiek, and from the south through the Riga Gulf. A prerequisite was to first sweep a passage through the multitude of Russian mine barriers that closed the Irben Straits tight.

At around 0315hrs the III and IV Minesweeper Divisions and three S-Flotillas departed Windau, followed by the tenders *Primula* and *Indianola*. The wind was a fresh southwesterly and there was a light mist. During the day the wind dropped and visibility improved slightly, but these conditions were favourable for minesweeping and progress was good, so that by early afternoon the chief of III Minesweeper Division was able to report that the gaps through barriers 1 and 2 were complete.

In the meantime, at about 0600hrs, the Commander-in-Chief of Reconnaissance Forces of the Baltic (BdAdO), Kontreadmiral Hopman, led his cruisers, *Kolberg*, *Strassburg* and *Augsburg*, out of Libau. They were preceded by boats of the 16th Torpedoboat Half Flotilla acting as minesweepers and anti-submarine protection. They proceeded northwards at about 14 knots. Shortly after 0800hrs, Battery No 43 at Zerel opened fire on these cruisers at a range of 24,000 metres with their 12-inch guns. Leitenant Bartinev, the commander of Battery No 43, gives the following description of the action:

> On the morning of October 14th it was reported to me from the lighthouse that smoke was visible to the southwest, at Lyserort. The horizon was clear and visibility to seaward was rather good. The Kurland coast could be well seen, although not clearly. One group of smoke could be seen from the lighthouse to the southwest at Lyserort, and two other groups were visible moving to the north.... It became possible to distinguish the masts of three units and their funnels as they approached.... About 8 o'clock it was learned that it was the light cruisers *Stralsund*, *Augsburg* and one of the *Stettin* type, taking course through the Irben Straits. Behind them a smoke cloud was visible moving from the southwest, but the masts and silhouettes of these were not visible. The distance on the rangefinder indicated a range of 130 cable-lengths and estimated speed was 23 knots. Fire was opened on the enemy head from two guns. The cruisers went in line ahead with a distance between them of 4 to 5 cable-lengths and a speed of 21 to 23 knots. The first salvo was to the side with a large spread, up to 30 cables. The range was corrected and fire resumed, but it was found that the shells fell short and therefore fire was ceased. A total of twelve shots were made. The cruisers turned towards the coast and began to disappear in the haze near Mikailovsk lighthouse.

According to the Germans the rounds fell between the cruisers and torpedoboats and, therefore, Kontreadmiral Hopman turned eight points, that is 90°, away to starboard and reduced speed to 7 knots. Ten minutes later he turned back to port and continued his advance. At 0845hrs the cruisers anchored near Mikailovsk Bank.

The minesweeping and clearing work continued into the afternoon and about 1400hrs, three nautical miles past Barrier 2, the 3rd S-Half Flotilla pushed onto a third barrier, consisting of pendulum-type mines. The III and IV Minesweeper Divisions set about clearing a gap in this barrier whilst the 3rd S-Half Flottille continued to search. Soon after, they discovered a fourth barrier, which they began to clear themselves. At about 1700hrs Kontreadmiral Hopman decided to call it a day and ordered the searching and clearing work to cease. The minesweepers anchored close in to shore.

During the course of October 14th the land battle around Thomel and the stone dam intensified. At 0800hrs in the morning the German troops were disposed as follows: the 1st Cyclist Company was at Saikla; the 5th Cyclist Company were at Thomel; the 3rd Cyclist Company were south of Thomel and Sturmkompanie 18 and the 6th Cyclist Company were at Orrisar. The 5th and 3rd Cyclists were supported by a machinegun Company. The 2nd and 4th Cyclist Companies were near Masik. Hauptmann von Winterfeld had ordered the 2nd Cyclist Company to move forward to the front at Saltak Manor. He intended to attack the Russians. The Russians, however, struck first.

At 0700hrs the Russian artillery began bombarding the 5th Cyclist Company near Thomel and Thomel Manor, and at 0800hrs their infantry and cavalry began to attack. To counter this attack a platoon of the 3rd Cyclist Company and a machine gun platoon were sent forward. The garrison at Thomel were sorely pressed but successfully beat off wave after wave of attacks, at times using hand grenades. However, the German situation was deteriorating rapidly and the commander requested reinforcements from Hauptmann von Winterfeld. By 1200hrs the first men from the 2nd and 4th Company arrived at Thomel Manor. The 4th Company was immediately ordered to attack Lewwal. They pushed the Russian forces, including a cavalry squadron, back. However, in the meantime the Saltak Manor was destroyed by fire. After this there was a lull in the battle.

The German forces were being stretched to their limit. The Russian right flank was threatening to link with the forces coming across the stone dam from Moon Island. These were under the command of Starchi Leitenant Prestin, who had previously been evacuated from Arensburg aboard the transport *Elba*. To contain this Russian bridgehead, Hauptmann von Winterfeld had only Sturmkompanie 18 and the 4th Cyclist Company.

Towards 0900hrs Hauptmann von Winterfeld ordered the 6th Cyclists to advance from eastern Orrisar towards the stone dam, and try to force the Russians back. However, after advancing just 300 metres from Orrisar, they were stopped by Russian machine-gun fire. Sturmkompanie 18 advanced in support, but the Germans were stopped by heavy fire from the stone dam and surrounding coppices.

Sturmkompanie 18 was then ordered to advance on the right flank of the 6th Cyclist Company, towards Turna. At the same time the V Cyclist Battalion arrived in Masik and was also ordered forward on the eastern flank, through the woods to Turna and Saltak. Soon after midday they reached positions between Saltak Manor and Mezarro, and stabilized the eastern end of the German line. The assault company was halted by heavy Russian resistance after advancing just 600 metres.

Meanwhile, the Russian line at Thomel was being reinforced by further troops coming from Arensburg. The 2nd and 5th Cyclist Companies were coming under increasing pressure. Then heavy artillery shells began landing around the German positions. The 25cm gun battery at Woi, on Moon Island, had entered the battle. Thus at 1400hrs the 2nd and 5th Companies and Sturmkompanie 18 were engaged in a serious battle along a line running from Saikla to Thomel, Saltak and Mezarro and the eastern precinct of Orrisar, a front some 10 kilometres in length. The line of the 2nd Company between Saikla and Thomel had gaps of several hundred metres, and between the 2nd and 5th Companies, that is between Thomel and Saltak, a 1 kilometre gap existed.

The Russian attack intensified and the II Cyclist Battalion had used their last reserves. Further reinforcements were desperately needed by the German line. These finally came at 1400hrs in the form of IV Cyclist Battalion. They had departed Karris at 0800hrs and had passed through Tagafer before arriving at Saikla at 1400hrs. The total distance covered was just 20km, but they had been delayed in passing the 65th Infantry Brigade, who were using the same road. They were immediately deployed at Thomel Manor estate, to support II Battalion, which was suffering losses from enemy fire. The IV Battalion entered the line between the II Battalion and V Battalion.

This reinforcement came at a critical time as the Russians attacked towards Lewwal in four consecutive waves. However, the German line held, whilst the commander of the IV Cyclist Battalion, Major von Frizen, assumed command of the II and V Battalions.

At the same time the situation on the eastern flank was also becoming critical. The Russian machine-gun fire intensified and reinforcements were arriving across the stone dam. German reinforcements from the 42nd Division had been promised for 1400hrs but at 1500hrs there was still no sign of them. Then two Russian armoured cars appeared across the stone dam and the 6th Cyclist Company and Sturmkompanie 18 were forced to retreat before the advancing Russians. The position had now become critical for the Germans and it was doubtful if the eastern flank could be held. Towards 1600hrs the communication officer from FK von Rosenberg's flotilla advised that the arrival of the 65th Brigade was imminent. The flotilla was therefore requested for fire support to bombard

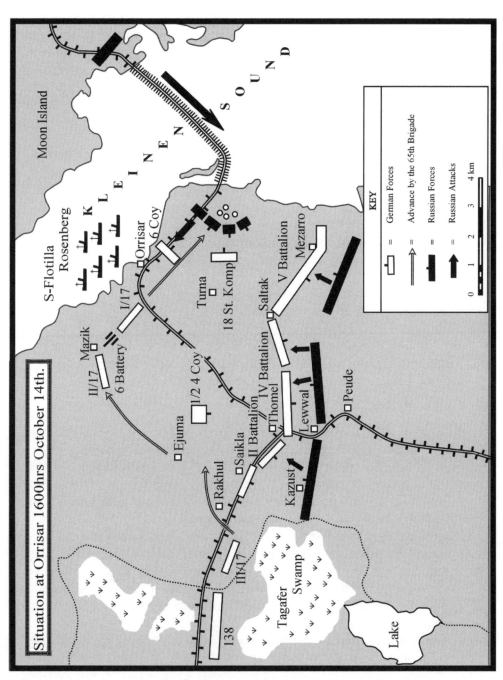

Map 9: Situation at Orrisar 1600hrs October 14th.

both ends of the stone dam. Soon afterwards the commander of I Battalion, 17 Regt, arrived in Orrisar, together with guns of 6th Battery.

On the morning of 13 October Generalleutnant von Estorff and his staff had still considered that the Russian ground forces would concentrate in Arensburg. In view of this he had ordered 65th Infantry Brigade to approach and cut off Arensburg from the north. However, on the evening of 13 October, an officer of 8th Field Artillery Regiment, Offizierstellvertreter Meyer, sent a report to the divisional staff headquarters which ran in part:

> Early today my regiment gained useful knowledge about Arensburg. After bypassing enemy patrols by skirting around them through woods my patrol and I reached Arensburg. We rode into the town and nothing was seen of the enemy, apart from some stragglers. Only the town commander, Colonel Popov, was still there....On questioning he remarked that the town garrison, approximately 10 to 12,000 men, had marched away towards Moon the previous evening.

He remarked further that another 5,000 men had gone to Sworbe. Offizierstellvertreter Meyer continued:

> As I sat down in a yard to put my report on paper and dispatch it, we were suddenly attacked by Russians. My companion was taken captive, I succeeded in escaping. Destruction in the town has taken place to only a small extent.

In the divisional headquarters it was understood that the enemy had been beaten at Uduvere during the day and that some Russians had been taken captive. It was thought that this had caused the Russians to retreat to the south. In relation to Orrisar the HQ only had a general report from a flyer that there was seemingly a vehement battle occurring near Orrisar and that the stone dam was firmly in Russian hands.

Generalleutnant von Estorff now gave consideration to immediately continuing the advance with the entire division (apart from 131 Regt) to assist Section Winterfeld and trap the Russian forces. However, he had to consider the condition of his troops. They had suffered a difficult time. They had been confined in steamers for two or three days, enduring a sea journey and landing, followed by two very exhausting days filled with marching and battle in bad weather. The march had been over soft ground, the catering had been sparse and the 'goulash cannon' (mobile field kitchens for hot food) were missing. The latrines and bivouacs in the woods were wet and windy and without comforts, which were with the still-absent baggage train. The men had not settled down to rest until 2300hrs and had only had a snack. Life in the field had been difficult. Now they were to be asked to conduct a 40km forced march. Generalleutnant von Estorff was faced with a difficult decision. He was responsible for the welfare of his troops, so should he allow them to rest, and bring them into action in a refreshed state, or should he continue to stretch his men further and march to the aid of their hard-pressed comrades at Orrisar? Von Estorff was already a veteran of campaigns in South West Africa and knew the demands being placed on him and his troops; after considering all the circumstances, he ordered the march to continue.

Shortly after midnight the three regiments broke camp and began the arduous march carrying only their combat equipment. They continued into the morning, when it began to rain. Towards midday gunfire could be heard ahead. The men now marched animatedly. Soon, a large number of cyclists, about a hundred, came into sight on the narrow road and quickly passed the column. It was the IV Cyclist Battalion.

The advanced guard of the 65th Brigade, battalions I and II of 17 Regt and 6th Battery of the 8th Field Artillery Regiment, under the command of Colonel von Kaweczynski, approached Saikla at the same time as the IV Cyclist Battalion, at 1400hrs. They approached across Tagafer swamp to enter the battlefield from the west and at Saikla met the flank of the II Cyclist Battalion, facing to the south. They could not continue to march along the road to Thomel, and thence to Orrisar, as this avenue lay under continuous machine-gun and artillery fire. Whilst the IV Cyclists went to reinforce the line the advanced guard turned off the road to the north, passing through the villages of Rakhul, Ejuma and Masik and then turned in the direction of Orrisar.

Meanwhile the Russians had intensified their attacks across the stone dam and towards Orrisar. Two armoured cars had advanced across the dam and began supporting the troops advancing towards Orrisar. The German cyclists were forced to retreat. Further Russian reinforcements arrived across the stone dam.

During the course of the day, the Russian Death Battalion, 600 men under the command of Captain 2nd Rank Shishko, arrived in Kuiwast from Rogekul. The previous day they had embarked aboard the transports *Buki* and *Vassian* in Reval. After receiving ammunition they advanced across Moon and at 1500hrs sent a reconnaissance patrol across the stone dam.

The appearance of armoured cars was of grave concern to the Germans and they were powerless against them without artillery support. Therefore the leader of 6th Battery found a suitable firing position in a park near Orrisar and ordered his guns to advance at the gallop. The guns took up their positions and were ordered to open fire on the advancing armoured cars. The park reverberated with the thunder of cannon fire and the Russian armoured cars were showered with earth from the exploding shells. Their advance towards Orrisar had been halted and they were forced back towards the stone dam.

It was beginning to grow dark, but the I and II Battalions, 17 Regt, under Hauptmann von Redern began an attack towards the bridgehead. The Russian infantry under Starchi Leitenant Prestin were now hard pressed. When the torpedoboats of Fregattenkapitän von Rosenberg opened fire on their trenches, the soldiers, and then the seamen, began to retreat towards the stone dam. Nevertheless, the first reinforcements from the Death Battalion were beginning to arrive across the dam. German reinforcements also began to arrive in the form of the III Battalion, 17 Regt. Towards 1730hrs the brigade commander, Oberst Matthiass, arrived in Turna to direct operations. He desired an attack towards the Russian bridgehead but it was already too dark to advance through the wooded area.

The main line of the II, IV and V Cyclist Battalions had been under attack all day but had held firm. When 138 Regt arrived the Brigade Commander dispatched them to the Saikla area to act as reserve.

At 2230hrs on 13 October, 255R Regt received orders from the 42nd Division staff to pursue the enemy, who would not accept battle, as quickly as possible. At 0130hrs on 14 October, the regiment set off through Karmel, Mustla and Odin, and were directed by local residents through Putla and Sal. At about 0900hrs the regiment was fed at Kel'yala. A further rest, from 1500hrs to 1730hrs, came 11km east of Kel'yala, before the 255R continued almost without stopping until, at 0100hrs on 15 October, they reached Kapra, just to the south of the Russian forces. There had been no contact with Russian forces until they approached Kapra. Their arduous march had covered 55 kilometers.

The situation was not clear to the commander of 255R Regt, Oberst Berring, and therefore, in consideration of the fatigued condition of his troops, he refrained from a night attack. The 80th Cyclist Company were dispatched to control the road to Arensburg.

In nine hours the 65th Infantry Brigade had marched 36 kilometers and the 255R Regt had marched 55 kilometers in twenty-four hours. They had marched over soft roads in torrential rain, with even the highway having mud 10 to 20cm deep.

The decision by Generalleutnant von Estorff to continue the march was thus fully justified. The 65th Brigade had arrived in the Orrisar area only just in time to save Sturmkompanie 18 and the cyclists from being defeated and retreating, which would have allowed the Russians a secure connection with Moon Island and the ability to provide reinforcements or retire, as they desired. Instead, however, the German positions had been held firm. The stone dam bridgehead had been retaken and the retreat of

Russian forces was thus prevented. The front line was occupied by the cyclist battalions, reinforced by the 17th and 138th Infantry Regiments. The line of retreat was blocked by 255R Regt. The Russians were indeed caught in a 'cauldron'.

In the meantime, after Generalleutnant von Estorff received the report about the abandonment of Arensburg, he had ordered the 6th Cyclist Battalion to immediately occupy the city. At around 0400hrs on October 14th the battalion arrived in Arensburg and occupied it. They took captive a colonel and 260 soldiers, who were hidden throughout the city. With that the capital had fallen.

During the course of the morning the 8th Army High Command (AOK8) decided, in consultation with the naval command, to include the island of Dago within the scope of the Ösel operation. Once sea mastery had been established in the Kassar Wiek, the further occupation of Dago would give complete domination of the Moon Sound and the entrance to the Finnish Gulf. With Dago in German hands, the defense of Ösel would be considerably eased. It was therefore planned to stage the landing on 16 October with the support of the S-Flotilla. General von Kathen decided to use 17 Regt, the II Cyclist Battalion, and a field battery under the command of Oberst von Kaweczynski. As soon as these troops became dispensable on Ösel they would move to Poka Bay for transport to Serro. The I FdT was to make the necessary arrangements, and during his absence the task was entrusted to Fregattenkapitän Freiherr von Gagern, commander of *Emden*.

Before returning to the Sworbe Peninsula and Zerel it should be mentioned that the Russian Naval Forces of the Riga Gulf were also reinforced during the course of 14 October. The armoured cruiser *Admiral Makarov* arrived in the Moon Sound from Lapvik in Finland, escorted by the torpedoboat-destroyers *Storozhevoi* and *Del'Nyi* . They remained in the northern Moon Sound channel during the night. In addition the torpedoboat-destroyer *Turkmenets Stravropolski* arrived in Kuiwast after concluding maintenance in Helsingfors. The transports *Izhe* and *Aktiv* arrived off Worms from Lapvik.

During the evening of the previous day, 13 October, 131 Regt, under the command of Oberstleutnant Fischer, had advanced to the northern end of the Sworbe Peninsula. The Russian garrison had retreated to Sworbe itself. The regiment was accompanied by its battle train and 5th Battery. The following day, they would continue their advance to the south, and for this they would require the support of the Navy. Therefore Oberstleutnant Fischer dispatched a wireless message to the IV Battle Squadron in Tagga Bay. Vizeadmiral Souchon put to sea at 0910hrs on October 14th with *Friedrich der Grosse*, *Kaiserin* and *König Albert*. They were screened against submarines by six boats of the IV and VI Torpedoboat Flotillas.

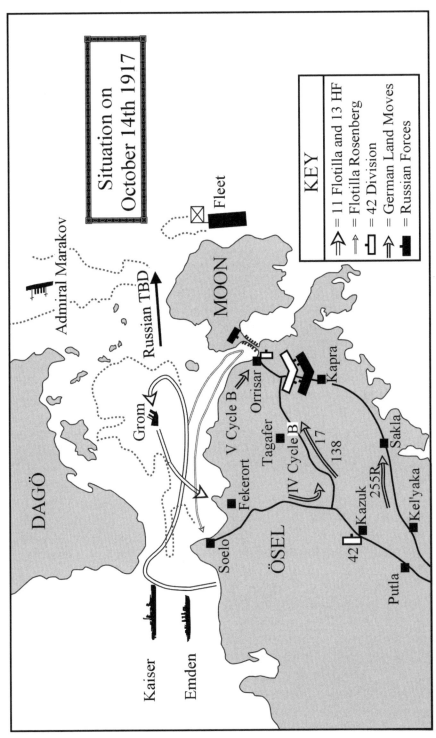

Map 10: Situation on October 14th 1917.

Nevertheless, Oberstleutnant Fischer thought that perhaps he could take the Sworbe Peninsula, and with it the Zerel battery, by negotiation, and thus avoid further bloodshed. He therefore decided to dispatch his ordinance officer, Oberleutnant der Reserve von Oppen, to the Russians to negotiate a surrender. He would take a note with him stating:

> Should the military buildings and the guns be handed over to the Germans undamaged, then the German vanguard commander guarantees that although the entire Sworbe garrison will be interned, they will not be forced to work against their will. In this case the entire garrison will be especially well treated. Immediate decision required.

At about 0830hrs, von Oppen departed the regimental staff, escorted by the battalion trumpeter, two hussars and a *gefreiter* (private) as interpreter. After half an hour the group encountered Russian forces near Ansekull and, although they were carrying a white flag and sounding a horn, they came under a vehement fire. They quickly took cover. However, Oberleutnant von Oppen was not deterred and with raised hands he and his interpreter were taken into Russian captivity. They were not well received and after a close search and a long wait they were blindfolded and taken on a three hour journey on a small wagon. They finally met the regimental staff of the 425th Kargopol Infantry Regiment at Torkenhof (17km southwest of Ansekull) at 1530hrs in the afternoon. They soon obtained the impression that it was not the commander, Colonel Borsakowski, but rather the twenty-strong soldiers' council that were in charge and making the decisions. One of the delegates later reported the contents of the German note to Battery No 43, and added that the Germans had said that if the battery was not surrendered intact then the Germans would take no prisoners and execute all the crew. To this the delegate replied, in his own words: 'The Russians will not surrender into captivity and will enjoin the fight until the end, to the last shell'. The delegate went on to say the German parliamentor had stressed that the Germans did not want bloodshed in the affair, and the delegate then questioned why they had begun the battle to take Russian soil, to which the German had replied that it was in order to obtain peace sooner.

In anticipation of a quick answer from the Russians, Oberstleutnant Fischer had ceased the advance, for the time being. Towards noon two naval flyers arrived with the regiment, which was now out of wireless contact. They notified the commander that there were Russian destroyers in the Riga Gulf. The presence of Russian warships in the vicinity of the coast led to the supposition that the Russians would be evacuated from Sworbe. This had to be prevented. On the other hand Oberleutnant von

Oppen was still not back after five hours. Fischer therefore gave the order: 'The regiment resumes the advance. The battalion begins immediately'.

The German advance resumed to the south, towards Ansekull. Shells fell ahead. Soon a violent firefight developed. The Germans found that the village of Ansekull was strongly occupied and two Russian batteries bombarded the path of the advance. The time remaining before darkness was too short to develop an attack, and Oberstleutnant Fischer determined a night attack was too risky, so the regiment settled down for the night.

When the Germans advanced and engaged the 425th Kargopol Infantry Regiment, Captain 1st Rank Knüpfer dispatched the torpedoboats *Ukraina* and *Voiskovoi*, which Vice Admiral Bakhirev had placed at his disposal, to Cape Merris to bombard the German positions. However, due to the inaccurate instructions from ashore, the torpedoboats did not open fire and the following morning returned to Mento.

After quitting Tagga Bay, the German IV Battle Squadron increased speed and by 1500hrs was in position to begin their bombardment. The task of *Friedrich der Grosse* was to fire against Russian ground forces as directed by the commander of the 131st Regiment, to support the German attack. The task allotted to *König Albert* and *Kaiserin* was to bombard the Russian heavy battery No43, at Zerel, when requested to do so by the infantry. The Germans believed the battery's 12-inch cannon had 360° traverse and, with their long range, were a threat to the German troops.

Before the battleships could take up their firing positions, their foreseen areas had to be swept for mines. This task was allotted to T170 and T169, but, due to frequently slipping their minesweeping gear on the bottom, they were unable to fulfill their task, so that by 1420hrs they had returned to the flagship and taken station ahead of her, once again with their sweeper gear set. By 1500hrs the battleships were in position, awaiting fire directions from ashore.

After firing on the cruisers of Kontreadmiral Hopman during the morning, the battery at Zerel had maintained their vigilance. However, the mist had intensified so that the visibility in the Irben Straits totalled no more than 30 cable-lengths, or 6,000 metres. Shortly after 1500hrs there was a renewed alarm. The report arrived: 'From the lighthouse they can see German dreadnoughts closing'. The commander of the battery, Leitenant Bartinev, went to the lighthouse, ordered the battle flag to be raised and sounded the alarm. Leitenant Bartinev later wrote:

To the northwest the fog had dissipated and close to the coast the funnels and masts of a large vessel were visible, with further smoke behind. By using the 15 foot stereo telescope a battleship of the *Kaiser* type could be recognized. The range to the dreadnought was

76 cable-lengths. By 'phone I ordered the diesel engine to be started and to make the guns ready. In view of the sudden appearance of the enemy from the fog the question was would we be able to prepare the guns to open fire in time? The enemy did not open fire and this allowed the crew to gather on the battery and prepare the guns for firing, and to turn them 180°. All this occupied a time of about 20 minutes. I transferred to the central command post: 'Central direction. Guns load. Battleships range 76. Aim. Salvo of 2'. I had personally measured the range with the rangefinder and determined it was 76 cable-lengths.

At 1600hrs the first salvo from Battery No 43 crashed out, and was thought by the Germans to be aimed at T170 and T169, which were still sweeping for mines. The boats prudently turned away to the north. In reality the fall of shot was simply wide. Leitenant Bartinev continues:

Our first salvo at 1600hrs from guns 2 and 4 lay far off to the side. The aim was corrected 50. The first correction was 8 cables since I did not trust the range finder. Sometimes it was necessary to measure the range again. The first salvoes were not bad. One of the salvoes lay thus: the first between the funnels not far away, and the second right under the stern, 30 to the side. It was similar to a hit, but I accepted that the shell fell short. Subsequently, in captivity, we learned that *Kaiser* [in fact it was probably *Kaiserin*] had been hit in the 6-inch battery. Probably it was a hit from this salvo. After that they quickly increased the range and because of that our shells fell short. The distance between the fall of shot was sometimes so great that both shots couldn't be observed in the field glasses. The guns were ready to fire a salvo every 2 minutes, but despite the fact that I fired in salvos of two, it was necessary to wait 2 minutes between salvos. There were misfires. All this created problems in management of the fire from the central direction position, and I assumed it was the reason for the large spread in the fall of shot. On my question 'is the target in sight?' I did not receive an answer and eventually heard 'the target is not visible'. Therefore I dared to order 'Cease' and checked on the guns.

After the second salvo, *König Albert* and *Kaiserin* returned the fire, whilst *Friedrich der Grosse* weighed anchor and approached her sister ships, as she was not yet required for her primary task, the support of 131 Regt. For the next hour the three battleships fired on the Zerel battery at ranges from 17,000 to 20,000 meters and fired a total of 120 projectiles of heavy calibre ammunition. According to the German report, the fourth Russian 12-inch salvo straddled *Kaiserin* amidships, so that after that she was obliged to steer a zigzag course to avoid being hit. The *König Albert* also made speed and course alterations to avoid being hit.

The results of the German fire were not so good. The first German salvo lay near the reserve magazine, about 1,500 metres from the battery. The salvos were closely grouped and began moving closer to the barracks. The shell falling closest to the battery impacted 64 metres from a gun and splinters struck the concrete mounting. The German salvoes followed at intervals of thirty to forty seconds in groups of three or four. After a short interruption of thirty minutes the German fire became more intensive. The salvoes lay near the Russian aircraft station and three aircraft took off through the columns of smoke and disappeared to the northeast. Further salvos fell near the light house. The nearest fell 30 metres away and showered the lighthouse with splinters. As the visibility and light conditions deteriorated the Germans ceased fire for a second time at around 1730hrs. During the action the Russian four-gun battery had fired 26 shells in reply to approximately 120 heavy shells fired by the Germans. During the night *Friedrich der Grosse* remained under way, whilst the other two battleships anchored.

However, all was not in order at Battery No 43. With the beginning of the German bombardment, many men from the second gun ran to the central post and caused great confusion. As the German shells landed near the central post and magazines the men sheltering there fled into the woods. Soon after, the lower crew of the first gun stopped work and some of those of the third gun fled. Only those of the fourth gun continued to fire until the order to cease fire. Those who fled were fired upon with rifles from the third gun and a machine gun from the second diesel generator. Leitenant Bartinev wrote: 'The chairman of the committee of Battery 43, Miner Savkin, came to me at the lighthouse and expressed his anger at the behaviour of the crew, and he demanded that all deserters be shot'.

The spirit of the crew during the battle is described by the commander of the third gun, Michman Goncharev:

Up until the enemy fired the crew performed their duty properly. When the first enemy salvo lay in the vicinity of the second magazine the crew began to exhibit signs of anxiety and were distracted from their affairs of observing the fall of the enemy shot and uttered displeasure, which is why the enemy units were allowed to approach to a range from where they could conduct battle with the battery. As the enemy approached there was increasing anxiety among the crew and reduced orderliness and work intensity. After the first fall of shot near the first turret, those on my turret began to call in panic:

'Second turret damaged!' The crew pushed me from the entrance to the ladder and fled the installation, and together with those from the third magazine and fourth turret, fled across a field in the direction of the forest. Remaining on the turret I observed that the first and second turrets had also been abandoned by their crews, and I went down from the installation and attempted to persuade the crew who had left to return to their places....only the threat that fleeing crew would be fired on caused the crew to return, running bent over, apparently only obeying fear.

Leitenant Bartinev continued: 'The role of the officers is not clear, probably they were confused. For me the flight of the crews was unexpected since the firing of the enemy was poor, and our crews had previously been bombed frequently'. Leitenant Bartinev determined to go to the battery to support Committee Chairman Savkin. After he arrived at the battery he gave a short speech and arranged a general meeting at the barracks. Then he spoke to Captain 1st Rank Knüpfer and made a report. He asked that those who had fled to Mento, about 125 men, be disarmed and detained there.

There had been several jammings and breakages with the battery. The first gun was serviceable, the second had broken loading rails; the third had a defective loading elevator, as did the fourth gun. In the gathering darkness, and despite the confusion, Leitenant Bartinev organized repair parties so that by 1900hrs the damage had been rectified, apart from the damaged rails.

At the assembly in the barracks Leitenant Bartinev made a fiery speech, following the committee chairman, and emphasized the extremely poor shooting of the Germans. The men responded enthusiastically. Leitenant Bartinev continued: 'There was a question about the arrival of our fleet and the readiness of transports to evacuate our garrison when all the shells were expended, and that they could be late, but in general it was possible to cheer up the men and all went well'.

After this Leitenant Bartinev again spoke to Captain 1st Rank Knüpfer and requested that the deserters be disarmed and detained. Captain 1st Rank Knüpfer dismissed this request. Now things took a turn for the worst. At 2100hrs Leitenant Bartinev was summoned and found himself in front of an armed mob. He wrote:

One of them addressed me, stammering, 'Mister Leitenant, we can fight no more. It is necessary to surrender. To resist further is useless'. Peering into this crowd I could see only senseless physiognomies grown completely dull from fear and finally demoralized. There were about 30 people. To persuade them and even to try to influence them was useless. Having weighed the situation, and seeing the confused silence of the committee I could only answer them: 'Be off, I do not wish to speak to you'.

Leitenant Bartinev thought it pointless to address them. It now became apparent that even those who had continued to fight were in danger of becoming unreliable. Frank conversation between the officers was impossible as sailors' committee members overheard everything and it was necessary to avoid provocation. Leitenant Bartinev explains:

I assumed the other batteries were under the same influence as Battery 43 and the others' actions would vary with the circumstances. Although the commanders gave me mostly good assurances about their batteries, from their general tone I understood that they could not be relied on as they had the same general basis for demoralization as Battery 43, i.e. the magazine explosion, the arrival of new crew, the obvious desire not to fight etc. They were already in a completely unstable condition. On the batteries the offers and intimidation of the German truce envoys were widely known. Mento was already flooded with fugitives and delegates from all the batteries and communication with them had become difficult. The general demoralization had begun to develop suddenly and extremely quickly. Only one Leitenant Lindeberg had correctly estimated the situation and frankly told me that he could not count on his crew. They had remained with him only out of shame. He considered the business as hopeless unless we were supported by the Fleet.

The breakdown in organization had happened so quickly because firstly the fugitives were allowed back, and also because of the unimaginable negotiations between all interested parties of the army and battery, and the difference of opinion of the 'supervisors' in Mento, which brought mess and chaos and undid the conscientious work of others.

The telephone operators, miners, electricians and the committee had kept their spirit. Around this time, the twelfth hour, I learned from the loyal crew that some mechanics had begun treacherous behaviour. They asked me for advice and instructions about what to do. I encouraged them to remain at their places and to try to keep the others there also. About this time I found out that from all the crews there were only sixty reliable men remaining – no more.

During the night there was a further general assembly of the crew and it was decided to send the following telegram to Admiral Bakhirev: 'Position at

Zerel is critical, await immediate aid by the fleet in the morning to save the position'. The majority of the garrison desired an immediate withdrawal, and only this telegram held them until morning. Then another message: 'Crew persistently pleads for prompt fleet help - please reply - Zerel'. Then a reply: 'Crew of Zerel garrison. Comrades, do not be unsteady. Assistance by morning'.

These messages caused a stir on the ships in Moon Sound and the crew of *Slava* requested Vice Admiral Bakhirev to send a battleship to Zerel's assistance.

CHAPTER FIVE

15 October: The Battle Around Zerel

Dawn on 15 October brought with it favourable weather conditions for minesweeping in the Irben Straits. The wind was a light northeast to northwest, the sea was quiet and there were showers and drizzle. Visibility conditions were not good, although they improved as the day progressed. Both the Germans and Russians dispatched some of their strongest forces to the Irben Straits. Towards 0700hrs the German minesweepers renewed their work, supported by Kontreadmiral Hopman's VI Reconnaissance Group (VI AG). The minesweepers worked on barrier gap 3 and then proceeded to work on barrier gap 4. However, at about 1125hrs, they observed smoke to the north and, assuming it emanated from Russian forces, they retreated.

On the morning of this day the Russians dispatched the torpedoboat-destroyers *Izyaslav* and *Avtroil* from the Moon Sound for reconnaissance in the Domesnas position area. With the reduced visibility it was not these boats that were observed from the German minesweepers of the 3rd S-Half Flotilla however.

The persistent pleas from the Zerel position for support did not go unheeded by Admiral Bakhirev. At 0600hrs on 15 October he ordered the battleship *Graschdanin* to Sworbe to support the failing spirits of the Zerel battery crews, and to provide fire support for the troops. The battleship's escort consisted of the torpedoboat-destroyers *Steregushtshi*, *Turkmenets Stravropolski* and *Amurets*, under the command of the chief of the VI Division Torpedoboat-Destroyers, Captain 1st Rank Ekimov. No other ships were available to be sent: *Bayan* needed to replenish her coal stocks; *Slava* was needed to defend the Kassar Wiek against German torpedoboats and to bombard the stone dam. Accordingly she was ordered to move nearer to Schildau Island. During the late morning the cruiser *Admiral Makarov* arrived at Kuiwast, but she had not been briefed and was low on coal. She was sent to the northern Moon Sound, near to Kharilaid, in order to prevent the German torpedoboats from exiting the Kassar Wiek to the north.

The smoke cloud that caused the German minesweepers consternation emanated from the torpedoboat-destroyers *Steregushtshi* and *Turkmenets*. The two opposing forces stood just 7 nautical miles apart but owing to the atmospheric conditions the vessels could not see one another.

In the meantime the battleships *König* and *Kronprinz* had completed their coaling in Putzig Wiek and in the early morning of 15 October were off the coast at Windau. There they were met by the *flottilleboot* (flotilla leader) of the VIII Torpedoboat Flotilla, V180, which would pilot them through the large ship channel. At about 0730hrs they began to advance at 10 knots, preceded by three M-boats of 8th Minesweeper Half Flotilla and two *sperrbrecher* vessels (literally 'barrier breaker', ships made as unsinkable as possible and used to enter mined waters first). The tender *Blitz* was attached. Two hours later the battleships under Vizeadmiral Behncke anchored south of point 'F', to the north of Pissen. A conference was then held aboard *König* between Vizeadmiral Behncke and Kontreadmiral Hopman and the following situation was revealed: the Russian mine barriers were proving extremely difficult to penetrate, the mine fields being laid closely together and the mines cunningly deployed. The minesweeping work was technically difficult and time consuming with some types of Russian mines causing considerable uncertainty as they either slipped through the sweeper gear or else were towed along. The gaps in barriers 3 and 4 were not yet unquestionably free of mines and the obstructions north of barrier 4 were still unknown. The situation of the Zerel battery was also unknown. The BdAdO only knew that 131 Regt was near Ansekull, about 24km from Zerel.

From intercepted Russian wireless messages it was known that Russian sea forces were hurrying to help at Zerel, and it appeared the Riga Bay Operations Group forces were intent on holding Sworbe and the Zerel battery. The German ground forces were therefore expected to be delayed and with clearer weather the Zerel battery could command the entire narrow Straits. Any German forces, that had earlier passed within 12,000 metres of the Zerel battery, would be endangered. Therefore, the chief of the III Battle Squadron, Vizeadmiral Behncke, with the agreement of the BdAdO, Kontreadmiral Hopman, determined to forgo the route to the north, and direct the minesweepers to breakthrough more to the east. This route, however, was even more difficult as there were three lines of Russian blockships at Jaunzeem, Klein Irben and Petragge. North of Jaunzeem and Klein Irben lay a long Russian mine barrier laid during June-July 1917. To save time the route east would be begun north of gaps 1 and 2. The mine search and clearing units were recalled from their work areas and during the early afternoon began work on a new route to the east.

The Germans were obviously totally unaware of the chaos reigning on the Zerel batteries 40, 41 and 43. The mere threat of the long barrels of Battery

No 43 was enough to influence the German leadership to discontinue the minesweeping to the north and choose a more easterly, more difficult route. However, the battery had to maintain a stubborn defense, but the will of the men to fight had faltered and finally failed.

As previously related, Vice Admiral Bakhirev wished to hold the Zerel battery at all costs. It was impossible for him to overstate the importance of the battery for the defense of the Riga Gulf and Moon Sound. Therefore he dispatched the battleship *Graschdanin* to Zerel early on the morning of 15 October. Another four 12-inch guns would be valuable in defending the Irben Straits against minesweepers, but a more important aspect was the moral support the battleship would provide for the garrison. However, the garrison had seriously undervalued their contribution not only to the overall defense of Moon Sound, but also to greater Russia at large.

During the morning of 15 October the two Russian destroyers *Ukraina* and *Voiskovoi* again approached Cape Merris and opened fire towards the German positions. In all they fired around 200 shells, but when the Russian field batteries also opened fire they were immediately ordered to cease fire. Similarly, when a German reconnaissance aircraft was taken under fire by Battery No 44 at around 0800hrs, the anti-aircraft battery was categorically ordered to cease fire by Battery No 43. Apparently the garrison did not want to antagonize the Germans. Soon after this Leitenant Bartinev received a message from the central exchange stating that it had been decided to abandon the batteries, and not give battle. This order included officers. With this Leitenant Bartinev said he could see the hopelessness of the situation and decided to assemble a demolition party to bring explosive charges to the battery. However, the garrison would not allow this and it was necessary to allow a period of time for the crew to leave, so he could work with freedom of action. Finally the crew agreed that, after they had arrived in Mento and had boarded transports and barges, they would allow the officers to destroy the battery. As the garrison departed Leitenant Bartinev began gathering explosives on the battery. However, he had not yet given up on the idea of getting at least one gun operational, either with crew from a torpedoboat, or with a crew of officers. He informed those in Mento that the guns could fire on the isthmus and that he had a fire plan map for this at the lighthouse. Nevertheless, there were still no clear instructions from Mento, and contact could not be made with Captain 1st Rank Knüpfer. Of those who remained with Leitenant Bartinev most were disillusioned and dispirited. Nevertheless, they were still able to lay explosive charges on the batteries, in the magazines and in the diesel engine electricity plants. Leitenant Bartinev said: 'I could not understand why Knüpfer had not found it necessary to talk to me. He had not spoken to me all day'. There was much confusion on the battery. Individual groups began to demolish minor emplacements, and an arsenal was fired. Leitenant Bartinev had expressly forbidden this, but now the flames developed quickly and rockets, shells and small arms fired in all directions and began to blow up.

At around 0600hrs on 15 October the German IV Battle Squadron again made for their bombardment positions to the west of the Sworbe Peninsula. Vizeadmiral Schmidt had ordered them not to open fire unless they, or the advancing troops, were taken under fire. However, Vizeadmiral Souchon had no direct contact with Oberstleutnant Fischer and 131 Regt. Towards 1250hrs a powerful, spiralling smoke cloud was observed in the direction of the Zerel battery, and Vizeadmiral Souchon believed that this marked the beginning of the destruction of the battery and emplacements by the Russians themselves. More likely it was the detonation of the arsenal located in a log hut near to the central post, near a village about 50 *sazhen* (106 metres) to the rear of the battery. Nevertheless, Vizeadmiral Souchon could see the German ships of the III Battle Squadron attempting to breakthrough the Irben Straits and he believed hurrying things along on the Sworbe Peninsula would be of great value. He therefore ordered his ships to open fire and from 1340hrs to 1420hrs Battery No43 at Zerel, other emplacements and buildings on Zerel and two steamers lying east of the peninsula were taken under bombardment. On this day the shooting was somewhat better than on the previous day. Leitenant Bartinev wrote:

> The first salvo fell about 50 sazhen (106 metres) from the battery and splinters fell all around. Ensign Tikhanovich, approaching me to request permission to destroy the battery, was thrown to the ground. The bombardment proceeded with great intensity for about half an hour. The salvoes followed one another at an interval of 15 to 20 seconds. The shells probably landed nearby since the whine of splinters was clearly audible. The crew were sent to the reserve magazine and took flight to Mento.

One 30.5cm shell wrecked the magazine of Battery No 40. Leitenant Bartinev now quickly decided to destroy the remaining battery and magazines, but both attempts to detonate the explosives failed, probably because the German shells had cut the wires. Therefore he set fire to a warehouse, a construction store and some oil barrels. The lighthouse was also set ablaze. Leitenant Bartinev decided to regroup before taking further action. His group then made off for Mento and were twice attacked by German aeroplanes. As they approached the town, towards 1800hrs in the evening, they could see *Graschdanin*. It was already beginning to grow dark. Upon arrival he finally met with Captain 1st Rank Knüpfer and others, but Knüpfer was preoccupied with evacuating his family. Leitenant Bartinev settled down for the night for a long-awaited rest.

The Germans observed the detonations and fires and assumed that the Russians were abandoning Sworbe. About 1600hrs Vizeadmiral Souchon reported to Vizeadmiral Schmidt: 'The enemy has abandoned Zerel and destroyed emplacements with explosives and fire'.

During the evening of 15 October the battleships *König Albert* and *Kaiser* were detached to coal in Putzig, whilst the flagship *Friedrich der Grosse* anchored for the night. The following day she would patrol the coast.

Meanwhile, in the Irben Straits, the minesweepers had scarcely begun work on the route to the east, when at 1340hrs the thunder of heavy cannon was heard to the northwest as the IV Battle Squadron opened fire on Zerel. Vizeadmiral Behncke now decided to await events, for if the Battery 43 was defeated then the less difficult northern route to Arensburg could be taken. The 3rd Minesweeper Half Flotilla and the II and IV Minesweeper Divisions were now recalled and valuable time was lost. Only one hour of good daylight remained, and then the cruisers would be forced to anchor on the intended breakthrough route. This was not advisable and therefore all thoughts of continuing the breakthrough were abandoned for the day. The remaining hour of daylight was utilized to broaden the already-swept channel, gap 4, to 400 metres. The 3rd Minesweeper Half Flotilla received orders to accelerate work on a mine-free channel along the coast in the small vessels channel. This was because the U-Boot UC78 had reported a battleship of the *Slava* class with two destroyers south of Abro Island, and Kontreadmiral Hopman feared these would attack his minesweepers which were pushing east. As the German minesweepers to the north began to retire they sighted the battleship to the east of Sworbe, firing her heavy artillery.

Earlier in the day, at 1100hrs (noon using Russian time), the battleship *Graschdanin* and her escorting torpedoboats raised anchor and went out into the Riga Gulf. They were following minesweepers and, as the sweepers turned to return to the Moon Sound, one of them exploded a mine just 400 metres ahead of *Graschdanin*. The commander of the battleship, Captain 1st Rank Rudenski, ordered a new sweep ahead, and this consumed a further hour, so that it was only at 1330hrs that *Graschdanin* could resume the advance. At 1500hrs the minesweepers were dismissed, speed was increased to 17 knots, and the torpedoboat-destroyers were set as an anti-submarine screen.

On approaching Arensburg roadstead, two bright lights could be seen on Zerel, which resolved themselves into the burning lighthouse and the large building nearby. The remainder of the area was obscured by dense clouds of smoke. Captain 1st Rank Rudenski wirelessed Vice Admiral Bakhirev over the situation and awaited further instructions. Vice Admiral Bakhirev wrote:

At 1700hrs, as the Zerel 12-inch battery could be used against us, I ordered the commander of *Graschdanin*, by wireless, to destroy the batteries with all available means. At the same time I sent a telegram to the Fleet Commander about our problems in relation to bombarding the Zerel batteries. [The reply was] 'In case of Zerel falling, I consider the Irben passage as strategically lost and it would be impossible to protect the rear of our forces in the Riga Gulf and on Ösel. With the absence of the battery at Zerel the supervision is now impossible and I now order: all measures to be taken to strengthen the defenses of the southern Moon sound, and secondly, lay mine obstacles to make it more difficult for the enemy to use the Riga Gulf; thirdly to strengthen the mine defenses of Pernau by means of barriers; fourthly, to assist as much as possible the forces on Ösel with our units, and fifth, to secure the inner waters of the Moon Sound. No1655. Rear Admiral Razvozov'.

On the face of it these measures might seem obvious, but this order reconfirmed the determination of the Russian leadership to hold the Riga Gulf and Moon Sound with all available forces, and to conduct a stubborn defence in depth.

After receiving her orders *Graschdanin* went to Cape Mento, proceeding along the narrow channel. On one side was the shoreline and shallows, on the other side were mine barriers. In the case of attack by aircraft with bombs, or submarine attack with torpedoes, it would be impossible for the battleship to take evasive manoeuvres. The mood aboard the ship was tense. This passage by Captain 2nd Rank Kosinski shows just how strained nerves were:

All attention was applied to watching the body of water, searching for the unexpected feather of a submarine periscope or a trace of mines. The command was in a highly nervous state when a hysterical voice was heard: 'Submarine on the left bow', and the ship, obeying the preconceived instructions, turned sharply away and began shooting from both sides. It was likely that the reported trace of the submarine was debris or some other item protruding from the water, and in the meantime the ship was turned inside the mine barrier. There was concern that the firing was dangerous for the escorting *Amurets* and she would be damaged, and shells flew over the torpedoboat at a low height. Therefore the bugler was ordered to play 'shot', in order to stop the shooting, but this proved no easy task. The signals from the bugler, over the phones and on the dials all turned out to be inadequate, and it was necessary for the Senior Officer to run from the conning tower and shout aloud at the gun's serving crews to get them to cease fire. In the words of the former Senior Officer, during these two to three minutes it was close to panic, and this was only just prevented.

Vice Admiral Bakhirev's flagship of the Naval Forces of the Riga Gulf was the armoured cruiser *Bayan*.

Left: Vice Admiral M K Bakhirev (marked by the arrow) on the bridge of a battleship earlier in the war.

The armoured cruiser *Admiral Makarov* arrived to bolster the Russian defences on 14 October 1917.

Top Left: The prototype of the Russian *Borodino*-class battleships was the French-built *Tsarevitch*, whose name was changed to *Graschdanin* (Citizen) after the first revolution.

Above: *Slava*, the last ship of the *Borodino* class, seen from astern.

Left: This fine stern view of the gunboat *Grozyashchi* shows three of her four 6-inch guns

The gunboat *Chrabry* at Riga.

The Russian destroyer *Grom*. The V100 and other large German torpedoboats were direct copies of these large Russian boats.

The shallow-draught mine layer *Pripyat*.

SMS *Kaiser*.

Vizeadmiral Ehrhard Schmidt (centr
marked with an 'x') and his Staff
aboard his flagship, *Moltke*.

The small cruisers *Frankfurt* and
Augsburg in Libau prior to the
beginning of the operation.

A minesweeper of II Minesweeper Flotilla. In the background the aircraft tender SMH *Santa Elana*.

A German A-type torpedoboat, used by the minesweeper flottillas.

A view of the damage caused when the minesweeper M75 struck a mine on 8 October, during preparatory mine sweeping for Operation Albion.

The *sperrbrecher* (barrier breaker) *Rio Pardo*.

The German torpedoboat V100.

The German net layer *Eskimo*, which began the war as an English merchant ship.

The minelayer *Nautilus* transfers mines to small minesweeper motorboats for laying in shallow waters.

The German battleship *Grosser Kurfürst*, just after completion in 1914.

The airship SL8 passes over *Grosser Kurfürst*. Operation Albion really was an all-arms affair; airships were used for long-range strategic bombing and reconnaissance; aircraft were used for bombing and reconnaissance; U-boats were used for mine laying, and the battleships, cruisers and torpedoboats used their guns to support the Army ashore and to do battle with the Russian naval forces.

A view of the damage caused when *Grosser Kurfürst* struck a mine at 0509hrs on 12 October.

SMS *Bayern* in Tagga Bay after suffering damage from a mine. The bows have sunk by approximately 1 metre. In the background, *Rio Pardo* and a torpedoboat.

The damage caused to *Bayern* by the Russian mine struck at 0507 on 12 October. The blast destroyed the forward broadside torpedo room.

The small cruiser SMS *Emden II* opens fire on the Russian battery at Cape Toffri on Dagö Island.

German troops board
a transport steamer.

Troops disembarking from
a transport steamer into
boats for the landing in
Tagga Bay.

A close-up of the
troops ready to
go ashore.

German minesweeping
motor launches were
pressed into service to
take troops ashore.

The scene at the disembarkation beach in Tagga Bay. A Friedrichshafen FF33 floatplane has pulled up at the beach.

German ships in Tagga Bay. The battleship *Bayern* is on the right, Vizeadmiral Schmidt's flagship, SMS *Moltke*, in the centre and the battleships *Prinzregent Luitpold* and *Markgraf* are further to the left.

The German torpedoboat B98 comes alongside the stricken *Grom*, which had to be abandoned after she was hit by the battleship Kaiser and torpedoboot V100.

The battleship *König* follows minesweepers and *perrbrecher* vessels through the mine fields of the Irben Straits on 16 October.

On 16 October the minesweeper A62 captured a Russian barge with 300 men aboard that was adrift in the mined area of the Irben Straits. A62 is shown here with her prize under tow.

The battle in Moon Sound, 17 October. Russian shells fall near *Kronprinz*, whilst *König* is further ahead. At first the German battleships were unable to reply because the 12- inch guns of *Slava* outranged their own 30.5cm pieces.

As the range closes, *Kronprinz* fires a salvo.

A German shell lands near *Slava*.

A Russian salvo falls near German minesweepers at work in the Moon Sound on 17 October. These vessels were handicapped by towing their sweeper gear.

An aerial view of *Slava*, scuttled after being heavily damaged by multiple hits.

The German torpedoboat S64.

S64, scuttled after striking a mine near Kumora Reef on the night of 17 October.

The German torpedoboat B111 is towed stern first into Libau after striking a mine on 18 October. Her bow was completely destroyed by the mine, yet she remained afloat.

The battleship SMS *Markgraf*.

One of the abandoned 12-inch guns at Zerel.

The famous lighthouse at Cape Zerel.
The building to the left still stands today.

The grave of a sailor
from the German
torpedoboat B111,
killed when she hit a
mine on 18 October.

Buried together: a
German soldier of the
Pioneer Landing Corps,
another from 7th
Company, 131st
Infantry Regiment, and
an unknown Russian
soldier.

Whilst these events were occurring, German torpedo-bomber aircraft chose this moment to attack. One aircraft flew over the ship at 1,500 feet from right to left, and dropped a stick of ten bombs. Three bombs fell on the right side and the remainder up to 50 metres to the left. The Germans reported that they had obtained a hit. *Graschdanin* continued to Mento. Kosinski wrote:

> In the process of *Graschdanin's* approach to Mento the sun began to disappear on the horizon and the picture of Zerel became fairytale-like. The fires were devastating. Against the evening background the picture of the ancient lighthouse and buildings at Zerel were explicitly conspicuous, and columns of flame and burning buildings reminded one of the incandescence of the brazier. All the sea room between the ship and the shore was filled with boats, launches, tugs, and under the near shore stood a small steamer and a large barge. All these were filled with people, some shouting, and conspicuously pleading to go aboard the torpedoboat *Amurets*.
>
> *Graschdanin* approached to within 30–40 cables [3.9 nautical miles, which is just off Mento] of the 12-inch battery and deployed her armament to the left side, and opened fire from her 12-inch and 6-inch guns. A closer approach was hindered by the shallow water depth. By the time of the first shot the sun had already set, and the last salvo was fired in semi-darkness of the quickly descending autumn twilight.

One of *Graschdanin's* crew, V Ogilvi, later wrote:

> Shooting in the semi-darkness on our own battery, that was constructed with such labour and quickness, and for the entire summer and autumn of the 1917 campaigns had successfully defended the Irben position, was to give it away too cheaply. Finally we were surrounded by a gloomy, but grand picture: fires, enemy aeroplanes, machine-guns firing, circled by boats and tugs with people, who in panic had deserted their posts on the batteries and had not even managed to demolish their weapons, and the valuable guns had been abandoned to the enemy. All this, captured together, is engraved in the memory of every participant of our campaign to Zerel.

It was now almost completely dark and time to begin the return journey to Kuiwast. However, first *Graschdanin* took aboard some eighty or so men, soldiers and sailors, from an overcrowded tug. The escorting *Amurets* took aboard 150 men, but only two officers. Then the battleship departed for Moon Sound, escorted by *Amurets*, and accompanied by the steamer *General Zimmerman* and several tugs, all overcrowded. One tug towed a barge with 200 men aboard. The speed of the curious unit was low, just 6 knots.

The torpedoboat-destroyers *Steregushchi* and *Turkmenets Stravropski* lowered their boats, taking fifty-seven and forty-six men aboard respectively. They rendezvoused with the *Graschdanin* unit south of Abro and followed in its wake. Previously that evening Kontreadmiral Hopman had sent the following wireless order to UC57, stationed off the southern Moon Sound: 'A ship of the *Slava* class is traveling from Sworbe to Moon Sound tonight. Attack!' Towards 0145hrs on a clear night, UC57 sighted two destroyers on an easterly course, obviously an anti-submarine screen of the Russian unit. As Kapitänleutnant Wissmann carried out his attack and the range reduced to 2,000 metres, one of the Russian destroyers suddenly turned towards the U-boat at high speed, forcing UC57 to crash dive. The Russians quickly passed out of range for a successful torpedo attack.

During the morning the Russian unit was met off the entrance to Moon Sound by the torpedoboats *Donskoi Kazak* and *Razyashchi*. At 0800hrs on 16 October, *Graschdanin*, the torpedoboats, the steamer *General Zimmerman* and four tugs entered Kuiwast.

At around 0530hrs on the morning of 15 October, Fregattenkapitän von Rosenberg assembled his S-Flotilla and ran into the Kleinen Sound to support the German troops near Orrisar and the stone dam. His leader boat, T144, drew too much water to allow her to proceed further so therefore the flotilla chief boarded the small torpedoboot A29. In the Kleinen Sound an Army liaison officer was put ashore to establish contact with Section Winterfeld. After about an hour the officer reported the situation ashore by wireless and requested immediate bombardment of the head of the stone dam on Moon and the dam itself, and at the same time requested munitions and provisions. The A-boats immediately began the bombardment. On this the Russian V Division Torpedoboat-Destroyers, consisting of *Vsadnik* and *Moskvityanin*, opened fire on the A-boats, whereupon the IFdT, Kommodore Heinrich, ordered them to pull back.

Furthermore, during the course of the morning, the reconnaissance seaplane 1590, a Friedrichshafen FF33L, passed a message to *Emden* stating that there were up to twelve Russian vessels in the eastern exit of the Kassar Wiek. They were supported by a large number of ships in the Moon Sound.

At around 0455hrs the larger German torpedoboats of II Torpedoboat Flotilla (eight boats) and 13th Torpedoboat Half Flotilla (four boats) had pushed forward into the Kassar Wiek and began to advance in reconnaissance formation. Shortly before 0800hrs the boats V46 and S50 reinforced them to make a total of fourteen boats. These were taken under long-range fire by the gunboats *Chrabry* and *Chivinetz*, and pulled back for the time being. Around midday, V Div TBD was sent reinforcements by the chief of II Div TBD, in the form of the destroyers *Samson* and *Leitenant Il'in* and the gunboat *Grozyashchi*, and somewhat after that by the torpedoboat-destroyer *Desna*. The gunboats and torpedoboat-destroyers entered into exchanges of fire with the German torpedoboats when they advanced to the east, and were supported by heavy shellfire from the Woi Battery, *Slava* and *Admiral Makarov*.

The see-saw battle across the Kassar Wiek was continuing along the lines of the previous day. Before long A29 had expended all of her munition outfit and was detailed to Tagga Bay to replenish and fetch ammunition for the other A-boats. By noon A31 had also depleted her stock and was likewise ordered to Tagga Bay. She returned the same evening and anchored overnight in Soelo Sound, before arriving in the Kleinen Sound early on the following morning and landing the requested Army munitions at Orrisar.

As the battle raged back and forth across the Kassar Wiek, at 1130hrs Kommodore Heinrich ordered his boats to stand away to the west, to give them some respite from the heavy fire. At 1205hrs, as the unit passed just south of the wreck of *Grom*, the boat V100 sighted a lead-capped mine some 200 metres away on the surface. Just as the next boot, S50, was ordered to investigate whether the mine was moored, a heavy detonation occurred on B98. The forecastle was rent off and sank to the bottom, though part of it remained conspicuous above the surface, but B98 remained afloat. As many men had been below deck for lunch, there was a heavy loss of life, with fourteen dead and seven wounded. The B-boats were of sturdy construction and B98's remaining forward bulkhead held, so that she was able to steam under her own power to Tagga Bay, escorted by V74. The following day she was ordered to Libau under tow of the steamer *Caurus*. The B98 was subsequently repaired and returned to service. She had fallen victim to one of the mines laid by the Russians the previous night – now the Germans regretted not mounting a guard near the entrance to Moon Sound, as Fregattenkapitän von Rosenberg had suggested. The I FdT now took his torpedoboats to the north but the water depth there was comparatively shallow and the Germans suffered further attrition when, at 1610hrs, B110 and B112 grounded. B110 damaged two propeller blades but her reduced speed was sufficient for operations in the Kassar Wiek. The B112 likewise damaged her propellers but also suffered considerable damage to an oil bunker, which leaked, and therefore she was detached for repairs. The II Torpedoboat Flotilla now consisted of six battle-worthy boats.

That night, the eleven boats of Kommodore Heinrich's group anchored in a guard position off the western exit to Moon Sound, but towards 2015hrs the main body of torpedoboats retired further to the west, leaving three boats on guard. This measure was adopted to prevent a confused mêlée should the Russians try to break through to the west. At 2130hrs there was a further commotion as S63 ran aground in a water depth of 3.5 metres. She was, however, able to work herself free.

Earlier in the day, the planned landing on Dago had been carried out. At about 0900hrs Landing Corps Ahlefeld had landed two sections near Toffri and established a bridgehead. According to local inhabitants there were three Russian field guns near Emmast and, therefore, *Emden* moved closer to Toffri and T141 anchored near Serro, to lend support if required. Towards 1100hrs, Fregattenkapitän von Rosenberg returned from the Kleinen Sound to personally supervise the remainder of his S-Flotilla, leaving Oberleutnant zur See Dietze, aboard A32, in charge of things in the Kleinen Sound. Towards 1230hrs an intense battle developed ashore as the Landing Corps met unexpectedly strong opposition, to the point where Kapitänleutnant von Ahlefeld doubted whether the bridgehead could be held overnight. Therefore, towards evening, the S-Flotilla embarked the Landing Corps and withdrew; nevertheless, the attack was to be repeated the following day, after a more vigorous bombardment had been conducted.

An interesting overview of the situation on 15 October is provided by Oberst von Tschischwitz, chief of the general staff of the Landing Corps, in his description of a reconnaissance flight undertaken by one of his fellow offiziers:

At midday of October 15th an officer of the General Staff arrived at Papensholm. He had disembarked that morning and found himself on the way to Arensburg. He inquired whether there was an opportunity for himself to procure a flight along the coast to survey the situation - most importantly over the Kleinen Sound and the Sworbe Peninsula.

'Yes indeed, Herr Major,' replied the Station Leader, Kptlt A, 'I have a machine ready to take off and will gladly fly you myself'. As they passed he quickly showed the major the beautiful hanger, which remained undamaged, just as were five flying boats, some motors, cars and motorboats.

The propeller was swung and the two officers climbed aboard the seaplane. It was then launched into the water, whereon the propeller revolutions were brought up. With gathering speed the aircraft was showered and slowly it climbed away from the waters surface.

Soon the flyer took course northeast over the southern tip of Tagga Bay. There, there was still a mixed bag. The entire transport fleet still lay at anchor, although six empty transports were to return to

Libau that evening. Easily recognizable were *Moltke* and the FMS *Santa Elena*. Further north lay two battleships, to the right of them a cruiser. On the landing position swarmed horses and vehicles. The bay formed a fascinating picture which quickly disappeared. During subsequent flight the coast remained in sight on the left, whilst below they passed over scattered woods, empty fields, small villages and numerous farms. The juniper hedges showed as a dark line which gave way to peaceful meadows and pastures. The rise of terrain was imperceptible and totaled only 50 metres – Ösel is a flat island that rises to the north and falls away steeply at the coast.

Before long the southern tip of Dago was visible. Before the Soelo Sound lay *Emden*, resembling a sheep dog on watch. The Pamerort Peninsula pointed north like a finger. There were no roads to see. Still, one did go south, to Arensburg. Over the last few months roads had been built from Arensburg to the northeast, north, northwest and southwest. Now the aircraft arrived on the southern shore of the Kassar Wiek. Small vessels were going in two directions, to the west and the east. 'They belong to Flottille Rosenberg.' Further out they could see a large number of torpedoboats running on a westerly course from the Moon Sound. 'There appears to be something out of order' remarked the pilot. Later we learned that B98 had at that time run onto a mine.

The increasing haze forced the aircraft to go lower in order to obtain a clear picture of the situation in the Kleinen Sound. 'The village ahead of us is Orrisar. There lay Rosenberg with his A-boats. He seemingly shoots on Moon. However, on the stone dam there is no traffic'.

'There, I can see the battle line,' called the major, 'they stretch right to the Kleinen Sound. Could we fly along it?' Overall, movement in a southern direction was recognizable. 'I see only two batteries firing, one near Thomel on the road. The western wing rests immediately on a marsh. Please, could you now fly along the road to Arensburg?' - 'There appears to be a considerable part of the Russians cut off from Moon. The road is indeed completely clogged with vehicles. And there, German troops attack both sides of the northward traveling Russians - that must be the 255! [255R Regt] No, the pocket is finished. It's a pity we cannot see the finale. We must away.'

And now the aircraft flew along the old postal road to Arensburg. Single groups of horses and carts came trotting along. 'That must be the baggage train of the 255th!' To the left stood the blue, shimmering Riga Gulf, to the right another road that went from Arensburg to Pamerort was visible. Now the 65th Brigade came in sight. 'What does that smoke ribbon to the left of Arensburg come from?' questioned the major. 'That is the Russian Fleet'. 'Yes, then they can fairly shoot on Arensburg?' furthered the major. 'We cannot prevent them from doing so, Herr Major, so long as Admiral Behncke cannot break through the Irben Straits. Would that I had a couple of bombs with me!' The aircraft cut a curved course over water towards Sworbe and steered towards Tehomardi. Clearly visible was a Russian battleship to the west of Abro Island, with a destroyer nearby. Other destroyers cruised a little further west near the coast. The aircraft flew along the west coast of Sworbe to the south.

'I am curious', said the major, 'as to whether today the Russians are also finished here, as it would appear. It is so important for the Navy to breakthrough and cut off Moon. This morning we still had no report from Regiment 131'. 'There is movement on the road. Is that the village of Ansekull? See our troops, they lay still. There appears to be no battle - Curious!' Generally the area was wooded with a few small villages on the road, which our troops filled. A peaceful picture.

In the distance, to the right were several dark smoke ribbons and several times gunflashes could be seen. 'That is the IV Squadron firing on Zerel', said the pilot. 'I must go higher now as near Lebara there are flak batteries. We have recently bombed the airstation there.' On the landing ground near Cape Mento a small crowd was gathered. The air station was conducting a funeral.

The southern tip of the island came in sight. The IV Squadron had ceased fire. In the woods fires burned in several positions. Now the Zerel battery could be discerned - the giant, long 30.5cm barrels climbed towards the heavens. The flak battery did not shoot. In the area surrounding the battery the craters of the heavy shells fired by Souchon's squadron could be seen - they left quite a mess. Had the Russians themselves blown up the battery?

Flames came from several positions, and the lighthouse burned - proof of the good shooting by Squadron Souchon. 'No, it appears the finale is near here, also', imparted the major, 'but I do not understand why Regiment 131 do not advance'.

The aircraft turned in a great curve to the left. 'The wreck there, right ahead of us is that of a Russian destroyer that one of my flyers from Windau hit with a 60kg bomb. And on Zerel a bomb caused a munition depot to explode.' And now it was time to return. The weather had cleared and the sun shone. The aircraft was already quite low, below was the deep blue water of the Riga Gulf and to the west the green scattered woods of the peninsula and the dull, flat open sea. 'Well, well! - there come the Russians towards us in their boats. Will they indeed rescue their brothers in arms before they are taken prisoners?'

The aircraft went lower, towards Ansekull. The 131 [Regt] still stood there, however, not in battle. They waved to the aircraft above.

'Could you take me to Arensburg and land?' inquired the major, 'there is still an airstation and I wish to report as soon as possible.' In the course of two hours the entire island had been overflown.

The situation on the narrow neck of Sworbe Peninsula that had confused the German fliers was as follows: by the morning of 15 October the German negotiator, Oberleutnant der Reserve von Oppen, had not returned. In fact he had been detained by the Russians and held overnight in a field hospital, guarded by no less than six sentries, which, as the Russians explained, were as much for his own protection as to prevent escape. Nonetheless, the broader German terms and conditions had become common knowledge on the batteries and amongst the Russian troops of the 425th and 472nd Infantry Regiments. After initial resistance, the knowledge of the terms served to undermine the Russian morale. The soldiers' council, although not considering capitulation at first, had since come to agreement on just that, on the basis that Sworbe could no longer be held. About 0600hrs Oberleunant der Reserve von Oppen departed the Russian regimental headquarters, taking with him the Russian request for a cease fire and their terms for surrender. The Russian officers had wished to continue the fight, but the soldiers' council had carried the argument.

Nevertheless, in the absence of news from the negotiator the regimental commander of the German 131 Regt, Oberstleutnant Fischer, had decided to continue the attack. He ordered the bombardment of the Russian fortifications near Ansekull, from which the Russians now retreated. Resistance on the west coast was also suppressed. At 1330hrs, after twenty-eight hours, the negotiator returned and said that the Russians were willing to surrender, but desired an armistice to allow time to discuss terms and conditions. Oberstleutnant Fischer, through his regimental Adjutant Oberleutnant Dormagen and Oberleutnant der Reserve Oppen, refused the armistice but said, nevertheless, that he could offer honorable conditions.

A meeting occurred about 1630hrs in a village 5 kilometres south of Ansekull. It was strongly put that no armistice existed. The Russians requested that their capitulation be delayed until the following day (16 October) at 0800hrs. Towards 1800hrs the two dispatched officers returned with the news that the Russians were ready to capitulate. Nevertheless, the negotiations had consumed a great amount of time, over thirty-two hours, and this had allowed the Russians on Sworbe great freedom of action, including allowing many of the garrison to escape. In addition, the unclear situation had delayed the minesweeping in the Irben Straits, and thus the advance towards the southern Moon Sound, the next serious Russian obstacle.

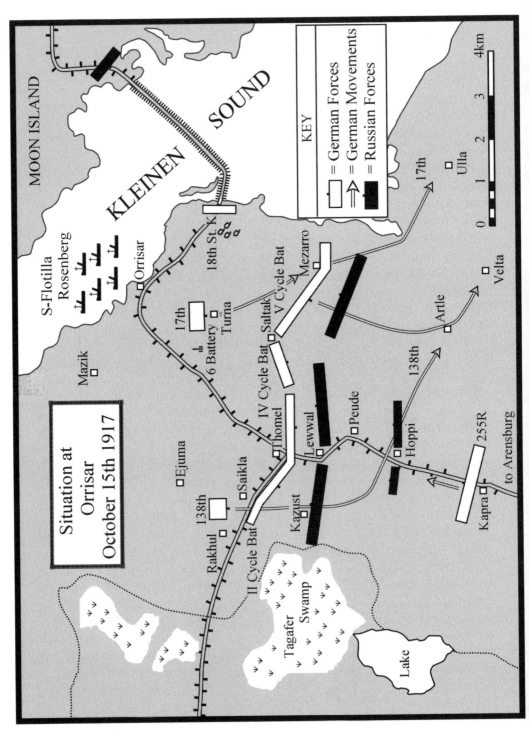

Map 11: The Situation at Orrisar, October 15th 1917.

Towards 2000hrs, the III Battalion, 131 Regt, reported that they had taken 28 officers and 1,200 men captive, together with 40 machine guns. During the night, at about 0200hrs, a Russian negotiator finally arrived and confirmed the conditions for the capitulation. In the meantime the commanding general of the Landing Corps, Generale der Infanterie von Kathen, together with Prince Joachim von Preussen, arrived at the headquarters of 131 Regt, to be personally briefed about the situation. General von Kathen then announced: 'I bring good news: still tonight a heavy battery will arrive here, and we have intercepted a Russian wireless message that states, "situation desperate, send ships!" Therefore the drama here is almost concluded! Preferably the battery at Zerel will be taken undamaged, and the ships can quickly go through.'

On 15 October the battle at Orrisar and Thomel was reaching a climax. During the night the heavy battery at Woi kept up a sporadic fire on the Germans and the Russian Death Battalion launched three unsuccessful attacks across the stone dam. The night passed quickly for the II, IV and V Cyclist Battalion.

The Germans were disposed with the II Cyclist Battalion on the western flank, the IV Cyclist Battalion in the centre and the V Cyclist Battalion on the eastern flank. This line occupied the entire front from the Kleinen Sound in the east to the Tagaffer Swamp. A reserve was formed in the west by 138 Regt, whilst 17 Regt formed a reserve in the east. The stormtroops of Sturmkompanie 18 held the base of the stone dam. The Russian regiments were arranged against this German line, but to the south of the Russians was the German 255R Regt. However, the situation during the morning of 15 October was still uncertain, and the regiments to the north were uncertain about the position of 255R Regt.

During the morning the Russians twice attacked the German line at Lewwal, but they were forced back under the fire of the II Cyclist Battalion. Then the V Cyclist Battalion was attacked by 200 Russian cavalry, supported by machine guns and artillery. This attack also failed under the fire of the cyclists.

With dawn the commander of 42nd Division, Generalleutnant von Estorff, arrived on the battlefield in a GAZ car. He feared that substantial Russian forces would be able to escape across the water to Moon or the mainland and therefore he ordered a general attack for 1100hrs.

At the appointed time, 138 Regt attacked on the right flank, advancing to the west of Kazust and Lewwal and then swinging to the east behind Peude across the main road to Arensburg. The II and IV Cyclists also attacked, supported by the 4th Battery. There was a lively firefight to the south of Thomel. After a short battle Kazust was taken, and then at about 1500hrs Lewwal was captured by the Germans. Apparently the accurate fire of the German battery seriously demoralized the Russian infantry. The right flank was broken and the 138 Regt turned east and continued to advance to Artle. On the eastern flank, the V Cyclist Battalion also attacked towards midday and advanced through Maikiul and Artle toward Velta, whilst 17 Regt advanced from Turna through Mezarro and Ulla. They met no resistance. Sturmkompanie 18 secured the base of the stone dam, preventing reinforcements from coming from Moon Island.

To the south, at around 1100hrs, the 255th Reserve Infantry Regiment also mounted an attack but had to halt near Hoppi because their shortage of ammunition would not allow them to participate in a lively exchange. However, towards midday the sound of artillery fire was heard in a northerly direction and Oberst Berring, commander of 255R Regt, took it to mean that 42nd Division approached. He therefore ordered an attack along both sides of the road to Peude. At this moment 2nd Battery arrived from Arensburg to support the attack.

Soon afterwards, the Russian fire was observed to weaken and confused shouting could be heard. At 1430hrs, 255R Regt launched an all-out attack and as the Russians recognized the advancing 65th Infantry Brigade they began to show the white flag. Towards 1500hrs the commander of the Russian 107th Division, General Ivanov, with two brigade commanders, sixty officers, the 426th and 472nd Infantry Regiments, and several field batteries all capitulated. Over 5,000 men, fourteen field guns and many machine guns and mortars were surrendered. There were many casualties, and in one position alone there were 100 Russian cadavers, whilst in one village lay 400 wounded. Only a few hundred Russians had escaped in boats across to Moon during the morning of 15 October. By evening that day the greater part of Ösel was in German hands and the majority of the Russians had been made prisoner.

Chapter Six

16 October: The Russians Falter

Early on the morning of the following day, 16 October, the attack on Dägo began again. At about 0800hrs *SMS Kaiser* began an hour-long bombardment of the bridgehead area, so that towards 0900hrs Landing Corps Ahlefeld could begin disembarking, according to plan. The steamer *Coburg* moved close inshore near Toffri to act as a breakwater to facilitate an easier landing. The German patrols pushed forward and between 1300hrs and 1400hrs skirmished with the Russians. The Germans did not know it but the only Russians in the immediate area were a few officers and thirty soldiers and sailors. Shortly before 1500hrs the landing corps re-embarked and thereon *Emden* moved inshore to undertake the planned bombardment.

The command of the Special Unit advised that a cyclist battalion would be embarked to support Landing Corps Ahlefeld on 17 October, whilst the remaining troops would be ready for the assault on Dägo on 18 October. A jetty, being constructed at Murrika, would be completed by the 18th and would assist in embarking the troops. Fregattenkapitän von Schlick completed the necessary arrangements for the transport of troops and stores.

In Mento on the morning of 16 October the situation at Zerel and condition of the batteries was completely unknown. At a meeting between the officers present Michman Larosh suggested that he, with Leitenant Bartinev and some others, should return to Battery No 43 and if there were no Germans present, they would destroy it. Leitenant Bartinev put this to Captain 1st Rank Knüpfer, who agreed, and the group set off. Leitenant Bartinev wrote: 'We went through Lebara and Mandu. The peasants we met on the road told us that the Germans were in Torkino and Gengi, and apparently were not present at Zerel'.

All the area of Cape Zerel was ploughed up by craters, but the battery itself was untouched by either the German guns, or those of *Graschdanin*. The guns, magazines and constructions all turned out to be in good order. The demolition charges had not detonated, only the charge on gun No 1 had partially exploded. As Leitenant Bartinev examined the No 1 gun a

German reconnaissance floatplane flew low overhead. It was found that the fuses were faulty and therefore it was decided that it would be easier to blow up the magazines and hope the explosions would damage the guns. The charges were laid and set and after just twenty minutes, as the Russian party ran to the No 3 magazine, there was a great explosion as magazine No 1 blew up. 'There was a huge column of black smoke and logs, rails, carriages and empty cases rose to a height of 100 *sazhen*....the magazine was finally destroyed', wrote Leitenant Bartinev. Next the No 3 magazine was fired, but only half the magazine was destroyed, whilst the remaining half lay smoking beneath a pile of earth. The No 2 diesel generator and some buildings were burned, followed by the No 1 diesel generator. Soon after, the other half of the No 3 magazine finally blew up. By 1400hrs the demolition party counted the business as finished and the group made its way back to Mento. Leitenant Bartinev was taken into captivity by the Germans.

At 0800hrs on 16 October, 131 Regt began to advance down the Sworbe Peninsula with orders not to fire on Russian columns on the road showing the white flag. SMS *Friedrich der Grosse* was also requested to hold fire, unless the Zerel battery opened fire. The situation remained unclear for the Germans.

Towards 1000hrs, 131 Regt pushed onto the approaching Russian 425th Infantry Regiment, at whose head marched the officer corps. Oberstleutnant Fischer called to the Russian commander: 'I regret your military misfortune, Herr Colonel'. Fischer's regiment captured 150 officers and 5,100 men. Also captured were 54 machineguns, 27 light and 8 heavy guns and supplies, 150 vehicles and horses, four 12-inch cannon, four 6-inch cannon, 20 anti-aircraft guns, 10 revolver cannon and huge amounts of provisions and war materials.

General von Kathen's chief of staff, Oberst von Tschischwitz wrote:

> The Russian garrison came up the Sworbe Peninsula onto the narrows at the north and took position near the sea. The prisoners were allowed to move freely about the German area. The officers were assigned to a special area; they were happy and appeared reconciled with the men. As evening came and the last rays of sunshine disappeared a happy picture emerged. The camp fires burned, the balalaikas spoke and the dances began. They played until well into the next day when the long prisoner column covered the road to Arensburg.
>
> If the Russian battle spirit was as of old, then how long could they have prevented the opening of the Irben Straits! This was the result of the revolution!

Admiral Bakhirev could not overstate the importance of the loss when he wrote:

The traitorous delivery of the 12-inch batteries had great significance not only for the defense of the Riga Gulf, but also for the Moon Sound. Therewith the Irben position lost any value; the supervision of our mine barriers ceased because of the insignificant number of our units, and we had to hold the better half of them in the Kassar Wiek. Our air reconnaissance service ceased as the air stations were lost. Due to the loss of our bases, our launches and shallow draught steamers did not have the opportunity to lay mines in the enemy's cleared routes. Thus the enemy could clear a passage along the coast and easily enter the Riga Gulf, and with excellent knowledge of our mine fields could operate freely. At the same time dispatching our ships to the Gulf had become extremely complicated.

Nevertheless, the Russian forces were still capable of counterattack. Vice Admiral Bakhirev asked the chief of I Division Minesweeper-launches, Captain 2nd Rank Chetverukhin, to undertake an operation with his shallow-draught minesweepers to render assistance to the Russian troops on the southeast of Ösel, at Kubassar. At midnight on the night of 15/16 October the minesweepers *Gruz*, *Kapsyul* and *Krambol*, together with some minesweeping motor launches, departed to land thirty-two light infantry. They were screened to seaward by the destroyers *Deyatel'Nyi* and *Del'Nyi*. When the infantry encountered German troops they were supported by the fire from the minesweepers. Further support was received from the 6-inch battery No 32 on Moon. From Russian stragglers it was learned that the 107th Division and General Ivanov had been surrounded at Peude.

Even if the revolution had debilitated many of the functions of the Imperial Russian Navy, it seems as if the Intelligence Service was still working efficiently. At about 1030hrs on 16 October the commander of the fleet, Rear Admiral Razvozov, advised the commander of the Naval Forces of the Riga Gulf, Vice Admiral Bakhirev, that it was expected that during the night German steamers would land 2,000 men on the part of Moon in the Kassar Wiek. It seems that the Russians had been able to intercept and decipher the following order, issued by General von Estorff on the afternoon of 15 October: 'If it is not possible to seize Moon by darkness tonight, I order the 17th and 138th Infantry Regiments, and Sturmkompanie 18, under the Command of Oberst Matthiass, to push forward onto Moon during the night of the 17th of October'.

Therefore Vice Admiral Bakhirev ordered all forces of the Riga Gulf to concentrate and attempt to cut off the landing force. Admirals Bakhirev and Stark gathered the division chiefs and torpedoboat commanders aboard the steamer *Libau* in Kuiwast, to discuss a plan of action. It was determined to dispatch paired groups of torpedoboats into the Kassar Wiek during the night. The ten coal-fired torpedoboats of the IV, V and VI Div TBD were to be used for this task. Nevertheless, the chief of the VI Division, Captain 1st Rank Ekimov, and the chief of the IV Division, Captain 1st Rank Postelnikov, met aboard *Steregushchi* and entered into further discussions with the torpedoboat commanders. They unanimously decided the planned operation was impracticable, due to navigational difficulties and due to the presence of large numbers of German torpedoboats on the Kassar Wiek. This decision was reported to Vice Admiral Bakhirev.

The coming of the morning of 16 October also saw a resumption of activity in the Kleinen Sound. At dawn the A-boats again pressed forward into the sound and just as on the previous day, the stone dam, its base on Moon Island and other positions on the island were taken under fire. The supply of munitions, provisions and materiel to Orrisar was maintained through the entire day. In addition preparations were undertaken to transport 2,000 men to Moon Island, although a message from the commander of the Special Unit, Vizeadmiral Schmidt, postponed the planned invasion of this island until 17 October.

Meanwhile, the larger torpedoboats were again occupied defending the Kassar Wiek against the Russian sea forces. At daybreak the 4th Torpedoboat Half Flotilla replaced the 13th Half Flotilla in the eastern part of the Kassar Wiek. Kommodore Heinrich had decided not to keep all the boats continuously on the move owing to navigational difficulties and hazards, danger from mines and the over-exertion of personnel and material. Therefore a squad of torpedoboats cruised to the east and the remainder anchored 1.7 nautical miles northwest of Keinast with short anchor chains. Here they were outside the range of Russian gunboats off Kumora Reef, but were near enough to intervene should the Russians move west.

During the night, the three Russian gunboats, *Chrabry*, *Chivinetz* and *Grozyashchi*, and the torpedoboats *Vsadnik*, *Moskvityanin*, *Samson*, *Leitenant Il'in* and *Desna* remained at the entrance to the Kassar Wiek. On the morning of 16 October *Chrabry* was detached to Kuiwast to replenish her supply of ammunition and *Desna* went to Rogekul for maintenance. When at around 0830hrs the squad of German torpedoboats advanced to the east, the Russian unit went to Cape Seanina and the gunboats *Grozyashchi* and *Chivinetz* opened fire. The two German boats developed a smoke screen and Kommodore Heinrich's remaining boats weighed anchor and moved east in support. After about an hour the action was broken off and both the Russian and German groups pulled back.

When Vice Admiral Bakhirev received notification about this skirmish he dispatched the III Division Torpedoboat-Destroyers from Kuiwast to the Kassar Wiek, fearing a landing on Moon was imminent. The armoured cruiser *Admiral Makarov*, laying to the north near Kumora Buoy, was likewise ordered to lend support. To increase the range of her guns *Admiral*

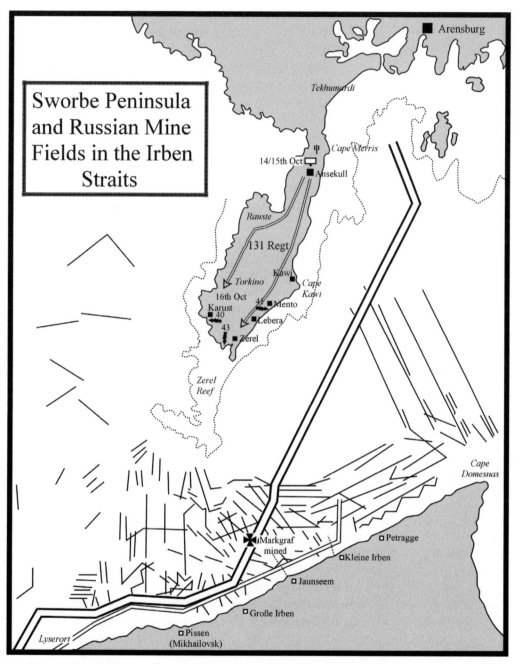

Map 12: Sworbe Peninsula and Russian Mine Fields in the Irben Straits.

Makarov could be heeled over 5°. Likewise, *Slava*, at Schildau, could be heeled to extend the range of her 12-inch cannon in support, just as she had done in defense of the Riga Gulf in August 1915. During her winter 1916 refit the range of *Slava*'s heavy artillery had already been improved from 88 cables to 115 cables.

Meanwhile, towards midday, the five minesweeper boats promised the previous day from the II Minesweeper Division, reported to the I FdT, Kommodore Heinrich. They were sent to clear a channel in the mined area in the middle of the Kassar Wiek, the barrier laid by *Pripyat*, which was greatly hindering the freedom of action of the German torpedoboats. The bow of B98 and the wreck of *Grom* were still conspicuous above the water and served as good navigation marks. Soon the minesweepers found a 'V'-shaped mine barrier beginning near *Grom* and stretching to the northwest and southwest. Most of the mines were of the 1908 type, spherical with lead caps and a charge of 150kg. At the beginning of the barrier were a few mines of the new 1912 type with a fat seam.

At about this time the small hospital ship *Viola* appeared on the Kassar Wiek, en route to the Kleinen Sound to evacuate the wounded of Section Winterfeld. The Russians took her for a troop transport and *Vsadnik* and the gunboats opened fire on her.

As the Russian destroyers of III Div TBD, *Izyaslav*, *Avtroil* and *Gavriil*, approached Raugen buoy they could make out *Viola* and the German torpedoboats. The I FdT had ordered his boats to withdraw to the west, but when the large Russian destroyers were reported he immediately took course towards them with his eleven craft.

At 1214hrs, as the range reached 65 cables (12,000 metres), Captain 1st Rank Shevelev's destroyers opened fire on the nearest German torpedoboats. As the range fell to 10,000 metres the Germans returned the fire. Shortly after, at 1220hrs, the III Division TBD turned eight points (90°) to port and moved away to the east, maintaining fire from their aft guns. During the turn *Avtroil* was hit three times: one shell struck an oil bunker and two shells struck under the bridge, wounding some of the crew.

The waters which the Russian destroyers were negotiating were shallow and extremely tricky. Their freedom to manoeuvre was restricted and they were forced to travel at slow speed. At 1225hrs, moving under fire, *Izyaslav* and *Avtroil* scraped their screws on the bottom at a speed of 15 knots. By 1230hrs the firing had ceased. *Izyaslav* was sent to Rogekul for an inspection of her propellers and *Avtroil* went to Kuiwast to have the shell hole closed up.

Towards 1300 Kommodore Heinrich and his boats returned to their old anchorage, whilst the A-boats in the Kleinen Sound continued about their business, despite fire from *Slava* and the Woi battery, some of which was falling quite close to the small vessels. *Slava* fired a total of eighteen 12-inch shells. With the Russian fire being so accurate, the Germans decided that their observation post must be close by. Therefore T144, T160 and the A-boats undertook an hour-long bombardment of the houses and other positions on the western end of Moon and near Kaggowa.

The gunboat *Grozyashchi* also continued to fire until 1415hrs, shifting fire to the German torpedoboats. After all the firing of this day there was damage to *Grozyashchi's* bow and stern guns; the first had its mounting damaged, the second had its mounting split, which was pulling it from the deck.

The battle on Ösel was drawing to a conclusion, with the last Russian resistance slowly being broken. Once the III Battle Squadron had broken through the minefields in the Irben Straits, the invasion of Moon Island would be able to proceed, probably on 17 October. Vizeadmiral Ehrhardt Schmidt still had the opportunity to further weaken the Russian sea forces in the Moon Sound and therefore he gave the following order by wireless to the I FdT, Kommodore Heinrich: 'During darkness attack the Russian forces in Moon Sound and Riga Gulf with all means: the A-Boats are first to complete their task in the Kleinen Sound'. The previous day, torpedoes from other T-boats had been taken aboard *Emden* and serviced before being delivered to the A-boats by T160, so the small torpedoboats were now fully armed.

Before darkness fell, Kommodore Heinrich, aboard V100, went to the western exit of Moon Sound to see where the Russian guard forces were located. To the northeast was the armoured cruiser *Admiral Makarov* and near Kumora Reef lay five destroyers. However, once again Kommodore Heinrich baulked at the prospect of a night attack. He justified himself in his war diary thus:

> I must refrain from a night attack by torpedoboats in the Moon Sound on this day. The A-boats have not yet completed their task in the Kleinen Sound: of the torpedoboat flotillas, the large boats of II Flotilla do not come into the question due to the difficult navigational conditions in Moon Sound, therefore only the 13th Half Flotilla remain. I hold it as premature to attack now - I must reckon on losses through mines or else stranding, without necessarily finding the enemy - I must for the moment employ myself with the security of the Kassar Wiek for Army operations.

It is odd that the I FdT discounted the B and G-Boats of II Torpedoboat Flotilla, as the majority of the Russian destroyers were of almost identical dimensions and displacement (although there had been several groundings of both Russian and German large types). Towards 1845hrs Kommodore

Heinrich and his torpedoboats anchored near Pavasterort, whilst a squad of boats from 13 TBHF patrolled near the channel to Moon Sound.

During 16 October the German Naval Air Arm was also active. Earlier Arensburg had been established as a base for seaplanes and during the morning two torpedo-bomber aircraft took off on a mission against land targets, escorted by two single-seat seaplanes. Each bomber aircraft carried eight 60kg bombs and at about 1000hrs they attacked the base of the stone dam on Moon. The bombs fell between the Russian guns and their ammunition lockers and an ammunition fire started and was visible for a considerable time afterwards. Two Russian single-seat aircraft took off but did not press home their attacks. Russian reports state that the flyer Shteven met an enemy aircraft over the Kleinen Sound, but, after his third pass, his machine gun jammed and he returned home.

Other German aircraft conducted reconnaissance over Moon Sound and were fired on by Russian torpedoboats. Still other aircraft overflew Moon at low altitude and exchanged fire with Russian ground forces. One German aircraft, which appeared over Kuiwast, was shot down by the Russian flyer Safonov and crashed on Moon, with both pilot and observer being killed.

Previously, during the early hours of 16 October, the airships had carried out an attack on Pernau, in the Riga Gulf. The first to attack was L30, and the airship commander, Oberleutnant zur See Vermehren, reported that his bombs had fallen in the town centre. The airships LZ113 and LZ120 (Kapitänleutnant Zaeschmar and Kapitänleutnant von Lossnitzer, respectively) followed and dropped a bomb load of 6,000kg amongst the roads and harbour buildings. Later, during the night, L37 (Kapitänleutnant Paul Gartner) repeated the attack on Pernau with a bomb load of 2,000kg, but this airship returned to Seerappen with the port midship engine gondola burnt out by a serious fire in the air. Airship SL8 (Oberleutnant zur See Ratz), did not reach the target, but was forced to return to Seddin after having trouble with three of her five engines. In Pernau ten people were killed and many houses were destroyed.

The German U-boats had also been active. The minelayer UC60 had the task of laying mines in the Nücko-Worms Channel and then moving to the Finnish Gulf. Early on 12 October the submarine approached Odensholm and spent the day on the bottom before laying her mines successfully in their allocated positions during the evening. Just before midnight she was accidentally rammed by UC58 and her port diving plane was bent, although the mission was continued. Early on 16 October, at around 1015hrs, UC60 came across a Russian transport of approximately 2,000 BRT near a reef by Povskär. The port tube was fired but the torpedo jammed, possibly due to the collision with UC58. The commander, Oberleutnant zur See Fischer, ordered the gun manned and fire to be opened. As the U-boat turned towards the ship, the torpedo slid from its tube and detonated on the bottom, about 15m ahead of the boat. There was some damage to the boat but most importantly about half the batteries were rendered unserviceable. However, UC60 was still able to force the crew of the Russian steamer, *Esti*, to abandon ship and she was then blown up with explosives. Nevertheless, because UC60, with her damaged batteries, could barely hold headway while submerged, the boat returned prematurely to Libau, returning via Dagerort and over points Gamma, Beta and Alpha.

During 16 October the Russians received further reinforcements in the form of the torpedoboat-destroyers *Emir Bucharski*, *Straschnyi* and the armoured cruiser *Diana*. During the early morning, at about 0520hrs, the U-boat UC58 sighted the cruiser in the southern part of the buoyed channel between the light houses of Cape Tachkona and Odensholm. The U-boat commander, Kapitänleutnant Vesper, thought the cruiser was *Bogatyr*, but it was in reality *Diana*, travelling behind the two destroyers as an anti-submarine screen, along with five minesweepers. UC58 attacked with her two torpedoes through the calm sea, and one torpedo was observed by the Russians to pass under the stern. Back on the German submarine a detonation was heard, which they took to be a hit. In reality the torpedo struck the bottom and exploded. The two destroyers counterattacked and unsuccessfully dropped depth-charges on the U-boat. For the following morning *Diana* was ordered to occupy a position guarding the northern entrance of the Moon Sound.

The previous day the minelayers *Zeya* and *Bureya* had arrived from Helsingfors and took on mines in Rogekul. From there they went to Kuiwast roadstead to join *Pripyat* that evening. They assembled with the minelayer *Volga*. Despite the resolution of the Russian torpedoboat commanders that the planned foray into the Kassar Wiek was impossible, the boats of the IV, V and VI Division Torpedoboat-Destroyers, a total of ten boats, nevertheless assembled near Cape Seanin in the evening. The *Novik* type destroyers of the I, II and III Divisions and the gunboat *Chrabry* supported them. As long-range support, the battleships *Slava* and *Graschdanin* situated themselves near Schildau and *Admiral Makarov* went to Severy Water, in the northern Moon Sound.

Therefore, because there were no spare ships available, the planned production of a new mine barrier in the Riga Gulf had to be cancelled. Admiral Bakhirev remained in complete ignorance about the position of the Germans in the Irben Straits. Nevertheless, during the night a patrol was advanced to Larina Bank, south of Moon Sound. It consisted of the torpedoboats *Deyatel'Nyi* and *Del'Nyi*. They were to advance into the Riga Gulf at day break.

During the evening Vice Admiral Bakhirev received notification from Rear Admiral Razvozov that the German landing on Moon had been postponed, and therefore he gave an order by wireless to the torpedoboat division chief to cancel the night operation. Admiral Stark then set the coal-fired torpedoboats along the edge of Moon Sound.

The weather on 16 October was particularly favourable for the continuance of minesweeping in the Irben Straits. Although late autumn usually produced bad weather, for the third consecutive day the weather was fine. There was a slight south-southwesterly wind, a light sea running and good visibility. Early in the morning, at around 0700hrs, the III Minesweeper Division, followed by the 3rd S-Half Flotilla and IV Minesweeper Division, advanced, sweeping a 400 metre-broad mine-free channel. Just north of barrier gap 4, more mines were found, forcing Kontreadmiral Hopman's cruisers, *Kolberg*, *Strassburg* and *Augsburg*, and Vizeadmiral Behncke's two battleships, *König* and *Kronprinz*, which were travelling in the wake of the minesweepers, to stop at about 1100hrs. During this pause the torpedoboat A62 sighted a barge to the north, which immediately showed the white flag. The barge, which carried 300 men of the Sworbe garrison, was taken in tow by Kapitänleutnant Doflein's minesweeper. During the previous day, as they were being evacuated from Sworbe, the barge had broken free from its tug and during the night had drifted into the Russian mined area. Fortunately they were now rescued and the II Minesweeper Flotilla chief received orders to tow them to Arensburg.

When the advance from barrier gap 4 towards Arensburg resumed, the German units found themselves in the following order: ahead was the III Minesweeper Division, then the 3rd Minesweeper Half Flotilla, both with sweeper gear set; 8th MSHF without gear, followed by the BdAdO's flagship SMS *Kolberg*; 3rd S-Half Flotilla and IV Minesweeper Division, both with sweeper gear set; two *sperrbrecher* vessels, followed by *König* and *Kronprinz*; then *Augsburg* and finally the support vessel group or 'train'. The buoy layers *Wilhelms* and *Mellum* marked the swept channel with buoys and the entire unit traversed the Russian mined area without incident, surely a credit to the tenacious minesweeper units.

During the journey across the Irben Straits, at around 1130hrs, *König* received a new order from Vizeadmiral Schmidt's staff by wireless: 'Attack the Russian forces in the Moon Sound and Riga Gulf with all possible means'. It was an important expansion of Vice Admiral Behncke's brief. Hitherto the primary task for the second phase of the operation had been to advance to Arensburg , make it a secure anchorage for the II Section of the transport fleet and to direct their unloading. Now the principal task was the accelerated attack on Moon Sound and the securing of Arensburg assumed a secondary importance. Vizeadmiral Behncke determined to push forward to the southern entrance to Moon Sound with his strongest forces that same day. He intended to anchor during the night and then to break into the southern Moon Sound on the following morning to attack any Russian forces he might find there. He therefore determined to use his two battleships, the small cruisers *Kolberg* and *Strassburg*, the VIII Torpedoboat Flotilla, the 20th Torpedoboat Half Flotilla and four trawlers of Coastal Protection Half Flotilla East. The cruiser *Augsburg* would supervise the occupation and unloading at Arensburg. The minesweepers would be split, the IV Minesweeper Division and 3rd S-Half Flotilla, whose motorboats were without a tender, would work off Arensburg, whilst 3rd and 8th MSHF and III Minesweeper Division and their tender *Indianola* would accompany Vizeadmiral Behncke.

At about 1430hrs the German unit, Gruppe Behncke, renewed its advance. The two half-flotillas of minesweepers led the way, one with broken out sweeper gear, followed *König*, *Kronprinz* and *Kolberg*, then *Strassburg*, *Indianola* and the four trawlers of Coastal Protection Half Flotilla East, the latter for use as marker boats for important turning points. The torpedoboats formed an anti-submarine screen. *Indianola* remained considerably removed from the lead ship of the group because she had to recover the motorboats of her III Mine Sweeper Division.

Meanwhile, *Augsburg* was detached to Arensburg with the support train, preceded by the IV Minesweeper Division and the 3rd S-Half Flotilla with their minesweeper gear broken out. The minesweeper M77 presented the captured Russian barge to a coastal defence trawler to be conveyed away with the train.

At the beginning of Operation Albion there had been two British submarines stationed in the Riga Gulf, based at Rogekul, C27 (Lieutenant Sealy) and C32 (Lieutenant Satow). When the German undertaking began, Captain Cromie, the chief of the English submarines in the Baltic, immediately dispatched another, C26 (Lieutenant Downie), from Hango to the Moon Sound. The evening of 16 October found Lieutenant Sealy to the southwest of the Moon Sound and it was here that he sighted Gruppe Behncke. Submarine C27 was able to get into an attacking position to port ahead of the German battleships, but, when Lieutenant Sealy raised his periscope to take final aim, he found that he had misjudged the speed of the German unit and that *König* was less than 300 metres distant. Nevertheless, at 1630hrs, C27 fired two torpedoes but both shots missed and to make matters worse, the submarine broke surface between the two German ships. The German ships did not open fire though, believing that the boat was one of their own. Fregattenkapitän Frank, Commander of *Kolberg*, which was traveling 500 metres astern of *Kronprinz*, explained the reason for not opening fire thus: 'It is one of our own that by chance is surfacing close to our line. Don't shoot. It has been run over. There indeed is misfortune!' Likewise, the torpedoboats did not drop any depth charges. However a curt signal from *König* removed all doubt as to the identity of the attacker: 'Two missed torpedo shots'. The range had been so low that the battleship's guns had been unable to depress low enough to take aim on the British submarine. Lieutenant Sealy quickly took his submarine to a safe depth and began reloading his torpedo tubes; he reasoned correctly that more German ships would follow. When he came to periscope depth again he was greeted by the sight of a large steamer and quickly he fired one of his two remaining torpedoes at a range of just over 700 metres. The target was *Indianola*, which was following the group after recovering two damaged motorboats of her minesweeper division, and at around 1645hrs she was struck amidships, beneath the funnel. The engine room and stokehold filled with water and the ship became unmanoeuvrable. She maintained positive buoyancy, however, and was in no immediate danger of sinking. Four torpedoboats were immediately dispatched to hunt the submarine but none of the depth charges they dropped was able to damage C27. The torpedoed tender was towed in to Arensburg.

Meanwhile, Lieutenant Sealy decided the time was right to quit the Riga Gulf, despite the fact that he had one torpedo remaining. After it became dark C27 surfaced but was immediately forced to dive again by German light forces. After a further unsuccessful depth-charging he was able to exit the Gulf and return to Hango.

The submarine C32 had been stationed 1 nautical mile north of Domesnas and during the same afternoon Lieutenant Satow sighted the German unit to the northwest, at a range of some 5 nautical miles. C32 dived and endeavoured to get into a firing position. However, as the submarine manoeuvred in the clear water she was spotted and bombed by a German seaplane, at which point Lieutenant Satow lost contact with the German unit. He correctly deduced that Gruppe Behncke was headed for the Moon Sound and accordingly steered for the southern exit of the Sound during the night. Luckily for the Germans he did not find them in the dark.

During the afternoon of 16 October, Gruppe Behncke pushed forward to the southern exit of the Moon Sound and at about 2026hrs dropped anchor. The German ships were anchored in one long line with torpedoboats at each end. To provide himself with some security, Vizeadmiral Behncke ordered the torpedoboats to extinguish the lanterns of the mine-free channel marker buoys; he then convened a meeting of the BdAdO and the ship and flotilla commanders onboard his flagship, *König*. The conference was later related by three of the participants. Kontreadmiral Hopman recalled:

Towards 9pm the unit anchored south of Moon Sound. In an immediately convened meeting Admiral Behncke made known his attack plans. The battleships would break through the blockaded area to the west and they would then defeat the Russian ships lying near Kuiwast and the shore batteries, whilst I with the small cruisers should penetrate the Kleinen Sound. The location of the Russian mine barriers was known to us from the map found on the captured Russian destroyer *Grom*, which two days before had been taken by our torpedobootes in the Kassar Wiek.

Kapitänleutnant Doflein related the meeting as follows:

> In the admiral's cabin on the flagship all the leaders were gathered in the dim light around the sea chart of Moon Sound. Briefly our leader, Vizeadmiral Behncke, outlined his program: 'With the day's dawn I will attack the Russian Fleet and shore batteries in the Moon Sound. I suppose, then, that they will give a hot battle and offer stubborn resistance from behind the mine barriers. Therefore the II Minesweeper Flottille should go forward first to pave a mine-free route to the enemy. If the boats come under fire they should continue the advance, however I will immediately push forward with the ships and attempt to surprise and destroy the enemy.

There was obviously some consternation about the English submarines after the attacks on *König* and *Indianola*, as reflected in Fregattenkapitän Frank's account:

> In the evening at about 9pm we all anchored in the middle of the sea, south of Moon Sound on a starless night. If a submarine travelled along the lights of the channel it would find us at their end. We were collected by a torpedoboat and taken to a sitting of admirals, commanders and naval staff officers on *König*. Despite the moonless night the dark ship's hull with its black smoke cloud was visible from far off. Admiral Behncke gave us sherry and cigarettes. He imparted our roles for the next day for an attack on the southern exit of Moon Sound. The battleships would push forwards towards Moon Sound and its fortifications, the cruisers against the Kleinen Sound and the battery at Woi. Indeed; and the submarines? 'I have dispatched torpedoboats to extinguish the buoy lights, gentlemen, but apart from that we must allow them to approach'.
>
> We returned aboard and slept well, the submarines did not disturb our night!

The final phase of the operation was about to begin.

CHAPTER SEVEN

17 October: The Battle in Moon Sound

The night passed quietly for Gruppe Behncke. The main concern for the German admiral was the Russian minefields at the southern exit of Moon Sound. The northernmost was rectangular in shape, measuring about 4 miles wide and 1 mile deep, whilst the southernmost was trapezoidal in shape and measured about 5 miles by 1 mile. The German U-boat mine barriers lay to the west of these fields. From the captured Russian pilotage book and the charts of *Grom*, the location of the Russian mine fields had become known but several mistakes had been made in relaying their positions to Vizeadmiral Behncke by wireless. The original German plan called for the unit to push forward to the west of the trapezoidal field then manoeuvre east between the two fields and give battle to the Russians. This route went uncomfortably close to the U-boat barriers, but the route to the east would take them very close to the 10 metre line and allow little sea room for manoeuvring. The cruisers of the BdAdO would follow and then strike northwest into the Kleinen Sound.

However, just before 0430hrs, an erroneous wireless message arrived, giving details of a narrow mine barrier running north-south between the two larger fields. Although the message was in error, as far as Vizeadmiral Behncke was concerned the situation had changed and now the minesweeper chiefs, Kapitänleutnant Doflein and Kapitänleutnant Weidgen, were called aboard *König* and given new instructions. The 3rd Minesweeper Half Flotilla would now sweep to the south of the trapezoidal field and then take course to the north from Larina Bank, followed by the battleships, whilst the 8th Minesweeper Half Flotilla and III Mine Sweeper Division would sweep west of the mine fields to clear a path for the cruisers. Valuable time was lost revising these arrangements and it was not until 0600hrs that the advance began in a freshening south-southwesterly wind.

About 0700hrs, the 3 MSHF took course east, sweeping a broad channel south of the trapezoidal mine field, whilst the 8 MSHF continued to the north. Shortly after, both groups slipped their gear, but whilst the 3 MSHF was able to continue eastwards without interruption, 8 MSHF had found mines and had actually pushed onto the southwest corner of the trapezoidal field. At about the same time, *König* sighted two Russian torpedoboats to the northeast, close under the Estonian coast. It was *Deyatel'Nyi* and *Del'Nyi* of XI Division Torpedoboat-Destroyers. However, the Russian torpedoboat-destroyers had sighted the German unit first.

At about 0600hrs *Deyatel'Nyi* had been patrolling near Larina Bank and had reported 'twenty-eight smoke columns in the southwest', and soon afterwards 'enemy force advances towards Kuiwast'. Upon receipt of this report Vice Admiral Bakhirev ordered *Graschdanin* and *Slava* to come south to Kuiwast Roads, where they arrived at 0700hrs. The cruiser *Diana*, which had arrived from the Finnish Gulf the previous day, was ordered to the north Moon Sound. The torpedoboat-destroyers and transports were ordered to weigh anchor and move to the north of Kuiwast Roads. Some steamers and tugs with civilian crews were released from service, whilst Kontre Admiral Stark boarded *Novik* where he was ordered to guard the Kassar Wiek and the deep dredged channel, and to prepare the steamers *Glagol* and *Pokoj* for scuttling in the channel should it be necessary to retire to the northern Moon Sound. Vice Admiral Bakhirev continued in his report: 'At 7 o'clock [9 o'clock Russian time], after the latest dispositions were given from ashore by telephone, I arrived on *Bayan*, and had at my disposal Captain 1st Rank Muromtsev and Flag Officer Leitenant Sokolov. The flag was raised and the order was given to weigh anchor'.

The commander of *Bayan*, Captain 1st Rank S N Timirev, reported that the battleships were reluctant to move. He wrote:

> A few agonizing minutes passed after the release of the signal. *Slava* and *Graschdanin* raised their anchors and raised their spheres to 'medium speed', but ...did not move. Not the slightest breaker was appreciable under their bows. Was it again the 'morale element?'... Bakhirev approached me and spoke through his teeth: 'They do not wish to go! What shall we do?'

Captain 1st Rank Timirev had an idea and the signal 'follow the admiral' was raised. Thereon the battleships followed *Bayan* down the Moon Sound to the firing position.

Meanwhile at around 0730hrs German seaplanes carried out a raid on Kuiwast roadstead. The seaplanes dropped a total of fifteen bombs, four of which fell in the roads, eight on the pier and command post, and three near the battery. Neither the command post nor any vessels were directly hit, but the effect of the bombs was impressive. Captain 1st Rank Timirev wrote:

The picture was graphic: all the water around our units literally boiled from exploding bombs, the high water columns mixed with rich black smoke, and the noise and crashing from the detonations was deafening, with splinters whistling in all directions - all this made for an impression of hell. This impression, however, was not related to the results. No damage was caused, short of several hits by fine splinters.

The decision by Admiral Bakhirev to accept battle in the Moon Sound was extremely courageous, but also calculated and aggressive. There was an overwhelming disparity between the opposing forces. The two Russian pre-dreadnought battleships could field eight 12-inch and twenty-four 6-inch pieces, against the two German dreadnought battleships armed with twenty 30.5cm and twenty-eight 15cm pieces. The dreadnoughts were much larger, almost twice the displacement, and carried much thicker armour. However, the sea room was strictly limited in the confined, shallow and narrow channels, and therefore there was no advantage in having superior speed. The mine barriers and shore batteries at Woi and Werder were also an asset to the Russians. Vice Admiral Bakhirev knew that the defence of the southern Moon Sound was the last chance to save the campaign and keep the Germans from the gates of St Petersburg. A stubborn resistance and repulse, or even delay, of the German attack would allow reinforcements to be ferried to Moon and enable further submarine attacks and minelaying to occur. Thus the German lines of communication would be stretched and the force in the Riga Gulf could only be supported for a few days. Then there could be some relief. On the other hand, surrender of the southern Moon Sound and Kuiwast would mean the certain loss of the islands and the enforced evacuation of the Sea Forces of the Riga Gulf. For an officer of the character and experience of Vice Admiral Bakhirev there could be only one decision: continue the defence with all means available, despite the odds.

After sighting the two Russian torpedoboats, the battleship SMS *König* opened fire on them with her heavy guns. The Russian torpedoboats quickly made off to the north. Soon after, the Germans could make out the Russian heavy units coming south from Kuiwast Roads.

Between 0722hrs and 0730hrs the 10-inch battery on Moon opened fire on the 8 MSHF, III Minesweeper Division and the *sperrbrecher* vessels. The barrier breakers were immediately ordered to the rear of the German line as, despite their relative immunity to mine damage, they were quite vulnerable to artillery fire. The 8th Minesweeper Half Flotilla was thereon ordered to leave the mine-clearing work to the III Minesweeper Division and to push into the Kleinen Sound.

After a short time the Woi battery ceased fire. As *Bayan* reached abeam Cape Paternoster she reduced speed and stopped, whilst the battleships continued a little further to the south to their firing positions. The three Russian ships stretched in a line running north – south and prepared to open fire. The guns of *Slava* could range to 116 cable-lengths (21,400 metres) and those of *Graschdanin* 88 cables (16,300 metres). The range of *Slava* would come as a particular surprise to the Germans.

At 0805hrs *Graschdanin* opened fire on the approaching German minesweepers of the 8 MSHF, under the command of Kapitänleutnant Erich Koellner. *Slava* and the Woi battery also opened fire. The shells landed all around the sweeper formation, with the Germans reporting the fire of the Woi battery as being particularly well laid. The minesweeper boats were bound by their sweeper gear and had to maintain a steady course without being able to return the fire. Nevertheless, none of the boats was hit, nor suffered splinter damage. When from time to time their gear slipped owing to the shallow water, the minesweepers covered themselves with a smoke screen and in this they were supported by two torpedoboats which Vizeadmiral Behncke had dispatched forward to them.

Meanwhile, the III Minesweeper Division also lay under continuous fire and they worked laboriously at clearing the located mines. Because of an error in relaying the position of the trapezoidal minefield to the III Battle Squadron chief, the Germans remained unaware that they had entered its southwest corner.

At 0800hrs Vizeadmiral Behncke ordered the cruisers to cease their advance so that they would not lay unnecessarily in the fire of the Russian battleships and coastal artillery. *König* and *Kronprinz* turned onto an eastwards course, into the channel swept by 3 MSHF under Kapitänleutnant von der Marwitz, south of the trapezoidal field. Meanwhile, *Slava* had slowly advanced to the south so that she lay between Cape Paternoster and Werder; at 0812hrs she shifted fire from the minesweepers to the eastward-steering German battleships. The German battleships replied with their heavy artillery at a range of 20,400 meters but, much to their chagrin, their shells fell short. The first salvoes were of three projectiles, but then subsequently of five shells. On the other hand, the fire of *Slava*, directed by her experienced gunnery officer, Starchi Leitenant Rybaltovski, was good, with some shells impacting just 50 metres distant from *König*. The Germans now found themselves at a severe tactical disadvantage - the 12-inch pieces of *Slava* outranged the 30.5cm guns on the German dreadnoughts and, moreover, the German ships were restricted to the narrow swept channel and were unable to manoeuvre. Under these circumstances Vizeadmiral Behncke was forced to reverse his course to a westerly heading and withdraw from *Slava*'s accurate fire.

Graschdanin meanwhile continued firing on the minesweepers with her 12-inch cannon and, when the range allowed, also opened fire with

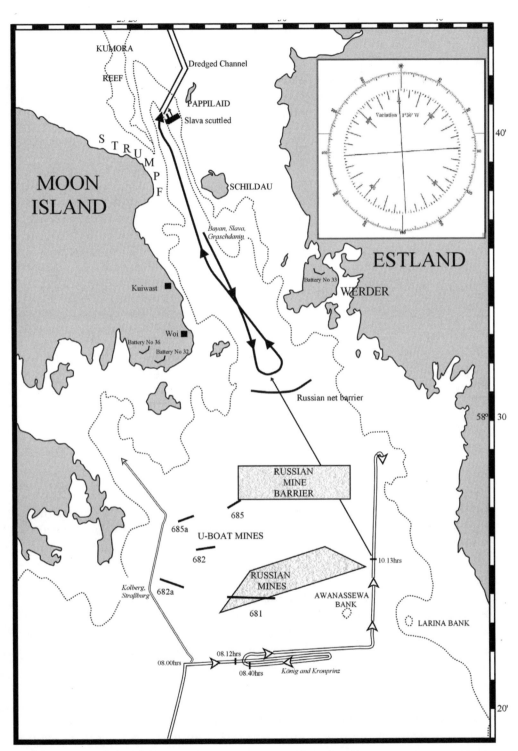

Map 13: The Battle in Moon Sound.

her 6-inch battery. The Russians were confined in a narrow channel with strong currents and they had to utilize their engines to hold position. At 0830hrs, as the Germans had retired, Vice Admiral Bakhirev ordered the battleships to maintain fire on the nearest enemy, the minesweepers. During this time the 3 MSHF continued its advance and at 0840hrs the minesweepers reached Larina Bank and turned north. With that *König* and *Kronprinz* resumed an easterly course at 0840hrs, following at low speed. *Slava*, meanwhile, repositioned a little more to the north, whilst to the west Kontreadmiral Hopman, on observing the squadron chief's movements, resumed his advance towards the Kleinen Sound. The Russians had resumed fire on the 3 MSHF at 0830hrs and held them under continuous heavy fire since. The shore batteries at Woi and Werder joined in the practice and it became obvious to the Germans that the Russians intended to stop the minesweepers, therefore stalling the entire attack. The minesweepers continued obstinately, M77 and M67 being slightly damaged by shell splinters in the process. Kapitänleutnant Doflein described the experience thus:

> the enemy fire began from the right and from far ahead. We were covered by a crossfire from *Slava* and *Tsarevitch* [*Graschdanin's* former name], *Bayan* and the shore batteries at Werder. House-high water spouts climbed amongst the half flotilla so that shrapnel and water rained on the boats. It was a wonder that with this hail of shot the half flotilla remained without heavy damage. My brave 3rd Half Flotilla was indeed courageous.

At about 0940hrs, the III Minesweeper Division was brought over to the eastern side of the Russian minefield to assist the 3 MSHF as they advanced to the north, whilst *König* and *Kronprinz* waited between Larina and Awanasewa Banks. It was Vizeadmiral Behncke's intension to allow the 3 MSHF to push north past the large rectangular field and then he would suddenly advance with his battleships and attempt to come to grips with the Russians.

Just before the cessation of fire the bow turret of *Slava* suffered multiple breakdowns. A double bronze gear wheel and pinion gave out, the shaft was bent and the gear wheel could not be moved. Both guns were therefore rendered unserviceable after the right gun had fired four shots and the left had fired seven shots. Both guns had been supplied to the ship in November 1916 and had fired a total of thirty-four practice rounds and forty-five battle shots. According to the opinion of specialists aboard *Slava*, the fault lay with the factory for manufacturing the gear wheel from defective material. Nothing could be done to remove or rectify the damage. There were now twenty 30.5cm cannon ranged against the two remaining

12-inch guns of *Slava* , the four shorter-ranged 12-inch guns of *Graschdanin* and the two combat-ready 10-inch guns of the Moon Island battery at Woi, which had a slow rate of fire.

There was now a pause in the battle and Vice Admiral Bakhirev signalled that the crews could go to lunch (Russian time being two hours ahead of German time, which is used here). The Russian units moved a little off to the north, where *Bayan* and *Graschdanin* anchored, and *Slava* held using her engines. The torpedoboat-destroyers *Ukraina*, *Voiskovoi*, *Donskoi Kazak*, *Turkmenets-Stravropolski*, *Sil'Nyi* and *Storozhevoi*, together with *Del'Nyi* and *Deyatel'Nyi*, guarded against U-boats.

Meanwhile, the German minesweepers continued their work to the east of the Russian minefields. *Slava* began to manoeuvre closer to them by going astern, though she could not utilize her 6-inch battery as the guns were loaded with anti-submarine plunging projectiles, even though the chance of a U-boat attack was remote.

At 0950hrs *Graschdanin* weighed anchor, followed soon after by *Bayan* and Vice Admiral Bakhirev ordered: 'If the enemy moves nearer, open fire'.

At 1004hrs *Graschdanin* opened fire on the eastern group of minesweepers. Then *Slava* also opened fire using her stern turret. Soon afterwards *Bayan* also opened fire and then *Turkmenets-Stravropski* and *Donskoi Kazak* also joined the target practice on the minesweepers at a range of 65 to 70 cables (11,800 to 12,800 metres). The minesweepers responded quickly and developed a smoke screen.

By 1000hrs the German minesweepers were abeam the northern edge of the rectangular minefield and Vizeadmiral Behncke gave the signal 'utmost power'. Now *König* and *Kronprinz* dashed forward, slightly *en echelon*, so that the latter could bring her guns to bear. At 1013hrs *König* opened fire on *Slava* to the right and at 1017hrs *Kronprinz* opened fire on *Graschdanin* to the left.[1] Further to the left was the armoured cruiser *Bayan* which remained untargeted by enemy fire until the conclusion of the battle, when *König* took her briefly under fire. The fire of *König*, under the direction of I Artillery Offizier, Kapitänleutnant Ernst Meusel, was rapid and well laid and three shells from the third salvo struck *Slava* below the waterline.

The first pair of projectiles struck the bow 10 to 12 feet below the waterline. The first hit the bow dynamo engine room and exploded either against the hull, or in a ventilation shaft, and produced a huge hole in the interior hull about 3.6 metres in diameter. The electrical power to the bow immediately failed. The crew in the dynamo room were quick witted but barely managed to escape through an emergency exit as the water flooded into all the compartments up to the battery deck. The hatch was torn to pieces, as was the door to the lower compartment of the bow 12-inch turret, and water flooded the bow 12-inch magazine. The other projectile of this pair made an underwater hole in the compartment of the wet stores and capstan flat, which were flooded. The bow immediately took on a total of 1130 tonnes of water.

As a result of these damaging hits the ship immediately took a list of 4 to 5°, which after several minutes increased to 8°. The chief engineer, Mazurenko, ordered counterflooding on the starboard side which reduced the list to 4°. He then went to report the extent of the damage to the commander, Captain 1st Rank Antonov. The bows sank 5 feet deeper, with an average increase of 2 feet, so that the draught at the bow was 31–32 feet, and aft was 29–30 feet. The bulkheads held nicely, with only a slight leakage through electrical connections.

The third shell from *König's* salvo struck the port side of the hull underwater, against the port engine room armour. Luckily however, the armour held and the explosive effect barely damaged the hull, so that the slight leakage could be controlled with the pumps available.

A short time later, at 1024hrs, another two projectiles struck *Slava* together. One struck on the port side near the forward funnel in the chapel flat, which was being used as a first aid station, and the other struck the battery deck. The first shell disrupted lockers, firefighting equipment (which caused flooding), ladders, a 6-inch magazine and the forward stokehold. A fire started on the upper deck. The forward dressing station was wrecked and there were dead and wounded sailors there. The executive officer, Starchi Leitenant Galler, arrived from the Central Battle Post and took charge of the firefighting. Despite difficulties locating the seat of the blaze because of the thick gas and smoke, the fire was extinguished after ten to fifteen minutes.

Flames, gas and smoke spread across the funnel and emergency exit to the conning tower. Gases from the exploding projectile also penetrated the bunker of the forward boiler room and the handling room of the left bow 6-inch turret. The stokers remained at their stations, but the 6-inch magazine was flooded as a precaution.

Finally at 1039hrs *Slava* received another two underwater hits. One projectile struck near the boiler room, the other on the armour outside the wireless-telegraphy cabin. In the boiler room compartment three men were killed, including one who was decapitated. The hit on the armour holed it and wrecked the bulkhead of a coal bunker.

In the meantime, *Kronprinz* had opened fire on *Graschdanin*. At almost the same instant as the first hit on *Slava*, two projectiles also struck *Graschdanin*. One hit on the stern and holed the upper deck before detonating underneath and demolishing several cabins. Splinters pierced the next deck and the battery deck. The resulting fire produced thick, dark poisonous smoke but the fire was quickly extinguished. The second shell struck the upper belt armour beneath the middle 6-inch turret at an acute angle and consequently only dented the plate before detonating. A large number of splinters holed the hull and damaged two dynamo engines and several steam pipes.

The Russian ships initially continued to fire on the 3 MSHF, before changing target to the German battleships. As the range decreased, the armoured cruiser *Bayan* also opened fire with her three 8-inch guns. Then, at around 1030hrs, Vice Admiral Bakhirev gave the VI Div TBD and XI Div TBD orders to retire to the north, to make way for the battleships. Subsequently the order was given 'MSRZ [Naval Forces of the Riga Gulf], withdraw'. *Slava* and *Graschdanin* now made their way to the north towards the dredged channel and passed out of range of the German battleships, the shortest range having been 16,500 meters. Accordingly, *König* transferred her fire to *Bayan*. Vice Admiral Bakhirev had decided *Bayan* would go last and in the meantime would offer herself as a decoy. Salvo after salvo, eight in rapid succession, now crashed around the Russian cruiser, whilst Captain 1st Rank Timirev used his engines and rudder to twist and turn his ship to evade destruction. He wrote:

> I shall never forget the next 15 minutes, conscious that the slightest malfunction of the engines or steering gear would make us an easy target, and one hit could send us to the bottom, it was difficult to preserve the coolness duty demanded. I was supported during this trial but the hero was M K Bakhirev, who maintained complete calmness on the bridge, not interfering at all with management, and only casting a sympathetic glance and smile as I played the mad 'game' on the engine telegraph. At last *Graschdanin* had disappeared towards Schildau Island and Bakhirev ordered me in a low voice: 'withdraw!'

With the last salvo from *König* a projectile struck the Russian cruiser. The 30.5cm shell struck to starboard near the bridge and penetrated the deck near the forward 8-inch turret, then penetrated the armoured deck and entered the cable compartment. The shell then exploded and set fire to much combustible material: rope, canvas, hemp and the like. The fire gave off a large volume of thick, suffocating, acrid smoke, which hindered visibility ahead from the bridge. The explosion also destroyed a bulkhead and wrecked the capstan room and some provisions, tore eight ribs and the internal plating of the double bottom and displaced several plates of the upper armoured belt. The proximity of the fire to the 6- and 8-inch magazines meant these had to be flooded and the draught forward increased to 26 feet. With the flooding and water entering through splinter holes around 1,000 tonnes of water entered the ship. The fire burned for around twenty-four hours before finally being extinguished. Two men were killed instantly, three died later of their wounds, and three men were wounded.

The Russian ships had lain under a continuous and well-directed heavy German fire. The salvoes of four or five projectiles lay close to the Russian ships and *Graschdanin* counted no less than twenty very close straddles, which caused enormously powerful vibrations through the hull, and loosened several armoured plates.

As the Russian ships passed abeam Schildau Island, the German battleships ceased fire on them and transferred their aim to the batteries at Woi and Werder.

However, at this moment six German floatplanes appeared and dropped around forty bombs, mostly on the smaller ships. The combined air and sea attack on the Russian forces must have been extremely daunting for the defenders, especially the minelayers with their highly-explosive cargoes, but nevertheless *Slava* succeeded in shooting down one of the seaplanes.

The casualties aboard *Slava* remain unknown, as does her expenditure of ammunition, whilst *Graschdanin* suffered five wounded, one of whom later died, and expended around fifty 12-inch high explosive shells and 114 6-inch shells. Vice Admiral Bakhirev later commended the commander of *Graschdanin*, Captain 1st Rank Rudenski, for the excellent handling and performance of his ship.

Previously Vice Admiral Bakhirev had ordered that mines be laid in the Kuiwast roads, but at 1120hrs Kontre Admiral Stark informed him that the V Division Torpedoboat-Destroyers had still not yet taken on mines. Therefore this plan was abandoned.

The hapless *Slava*, for so long a thorn in the side of the Germans in the Riga Gulf, was now mortally wounded. Unluckily, five out of the seven 30.5cm projectile hits had been below the water line and her 2.5 metre increase in draught made the passage through the dredged channel impossible. Captain 1st Rank Antonov therefore requested the admiral's permission to save his crew and scuttle the ship. As *Bayan* passed close to *Slava*, orders were given for her to be scuttled across the entrance of the dredged channel after *Bayan* and *Graschdanin* had passed. At this time some panic-stricken voices could be heard from aboard *Slava*.

At 1115hrs *Bayan* and *Graschdanin* entered the dredged channel. To render assistance for manoeuvring in the narrow channel, the commander of *Graschdanin* requested the tug *Chernomorski 2* and the guard vessel *Laski* to stand by the bow and stern of his ship. Captain 1st Rank Timirev refused the assistance of a tug for *Bayan*.

Vice Admiral Bakhirev ordered 'torpedoboats render assistance to the stricken ship' and the torpedoboat-destroyers *Sil'Nyi, Voiskovoi, Donskoi-Kazak* and *Storozhevoi*, the tug *Moskito* and a minesweeper were dispatched towards the stricken battleship. However, some degree of panic broke out aboard *Slava*. She was proceeding at low speed and Captain Antonov gave orders to stop, to allow the other vessels to enter the dredged channel. However, the engine room did not respond to the engine telegraph and it was found that the engine room had been abandoned on the orders of the Sailors' Committee. Engineer Mazurenko took some men to the engine room to respond to the commands from the bridge, but they could not stop *Slava* from being beached on a shoal to the southeast of the dredged channel, instead of in the channel itself.

The artillery officer, Starchi Leitenant Rybaltovski, reported: 'During the battle all crew strived to conduct themselves ideally, but in part some of the young put on life belts and panicked - shouting until they numbered about 100 men'.

The first of the torpedoboats came alongside and the commander ordered the crew to transfer across to them, after transferring the wounded first. There was increasing panic as *Slava*'s crew feared the imminent detonation of the battleship's magazines. Michman Kovshov wrote: 'When the torpedoboat-destroyer *Donskoi-Kazak* approached, many sailors wanted to jump down the gap, but the watch-chief of the torpedoboat, Michman Gedle, threatened them with a pistol, and ordered the transfer of the wounded first'.

The last to leave the ship was Captain Antonov. He found time in his report to excuse the behaviour of his crew: 'The behaviour of all officers and men during the time of the battle was above all praise, and only after the ship went aground, and in consequence of the order from me to blow up the ship being misunderstood, did part of the crew, the exceptionally young, panic'. After a final inspection Antonov boarded the torpedoboat *Storozhevoi* and she pulled away. Shortly afterwards, at 1158hrs, the Bickford fuses that had been lit detonated charges which exploded the aft 12-inch magazine. There was an enormous detonation followed by others and a huge explosion cloud climbed towards the heavens, which was visible to the I FdT and Leutnant zur See Ruge in the Kassar Wiek, some 25 kilometres distant.

To complete the destruction, the VI Division chief, Captain 1st Rank Ekimov, ordered *Moskvityanin* and *Amurets* to approach *Slava* and torpedo her. On *Moskvityanin* two torpedoes were launched, one of which struck between the funnels but did not explode, the other ran in circles. Two torpedoes from *Amurets* hit but likewise failed to explode. *Turkmenets* now launched two torpedoes and whilst one failed to detonate the other struck the starboard hull side near the forward funnel and exploded. Of the six torpedoes fired, only one had functioned properly, which vindicated Vice Admiral Bakhirev's poor opinion of materiel in the post-revolutionary navy. Fires continued aboard *Slava* throughout the night.

After the passage of the last Russian sea forces to the north, the steamers *Glagol* and *Pokoj* were scuttled in the dredged channel. *Glagol* was sunk in the southern part of the channel with nine 4-inch shells from the torpedoboat-destroyer *Zabaikalets*. *Pokoj* was scuttled near the first buoy by shots from *Turkmenets* and *Zabaikalets*.

Whilst the Russian sea forces were covering their retreat the Germans continued to advance, and at 1046hrs the Werder battery opened fire on the German battleships. The *König* returned the fire and after a short time the Russian battery ceased fire. Apart from some disciplined crew, the gun teams were fleeing without restraint. Battery No 33 had been abandoned. Soon after, flames could be seen coming from the signal station and other buildings and further detonations showed that the area was being abandoned.

At 1109hrs the two German battleships anchored with short chains abeam Selglaid, whilst 300 metres ahead the 3 MSHF investigated Fass Bank. The battleships were now taken under fire by Battery No 32 at Woi, but in contrast to the Russian battleships and the 10-inch battery at Woi, the 6-inch guns fired poorly and soon ceased. *König* returned the fire between 1115hrs and 1135hrs.

Of the five 10-inch pieces of Battery No 36 at Woi on Moon Island, three were mounted on a wooden base and could not fire to seawards, but could fire on the stone dam. The other two guns were mounted on concrete foundations and were behind wooden parapets, and could fire a salvo every 1½ to 2 minutes. When the German torpedoboats and battleships approached, many of the gun crews lost heart and almost all fled. When the Russian forces retired past Schildau, the guns were demolished and the crews that remained went to Kuiwast pier, to be evacuated to the continent.

Towards 1128hrs a false submarine alarm was given on the German battleships when a boat hook was mistaken for a periscope. After the attack by C27 the previous day, the Germans were acutely aware of the danger from submarines and, therefore, at noon Gruppe Behncke weighed anchor and proceeded up and down the eastern swept channel at low speed, under the protection of an anti-submarine screen. At around 1208hrs another submarine alarm was given, to port ahead, bearing 350 degrees. This time the alarm was real for it was C26 (Lieutenant Downie), which was manoeuvring to attack the German battlegroup. At the beginning of Operation Albion, C26 had been in Hango, but in the meantime had proceeded south and now found herself south of the Moon Sound in a favourable position to carry out a torpedo attack. Unfortunately, Lieutenant Downie was hampered by the shallow water depth and before arriving in a firing position found himself hard aground. C26 was unable to come free by going astern and therefore had to blow her ballast tanks to release herself. In doing so the boat broke surface with her conning tower and was seen by the Germans, so that the torpedoboats immediately took up the hunt for her. The torpedoboats opened fire with their guns and depth charges and continued the hunt for over two hours, at one stage forcing C26 into a net where she damaged her propeller. After darkness, Lieutenant Downie was able to surface and found that his hydroplanes had been damaged and jammed, rendering his boat unseaworthy, so he took his crippled submarine to Pernau, hoping to be able to effect repairs there.

In the meantime, the Gruppe Behncke had continued to press forward, although the way was not easy. The south-southeast wind and rising sea made the work of the advancing minesweepers difficult and they frequently slipped their gear on the rocky bottom. The motorboats of the III Minesweeper Division were forced to cease their activity because of the deteriorating weather. The 3rd Minesweeper Half Flotilla, led by A62, continued towards Kuiwast Roads. However, they soon ran into a heavy net barrier, supported by iron barrels, running in a semicircular arc between the islands of Wirelaid and Werder, directly across the southern entrance to the Moon Sound. The minesweepers were unable to penetrate this barrier, so, towards 1540hrs, Vizeadmiral Behncke ordered the work to be broken off and at about 1700hrs the battleships, screened by torpedoboats, anchored southwest of the trapezoidal minefield. At 1730hrs, A62 and the 3rd MSHF anchored with them.

Towards 0900hrs, when Vizeadmiral Behncke had resumed his advance towards the southern Moon Sound, Kontreadmiral Hopman had, likewise, again begun to press forward with his small cruisers into the Kleinen Sound. The minesweepers of the 8 MSHF were nevertheless encountering difficulties because of the error in communicating the locations of the Russian minefields learned from *Grom*'s captured charts. Having clipped the southwest corner of the trapezoidal minefield, the sweepers' progress was slow and it was not until towards noon that the cruisers, minesweepers and *sperrbrecher* ships arrived in the northwest of the Kleinen Sound at the 10 metre line. The minesweepers then went ahead to take soundings but T53 and A35 briefly went aground. *Kolberg* briefly took the Woi battery under fire for ten minutes from 1335hrs, but the Russian battery did not reply, so that Kontreadmiral Hopman had to ask the I FdT what the situation was.

Towards 1425hrs *Kolberg* and *Strassburg* anchored in the southern entrance of the Kleinen Sound. Then Kontreadmiral Hopman's flag lieutenant, Oberleutnant zur See Kelm, suggested that the two batteries on Woi could be captured by a landing party and offered to lead the group. A landing party of forty men and two machine guns was quickly assembled and made ready and at 1545hrs they were landed under the cover of two M-boats that had moved close inshore. At 1730hrs a white star shell was observed, the signal from the landing party that the battery had successfully been taken, though the guns had been rendered unserviceable. This small band were the first Germans to arrive on Moon.

The Landing Corps on Dago had a much more difficult time of it. At 0925hrs SMS *Kaiser* carried out a preparatory bombardment of the bridgehead area at Serro, which continued for thirty-five minutes. Section Ahlefeld was landed immediately afterwards and during the day patrols penetrated far inland, but nevertheless suffered some losses. At midday the transports *Oswald*, *Sangara* and *Borderland*, together with horse transports and barges, arrived off Cape Toffri, but the anchorage was not yet ready to accommodate them. Similarly, a cyclist battalion was delayed and only arrived at Pamerort around midday, so that all intended support for Section Ahlefeld was delayed and the Landing Corps was again forced to retreat to the bridgehead towards evening. Because of the difficulty in transporting the wounded it was decided to occupy the bridgehead overnight, although trawlers stood by, ready to evacuate the German troops should the Russians press home an attack. Although the fighting had been lively during the day, the night passed quietly for the Germans.

Nevertheless, although Section Ahlefeld was being sorely tested the Russians themselves were having problems. The force that had attacked the Germans had been a unit of 35 Jagers, whereas the 427th Grenadier Regiment had refused to go on the offensive and had retreated to Kertel, and some went to Helterma. Likewise, there was unrest amongst the crews of the gun batteries. The crew of Battery No 38 held a general assembly and determined to request support from the sea. If this was not forthcoming then they proposed to retire to the rear. They asked the crews of batteries No 39 and No 47 to join them, but these crews rejected their proposal. Nevertheless the commander of Battery No 47 was ordered to immediately render his guns unusable without making detonations, fire or noise, and the crew then retreated.

For the German forces in the Kassar Wiek, 17 October was a relatively quiet day. During the morning the craft of the II Torpedoboat Flotilla and the 13th Torpedoboat Half Flotilla were resupplied with 1,830 rounds of 10.5cm ammunition from V45, V44 and T139, whilst at the same time a continuous watch was kept on the entrance to Moon Sound. Five minesweepers of the II Minesweeper Division searched for mines in the Kassar Wiek, the 'Pripyat' barrier, but a shortage of fuel forced them to return to their tender in the Tagga Bay at around noon.

When the thunder of cannon was heard during the morning, the I FdT, Kommodore Heinrich, pushed forwards towards Moon Sound with V100 to investigate. At about 1154hrs the Russian forces in the Moon Sound were observed to begin lively movements, mostly in a northerly direction.

At about 1155hrs a huge smoke cloud from an explosion was observed on a battleship east of Kumora, which was in fact the detonation of *Slava's* aft magazine. Towards 1500hrs, Kommodore Heinrich took V100 forward into the channel that led to Moon Sound but he immediately came under the well-directed fire of *Chrabry* and the torpedoboat-destroyer *Konstantin*.

When the commander of the Sea Forces of the Riga Gulf had signalled 'Retreat', Kontre Admiral Stark signalled 'Rendezvous at Worms', and moved near to Kumora Reef with *Novik*. He ordered the minelayers *Bureya* and *Pripyat* to prepare to lay mine fields. *Bureya*, under Leitenant Semenov, was ordered to lay a mine barrier north of Seanin buoy, between there and the shore, in the 16 foot-deep channel between the Kassar Wiek and the Moon Sound. Leitenant S I Medvedev and *Pripyat* were ordered to produce a mine barrier near Schildau Island in the Moon Sound. The III Division Torpedoboat-Destroyers was to screen the operation. Kontre Admiral Stark considered it too risky for these shallow-draft minelayers to operate on Kuiwast Roads.

At 1230hrs the minelayers were dispatched to complete their missions and by 1320hrs they had completed their allotted tasks. *Bureya* laid eighty-four mines in four lines to produce an effective field.

Meanwhile *Bayan* and *Graschdanin* had anchored in the dredged channel. Vice Admiral Bakhirev convened a conference, which Kontre Admiral Stark attended, to coordinate further action. The chief of the VI Div TBD aboard the torpedoboat-destroyer *Turkmenets Stravropski*, was dispatched to Rogekul with orders to assemble all shallow-draft vessels to evacuate the garrison of Moon. Major-General Hendrikson had authorized the abandonment and destruction of this base, and had already determined that it would be impossible to retake Ösel, in light of the breakdown in discipline among the troops, and therefore the further defense of Moon was pointless. Therefore he instead determined to evacuate the island and requested that it be done during the night. Consequently Kontre Admiral Razvozov sent a wireless-gram to Vice Admiral Bakhirev reading 'Get all measures underway for the troops on Moon'. The admiral understood this as an order to evacuate Moon and he replied, 'This situation allows this at dawn'.

When the I FdT returned to his flotilla with V100, he held a conference with Kapitänleutnant Zander to discuss the possibility of making a night torpedoboat attack into the southern Moon Sound, with the 13th Torpedoboat Half Flotilla, later that night. Kapitänleutnant Zander agreed that a torpedoboat attack was possible through the narrow channels into the Moon Sound and also suggested that he push north to hinder traffic between Moon and the mainland. However, he only had four boats available for the task as S63 was in the Tagga Bay, and one of those, S50, would have to remain in the entrance to the Moon Sound as a navigation mark. That left just S61, S64 and V74 to conduct the raid. Kommodore Heinrich justified himself in his war diary as follows:

> Firstly the attack of the torpedoboat group would hinder the escape of *Slava*. I supposed that owing to her draught she could not pass into the northern Moon Sound, and was being repaired to reduce her draught ... If the Russian escaped I feared eternal reproachment for not ensuring her destruction. Therefore my orders to Kapitänleutnant Zander. A torpedoboat thrust into the northern Moon Sound during the clear night against the gunboats in the narrow channel east of Krukhlom, observed during the day, was considered by me as hopeless.

At about 2200hrs Kapitänleutnant Zander began his advance into the Moon Sound. Earlier he had questioned Vizeadmiral Behncke as to whether any of his forces were in the southern Moon Sound and received an answer in the negative, therefore any forces he might encounter would be Russian and he could attack without hesitation. The marker boat, S50, took up her position. The sea was quiet, the wind from the southwest and the visibility good as the torpedoboats advanced in line ahead in the order S61, S64 and V74, at low speed and taking continuous soundings. Towards 2230hrs they sighted a light to starboard ahead, seemingly one of the navigation marks on Schildau Island. Then just after midnight, the second boot, S64, was shaken by a heavy mine detonation, between the second and third boilers; she had run onto one of *Bureya*'s mines. The boat was immediately rendered unmanoeuvrable but was still capable of remaining afloat. The half flotilla's chief immediately turned S61 back towards the damaged boat, with the intension of towing her from the minefield stern first. Now several floating mines were sighted from the crow's nest where previously none had been seen; it seemed likely that the detonation had rent them free and they had floated to the surface. Despite this, a tow line was successfully passed and S61 began towing the crippled S64 towards the west, where the other boat, V74, had anchored as a marker, clear of the dangerous area. However, after making just 100 metres, S64 ran aground and it was decided to abandon her. Now, despite the danger from floating mines in the vicinity, S61 went alongside and took off the crew. Considerable skill was required to complete this manoeuvre. As S64 was not completely sunken, two explosive charges were detonated towards 0100hrs and the boat finally sank. The crew of the first boiler room, a total of six men, lost their lives and a further five were wounded. To Kapitänleutnant Zander it appeared that the western part of the channel was totally blocked with mines and therefore he abandoned the undertaking and returned to V100.

When S61 went alongside S64 she suffered a slight leak on the waterline, whilst V74 had damaged a propeller blade, so that both boats were no longer capable of unlimited action, especially not in the open sea.

The chief of the Special Unit, Vizeadmiral Schmidt, remained in full support of the torpedoboat operation and later wrote in his war diary:

> The sortie was, and remains, necessary as only with the full command of the Kassar Wiek can the Army's assault on Moon be given the required support. The sortie also had a reward. Without the support of the A-boats of Flotilla Rosenberg, Section Winterfeld could not have held the bridgehead at Orrisar. The Russians were pushed southeast to Moon and the fleeing Russians were then encircled. The appearance of the A-boats in the Kleinen Sound was, however, only possible as long as the torpedoboat forces of the I FdT held the eastern side of the Kassar Wiek.
>
> Finally it was of greater significance to hold the Kassar Wiek and Kleinen Sound whilst the III Squadron pushed into the southern Moon Sound so as to fully encircle Moon and hinder the escape of the Russians across the sea....only by battle and similar operations is the advantage of sea mastery obtained.

This day, 17 October, also saw events in the Kleinen Sound progress well for the Germans, and they realized their secondary objective of landing on Moon Island. During the morning Fregattenkapitän Rosenberg, aboard T144, escorted the hospital ship *Viola* into the Kleinen Sound where she immediately began the embarkation and evacuation of the wounded. The S-Flotilla chief then transferred to A28 and began preparations for a further bombardment of the stone dam that ran between Ösel and Moon. By about 0800hrs, the boats A32, A27 and A29 had completed replenishment of their ammunition stocks and were in position in the Kleinen Sound, so that at 0850hrs they were able to comply with a request from 138th Infantry Regiment for an immediate bombardment of the base of the stone dam on Moon. The Russians reported that the fire was directed by two seaplanes and was very accurate. Many were killed or wounded in the trenches and the telegraph connection to the Death Battalion, under the command of Captain 2nd Rank Shishko, was cut.

During the course of the morning, German reconnaissance aircraft reported that there were only small concentrations of Russian troops remaining on Moon. Therefore preparations to land on the island were accelerated. The attack was to be under the command of the commander of the 65th Infantry Brigade, Oberst Matthiass, and was to consist of the following units:

138th Infantry Regiment

255th Reserve Infantry Regiment (except I Battalion)

Sturmkompanie 18 (Section Winterfeld)

V Cyclist Battalion

1st, 2nd, 3rd, 4th, 8th (half of), and 9th Batteries of the 8th Field Artillery Regiment

7th Battery Heavy Howitzers

4th Reserve Heavy Artillery Regiment

3rd Company, 27th Pioneer Regiment

78th Reserve Pioneer Company

Half a platoon of the Telephone Section with two medium and two small wireless stations

At midday General von Kathen gave orders to immediately ferry the forces to Moon Island. At 1645hrs the artillery batteries opened fire and 6th Company, 138 Regt began to cross to Moon in rowing boats and land in the area of Kegova. The boats were screened from the enemy by a smoke screen and were supported by the fire of the A-boats. The landing did not meet any resistance and the troops began to advance, but immediately came upon the northern positions of the Russians to the west of the highway that crossed Moon.

Other parts of the II Battalion, 138 Regt, crossed behind 6th Company. They set up a bridgehead to cover the landing of subsequent battalions of the same regiment. An assault by the companies of the II Battalion was made during the evening. In the twilight the infantry advanced but were halted by Russian machine gun fire and a bombardment. The firing continued for about an hour.

Meanwhile, Hauptmann von Winterfeld's Sturmkompanie 18 lay in readiness to attack across the stone dam, in coordination with the 138 Regt. The agreed signal from the 138 Regt that the *sturmkompanie* was to attack was to be three white star shells.

For support of the 6th Company, 138 Regt, and also to create a diversion, the German artillery conducted a fire raid on the bridgehead on Moon at 1645hrs. A house at the base of the stone dam which contained ammunition was soon set ablaze. A huge explosion followed which half destroyed a Russian armoured car hidden behind the house.

The agreed signal was yet to be seen, but ambition got the better of the *sturmkompanie* and they began to advance across the dam. As they neared to within 500 metres of Moon a murderous Russian fire was opened on them from several sides, which forced Hauptmann von Winterfeld's men to ground. They were trapped on the 4 to 5 metre wide dam in a vicious firefight. The flames from the house illuminated the dam leaving the Germans no chance of advancing further.

However, the Russian bridgehead on Moon was under great pressure, caught between Sturmkompanie 18 and the 6th Company, 138 Regt. Finally at 0145hrs they began to retreat to positions between Linust and Nauze. At last the star shell signal was given and Section Winterfeld advanced onto Moon, capturing two guns, a machine gun and a burnt-out armoured car.

The Russian resistance by the Death Battalion had been resolute. When, during the day, the commander of the Moon garrison, General Martynov, had observed the retreat of the naval forces from the southern Moon Sound, he had requested permission to retreat, but the reply came that all forces should hold on. Then at 1600hrs Martynov repeated his request, and this time permission was given to retire to Rauga. Nevertheless, despite some of the Death Battalion also retreating from the dam to Rauga, the stubborn defence had continued well into the night and morning. However, as previously related, Vice Admiral Bakhirev had already been ordered to implement measures to evacuate the garrison.

The evening of 17 October saw the German sea forces in command of the southern Moon Sound, the north and south Kleinen Sound and the Kassar Wiek. Unloading work in the Tagga Bay was complete and all subsequent transport would be via Arensburg. A bridgehead had been established on Moon and preparations were complete for a further landing on Dagö. In addition there now seemed a possibility for German sea forces to push north to the entrance to the Finnish Gulf and completely cut off Vice Admiral Bakhirev's forces in the Moon Sound. Therefore, at 1900hrs on 17 October, Vizeadmiral Schmidt gave the following order to the Special Unit:

> The IV Squadron, II AG, VI TBF, 13th Half Flotilla, 4th Minesweeper Half Flotilla and II MS Div should cut off the line of retreat of Russian forces in the northern Moon Sound exit. The IV Squadron and 19th Half Flotilla are to hasten reprovisioning and march to point Gamma. *Kaiser* remain in Soelo Sound. Withdrawal of 13th Half Flotilla and VI Torpedoboat Flotilla boats from Kassar Wiek ordered. Refer to Leader II AG for positions for Sweeper Flotilla marker boats.

At the same time as the staffs began detailed preparations, the plan was referred to the Admiralty Staff (Admiralstab), as the Kaiser's approval had to be obtained for this further extension to the terms of the operation.

Note
1. By a curious turn of fate *Kronprinz* and the former *Tsarevitch* both shared the same name: Crown Prince.

CHAPTER EIGHT

18 October: The Capture of Moon Island

During the night of 17/18 October the Russian Sea Forces of the Riga Gulf remained at anchor in the northern Moon Sound. The torpedoboat *Razyashchi* patrolled near Kumor buoy with the three gunboats, *Chivinetz*, *Chrabry* and *Grozyashchi* anchored in single file along this meridian. Further to the north the, I, II, III and IV Division Torpedoboat-Destroyers were anchored on this meridian in two lines. The four torpedoboats of the VI Division Torpedoboat-Destroyers patrolled the dredged channel to the north of the scuttled steamers. After taking mines from the minelayer *Volga*, the V Division Torpedoboat Destroyers spent the night near Rukeraga. The cruiser *Admiral Makarov* and torpedoboat-destroyer *Likhoi* remained near the entrance to the Kassar Wiek. *Bayan*, *Graschdanin* and the minelayers *Amur* and *Volga* lay near Rukeraga with Kharilaid to the east. The hospital ship *Tovarishch* also lay near Kharilaid together with the II, III, IV and V Division Minesweepers and the XI Division Torpedoboat-Destroyers.

In the early hours of 18 October, Vice Admiral Bakhirev received orders from Kontre Admiral Razvozov to begin evacuating his forces from the Moon Sound, remove everything valuable from Rogekul and prepare the base for demolition. Then at 0300hrs he received another wireless message from the fleet commander: 'The enemy intends to baffle you by appearing in the north'. The Russian intelligence service had obviously deciphered the wireless message of Vizeadmiral Schmidt at 1900hrs the previous evening ordering preparations for the operation in the north. Vice Admiral Bakhirev said of this message: 'This telegram soon became known to the men, and certainly did not bring calm to the nervously-adjusted crews'.

At dawn on 18 October the German torpedoboats again took up their patrol positions in the Kassar Wiek and the minesweeper divisions resumed their minesweeping work. The Germans could see the cruiser *Admiral Makarov* and the gunboats in their positions. Shortly before 1200hrs Kommodore Heinrich took V100 to Tagga bay to personally report to

Vizeadmiral Schmidt and to receive further orders. Whilst he was absent the boat B111 ran onto another of the mines laid by *Pripyat*. The foreship was rent off, but the boat remained afloat with the loss of two dead, three missing and sixteen wounded. Although the German boats had frequently passed over this area previously without loss, it is certain that the mine was one from the northwest wing of the mine barrier. The crippled boat was brought to anchor near Pavasterort and the following day was towed to Libau by a tug. In the meantime, Vizeadmiral Schmidt granted the I FdT full freedom of action to undertake such offensive operations as he thought appropriate.

On this day the landing operations on Dago gained momentum. Before dawn *Emden* weighed anchor and took up a bombardment position so that from 0715hrs to 0800hrs she was able to take the area around Emmast under fire with 170 shells. This bombardment forced the Russian defenders to retreat. Later on in the morning T144, A-boats, trawlers and drifters landed the II Cyclist Battalion near Serro so that the toehold on Dago was secure enough to begin landing field batteries and other heavy equipment.

Nevertheless, there were still difficulties and towards midday the torpedoboat S50 became stuck fast in the Serro Channel. Generally speaking the increase in traffic in the narrow channel caused more accidents and now four vessels had grounded. Therefore the chief of the S-Flotilla, Fregattenkapitän von Rosenberg, ordered better marker indications to be laid out and appointed an officer to oversee management of the Söelo Sound.

Meanwhile, the advance progressed rapidly so that by 1700hrs von Rosenberg could report to the Special Unit that after a successful battle the bridgehead was secure and that the Russian forces had begun to retreat towards Heltermaa. The commander of the defences, Colonel Veselago, reported: 'The military parts, under the influence of panic, retreated to the piers at Heltermaa and Kertel'. Colonel Veselago requested that barges be sent to Heltermaa and Lekhtme to evacuate the troops. There was astonishing confusion about the situation and Starchi Leitenant Elachich wrote:

The garrison state was characteristic; stupid people, and nobody would reveal their unit, platoon, or company, and did not want to know the where or why, nor listen to speeches. The officers and the Chief of the Island Defence himself seemed to fear the soldiers, and yes in truth, these people were able, during the night, to break into the stores and steal from the local inhabitants: flour, butter, and sugar by the cart full, and generally everything that was in the stores, which the Chief of the Island Defence had ordered demolished, was

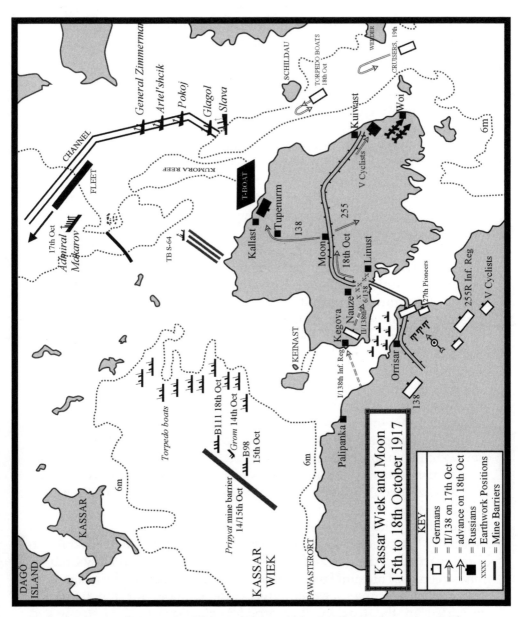

Map 14: Capture of Moon Island (Kassar Wiek and Moon 15th to 18th October 1917).

taken. Nobody knew what was happening abroad, and chaos ranged over everything.

During the evening, the Russian Colonel Veselago received a telephone message from Kontre Admiral Razvozov ordering him to demolish the 12-inch gun battery, No 39, at Tachkona. Thereon the battery was prepared with explosives. However, the moral effect of destroying the battery was taken into consideration and the Fleet Commander revised his orders, saying they should only be destroyed in the case of necessity.

At dawn on 18 October, the V Cyclist Battalion, 255R Regt, and 138 Regt (without its II Battalion) started across the stone dam to Moon Island, after the 3rd Company, 27th Pioneers, had prepared the dam for movement by wheeled vehicles. The Russians were not encountered and the column continued uninterrupted.

The V Cyclists pushed ahead and near Kuiwast they encountered a large Russian force. They surrendered without a fight. However, the main Russian forces departed in a northern and northeasterly direction. The 138th Infantry Regiment was given the task of taking the north of Moon Island. Soon a hussar patrol reported a Russian battery and troops near Tupenurm. A little later, some Russian officers and delegates from the Soldiers' Committee appeared to parley with the 138 Regt. It soon became apparent that they were willing to surrender on any terms, however, the delegates of the Death Battalion demanded that they be allowed to retreat to the continent. The Germans were in no mood to negotiate and demanded: 'Surrender! Otherwise we attack at 1300hrs'.

As no answer was received by the appointed time, the 138 Regt began an advance on a wide front. The attack of the regiment's 3rd Company bypassed Tupenurm to the northwest and proceeded towards Kallast, where strong Russian forces were reported. As they approached the town they were taken under heavy enemy fire. The regiment now swung the main thrust of their attack to the Russians flank and it was only after the Russians had been outflanked that they were finally forced to lower their weapons.

Meanwhile, Vice Admiral Bakhirev had ordered the chief of the I Division Minesweeper-launches, Captain 2nd Rank Chetverukhin, to begin evacuating the garrison of Moon Island with his shallow-draught minesweepers. The minelayer *Pripyat* and torpedoboats of the XI Division Torpedoboat-Destroyers would give close support for the operation, supported in the rear by the torpedoboats *General Kondratenko* and *Pogranitsnik*.

As the torpedoboat-destroyers *Izyaslav* and *Avtroil* had been damaged during the morning, they had been detached to Helsingfors, leaving III Division Torpedoboat-Destroyers with just one boat, *Gavriil*. Therefore,

Captain 1st Rank Shevelev was assigned command of the gunboats and at 12.35hrs he hoist his broad pennant on *Chivinetz*. The gunboats then moved to support the evacuation operation by taking up positions near the entrance to the Moon Sound channel.

During the afternoon, Captain 2nd Rank Chetverukhin approached the northern shore of Moon near Kallast and his launches began transferring troops from the pier to the larger minesweepers *Gruz*, *Minrep*, *Udarnik* and *Kapsyul*. During this evacuation the pier was kept free by the embattled Death Battalion, under the command of Captain 2nd Rank Shishko, who held the encircling German 138 Regt back. About 20 officers and 400 men were successfully taken aboard the boats, but Captain Shishko refused to depart, claiming that his battalion would be the last to quit the island. He continued to fight and was wounded and taken captive. From those evacuated from Moon Island, Vice Admiral Bakhirev learned that General Martynov had surrendered and that only the Death Battalion had offered resistance.

Of the garrison of Moon Island the following were taken into captivity: two battalions from the 470th and 471st Infantry Regiments, the 1st Estonian Regiment and some men from the Death Battalion, in total some 6,000 men. A significant number of vehicles and guns were also captured. Von Tschischwitz wrote later:

> A large number of guns, the coastal batteries, provisions, large quantities of ammunition and war appliances fell into our hands. Everywhere lay gun parts, vehicles, crates of ammunition and provisions and it formed such a picture of destruction that only those in the eastern theatre could experience.

If the operations ashore on Moon and Dago were progressing comfortably for the Germans, then the advance into the southern Moon Sound was progressing only with difficulty. The morning had brought a freshening wind from the south-southeast at strength 4 to 6 so that the motorboats of the III Minesweeper Division were unable to continue their minesweeping work. Therefore the 8th Minesweeper Half Flotilla began advancing into the southern Kleinen Sound, whilst Kontreadmiral Hopman's cruisers and torpedoboats remained anchored.

By 0830hrs the minesweepers had worked forward to a point about one nautical mile south of Paternoster lighthouse, sounding and laying buoys as they went, when the lead boat sighted the buoys of the Russian net barrier to the north. As the leader boat, A62, manoeuvred to investigate the barrier, the other boats, owing to a misunderstanding of orders, turned to the south at low speed. Kapitänleutnant Doflein therefore dispatched the boat that had been laying the marker buoys,

T66, to fetch them back. Soon afterwards a heavy detonation occurred as T66 ran onto the western wing of one of the U-boat mine barriers. T66 immediately sank by the stern with the loss of seventeen men, only the commander and six men being saved. Astoundingly the positions of the known mine barriers were marked on the charts of the leader boats, but not, however, on the charts of the other boats! Towards 0940hrs Kontreadmiral Hopman's cruisers anchored to the south of the buoyed channel.

Gruppe Behncke had quit their anchorage southwest of the trapezoidal minefield at about 0800hrs and proceeded to steer for the eastern swept channel behind the 3rd Minesweeper Half Flotilla. However, because of the heavy swell the motorboats of the Minesweeper Division could not be utilized. The heavy ships retraced their course of the previous day, travelling south of the minefield and then northwards between Awanasewa and Larina Banks, following Kapitänleutnant von der Marwitz's minesweepers which had their sweeper gear set and took continuous soundings. Shortly after 1000hrs Vizeadmiral Behncke decided to concentrate his push forward on the eastern flank and therefore ordered Kontreadmiral Hopman to dispatch *Strassburg* and the 8 MSHF to the III Battle Squadron, whilst *Kolberg*, the torpedoboats and barrier-breakers would remain to the west to cover the troops ashore.

At about 1240hrs a report arrived from the advancing *Markgraf* that she had run aground near Kalkgrund, but had since worked free and was still battle-worthy. Apparently, some of the buoys marking the mine-free channel had drifted owing to the strong wind and swell. This constituted an insidious danger.

Meanwhile 3rd MSHF and two boats of the VIII Torpedoboat Flotilla had pushed past the eastern wing of the Paternoster trapezoidal-shaped mine barrier and were advancing to Kuiwast Roads. They confirmed that *Slava* was sunken to the west of Pappilaid Island and was still burning. Nearby were two sunken freight steamers. To the north of there two Russian destroyers could be seen laying mines.

It was the Russian torpedoboats *Zabaikalets* and *Sil'Ny* which had been ordered to lay mine barriers along the deep channel after *Voiskovoi* had discovered the German boats on Kuiwast Roads during the morning. The German boats V180 and V184 rushed ahead at full speed and opened fire on the Russians before they made off to the north. A further Russian destroyer and six small vessels now came in sight north of the Strumpf Channel, whilst further north a large smoke cloud was conspicuous. These were the shallow-draught vessels Admiral Bakhirev had dispatched to evacuate the troops on Moon and the gunboat *Chivinetz* to the north was supporting them. This unit was already retiring to the north as the German torpedoboats opened fire at a range of 9,500 metres.

As the Germans continued northwards the three Russian gunboats, and destroyers *General Kondratenko* and *Pogranitschnik*, weighed anchor and advanced. As the range reduced the Russians opened fire at 1415hrs, so that with medium-calibre shellfire falling accurately about them the Germans made off south at high speed and under the cover of a smoke screen. During the action *Chivinetz* fired about twenty-five shots, whilst the torpedoboats had also joined in. After that the gunboats moved off to Kumora Bank, and the shallow draught units went to Rogekul.

In addition to the mine barriers, two more blockships were scuttled in the dredged channel. The run-down *Artel'shchik* and *General Zimmerman*, which had previously been damaged by bombs, were scuttled near Kumora Reef.

When Vizeadmiral Behncke received the battle report from the two torpedoboats he immediately dispatched *Kronprinz* and *Strassburg* forward to their support, but the Russian net barrier still barred the passage into Kuiwast Roads for the larger ships. The channel east of the barrier was only 4 metres deep, whilst the channel west of the barrier, which V180, V184 and the 3 MSHF had utilized to enter the roadstead, was 7 metres deep. Nevertheless, the ships advanced in the swept channel but before long both had grazed the bottom, *Kronprinz* in 9 metres of water. Luckily, neither ship was damaged.

Towards 1415hrs Kapitänleutnant Doflein, aboard A62 , found a 200 metre-broad 'gate' in the Russian net barrier, obviously to allow large ships through: after some skillful manoeuvring the gate, supported by iron barrels, was jerked open by A62. Kapitänleutnant Doflein later wrote:

> The commander skillfully manoeuvred his boat close to the barrier. Two brave men were allowed onto the pontoons and working up to their waists in water hooked a steel wire fast to the barrier and quickly climbed back aboard. Slowly A62 went astern with her propellers, the steel grill went tight and then – hurrah – the closed gate came open with a jerk. A group of the 3rd Minesweeper Half Flotilla was waiting nearby and quickly passed through the entrance and once through deployed their gear and found no mines. Then a signal went from A62 to *König*, 'Channel is free!'

The water depth here was 14 metres. The other minesweepers had meanwhile continued their work but to their great surprise (and joy) had found no mines in the Kuiwast Roads as far as Schildau Island. The minesweeping work continued until nightfall and then Vizeadmiral Behncke brought his unit to anchor off the southern entrance to Moon Sound.

As the evening of 18 October approached, the situation for the Germans was as follows: Arensburg had been established as a supply base with the II Transport Section already proceeding there; the southern part of Dago was in the hands of the II Cyclist Battalion and the S-Flotilla landing section. The Admiralty Staff had approved the operation to the north, but the Kaiser's approval was still wanting. Preparations for this operation were still not well advanced and commencement the following day seemed unlikely. The capture of Moon Island was almost complete and it was only to the northeast, where the Russians expected to be evacuated from, that resistance had been encountered. Ösel and Moon were now firmly in German hands.

Meanwhile the Russian fleet commander, Kontre Admiral Razvozov, was having difficulty deciding whether to order the withdrawal of the Riga Gulf forces. It was only after discussion at fleet headquarters, during which the proposed German objective of cutting off the Russians from the north was discussed, that the commander of the fleet finally decided to quit the Moon Sound: 'The timely removal of ships, in case the aim of the enemy is to cut off Moon Sound from the north, is approved'. He was genuinely concerned about the fate of the ships and crews and he telegraphed Admiral Bakhirev: 'In the case of necessity preserve all forces until the arrival of the First Battleship Brigade'. Kontre Admiral Razvozov was promising to provide support with the powerful squadron of dreadnought battleships.

CHAPTER NINE

19 October: The Landing on Dago

During the evening of 18 October the commander of the defences on Dago, Colonel Veselago, reported that morale on the island was deteriorating. He reported, 'The military parts, under the influence of panic, retreated to the piers at Helterma and Kertel. Apparently the enemy consisted of only a few'. There was disorientation amongst the Russian troops and they wandered along the coast between Helterma and Kertel, looking for boats to transport themselves to the mainland. The fleet commander authorized Colonel Veselago to demolish the 12-inch battery, No 39 at Tachkona, and preparations were made. Later these orders were modified to only destroy the batteries in the case of necessity.

On the following morning at 0500hrs Colonel Veselago urgently requested that barges be sent to Helterma and Lekhtma for the evacuation of troops. Accordingly Kontre Admiral Razvozov ordered the steamers *On*, *Pregrada*, *Tor*, *Toledo* and *Elba* to proceed from Rogekul to Dago Island. The first three anchored near a torpedoboat division, but did not report that they were acting under the authority of the fleet commander. Therefore, in light of the order to withdraw, *On* and *Pregrada* were dispatched to Reval. The latter ran aground near Cape Spithamn and was set afire and abandoned by her crew. *Tor* was abandoned for scuttling near Rukeraga and the English steamer *Toledo* grounded on a shoal between Dago and Worms.

The weather on the morning of 19 October was unfavourable as there was a fog. Nevertheless, during that morning the German 17th Infantry Regiment was dispatched to Dago, supported by 7th Battery, 8th Field Artillery. These forces were under the orders of the commander of 17 Regt, Oberst von Kaweczynski. The units were to be transported in two parts from Ösel, near Murrik, to Serro, on Dago. However, due to the bad weather, ferrying the troops was delayed and they only began arriving on Dago Island during the afternoon. Luckily there was no serious clash with the Russians. The advance proceeded rapidly and before dark the I and III Battalions, 17 Regt, had reached Vaimel, and the II Battalion

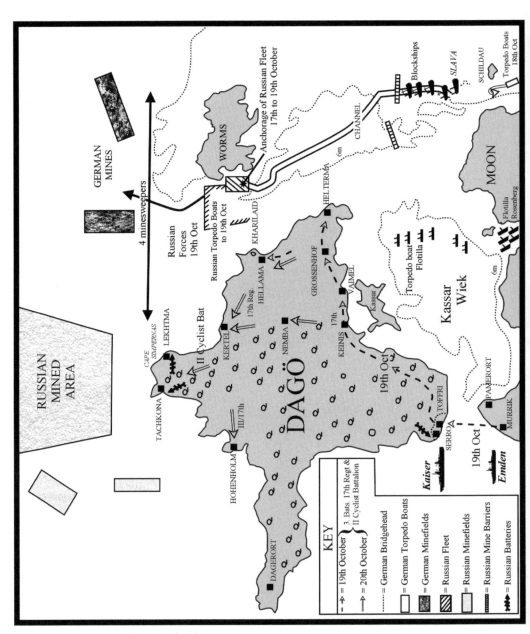

Map 15: Capture of Dago Island.

reached Keinis. The previously-landed II Cyclist Battalion also continued their advance and by nightfall they had reached Grossenhof, whilst one company had penetrated to the east coast at Helterma, and another had even reached Hellama.

Kontreadmiral Razvozov fully realized the importance of holding Dago, for not only was it the last foothold on the Baltic Islands, which commanded the entrance to the Riga Gulf, it was also the cornerstone of the defence of the 'Forward Position', and therefore the outer defense on the Finnish Gulf and St Petersburg. Razvozov then telegrammed the commanders of batteries No 38 and No 39: 'While the fleet remains in Moon Sound, its security depends exclusively on the fortitude of your batteries'. However, the fleet commander had greatly underestimated the situation and his order at 1100hrs to the battery, 'If the enemy appears before the batteries, immediately open fire and fight up until the last shell', was ill judged.

At the same time he dispatched a message to Senior Lieutenant Elachich and Colonel Veselago:

Convey to the troops, that they must hold up the enemy's advance to the Tachkona batteries, for the fate of the fleet in Moon Sound depends on this. That is why everything transportable has been transferred to Lekhtmu, and in the case that it is hopeless to hold the south, the regiment [the 427th] is to withdraw to Simperness, and defend it, where it may be supported by the fire of the fleet units.

Lieutenant Elachich replied with the following:

The regiment no longer exists, there remains only a riotous gang, ready to raise their bayonets against their officers in their anxiety to get across to the mainland. If possible it is necessary to evacuate them from the island soon. They will prevent the crew collected from the batteries from holding back the enemy. The batteries are ready for action with people enough to send a company, battle ready and with machine guns, to do as much as possible.

And Colonel Veselago reported:

The regiment no longer remains on the island. Several hundred men of the command begin rebellion and it is necessary to immediately cancel the orders and forward transport to Helterma and Kertel. Vehicles, machine guns and field guns have been abandoned. Stores are devastated. Only the new part of disciplined troops can save the battery position. The fate of the officers is dependent on this decision, and all around death rages.

However, Admiral Razvozov's fears that the Naval Forces of the Riga Gulf would be cut off in the Moon Sound were not realized on this day. Owing to the poor weather on 18 October, the minesweeping that was a necessary precursor for the operation in the north had been postponed by one day. The failure to sweep a route to the north meant that a quick appearance by the IV Battle Squadron was not possible. The 'Northern Operation' was only to be conducted under favourable circumstances. At about 1800hrs on 19 October the Special Unit received a wireless message from the Admiralty Staff stating that on orders from the Kaiser the 'Northern Operation' was not to be carried out. The Russian sea forces had been let off the hook.

Nonetheless, Kontreadmiral Razvozov was unaware of this development and the dangerous situation of the forces in Moon Sound forced him to a difficult decision. He came to the conclusion that if the Germans appeared off the Forward Position of the Finnish Gulf then he would enter into battle with them. With this in mind he ordered the 1st Brigade of Battleships from Helsingfors to Porkala Udde, the 2nd Cruiser Brigade to Lapvik and the 2nd Brigade of Battleships were dispatched to Reval. These orders were relayed to the Tachkona batteries to bolster their faltering spirits. The orders were also sent to the Commander of the Northern Front, General Cheremisov, who entirely approved of this decision.

The Supreme Commander-in-Chief thought otherwise and Kontreadmiral Bubnov telegrammed the fleet commander's staff:

> The key problem of the Baltic Fleet is to fight on the Central Position, with its flank cover. By accepting the fleet commander's noble decision, a disadvantageous outcome of the battle would have effect on all our positions in the Finnish Gulf and bring about the capture of the Central Position by the enemy. The noble purpose of the rescue of the small battle units is not absolved by the risk of catastrophe, with the power to affect the outcome of the war. Without the participation of those on Dago the Forward Position does not exist, and actually the fleet commander would be forced to accept battle in the open sea, and as has happened in the Riga Gulf, the likely outcome can not be favourable for us.

Rear Admiral Bubnov and the Supreme Command were therefore acknowledging the importance of holding the Baltic Islands, and their immense strategical value.

On the other hand, Vice Admiral Bakhirev had a different opinion about abandoning the Moon Sound. He believed that at least some of the forces should remain there. He thought that leaving the gunboats, some older torpedoboats and shallow-draught vessels behind represented little risk, as if they were lost it would not be significant for the fleet. From this position they could impede German minesweepers, and lay defensive mine barriers. The Germans were hardly likely to risk important forces to deal with these obsolete units. Vice Admiral Bakhirev thought that even larger units should remain behind and later wrote:

> In general I considered that the loss of the northern part of the Moon Sound by us would greatly affect the defence of the Finnish Gulf and our 'Forward position' would lose any value. The departure of all the fleet from Moon Sound would certainly affect the morale condition of the local armies. In my opinion it was possible for even the large units to remain there, certainly with the support of the fleet.

Nevertheless, in view of the categorical orders to withdraw, at 1400hrs the general signal 'B' was hoist on *Bayan*, ordering the Naval Forces of the Riga Gulf to raise anchor and depart to the north. The order of march was as follows: four minesweepers escorted by torpedoboat-destroyers of the I Division Torpedoboat-Destroyers leading; all the remaining torpedoboat-destroyers of the *Novik* type, that is *Desna*, *Samson*, *Leitenant Il'in*, *Pobeditel*, *Zabiyaka*, *Gavriil* and *Konstantin*; the cruiser *Bayan* as flagship, accompanied by the torpedoboats *Donski Kazak* and *Zabaikalets*; the cruiser *Admiral Makarov* with the torpedoboats *Steregushchi* and *Voiskovoi*; the cruiser *Diana* and the torpedoboat *Moskvityanin*; the battleship *Graschdanin*, escorted by the torpedoboats *General Kondratenko* and *Pogranitschnik*; then came the gunboats *Chivinetz*, *Chrabry* and *Grozyashchi* with the torpedoboats *Deyatel'Nyi* and *Storozhevoi*; the minelayer *Volga* and the transports *Olga* and *Izhe* in company with the torpedoboats *Lichoi* and *Sil'Nyi*; and finally, bringing up the rear was the minelayer *Amur* escorted by the torpedoboats *Turkmenets Stravropolski* and *Ukraina*.

The units would proceed independently under the cover of darkness and rendezvous at Ayaks Bank, then proceed to Lapvik. *Novik* was to mark the position of Ayaks Bank with a searchlight. After the departure of the gunboats from near Moon, the torpedoboats *Steregushchi* and *Donskoi Kazaks* laid mines in the area of Kumor buoy and north of there.

The Russian units passed the area of the German U-boat mine barriers and then at 1600hrs, 5 miles north of Stappelbotten, the minesweepers were dismissed. The weather was quiet and hazy. The destroyer *Desna* observed a submarine and *Samson* and *Leitenant Il'in* were sent to investigate but the submarine turned out to be Russian. Towards 1800hrs *Novik* illuminated her searchlight in fog and the Russian units all passed safely into Lapvik Roads by morning.

The V Division Torpedoboat-Destroyers was ordered to exit the Moon Sound via the Nukko-Worms channel. After the other units had passed, the boats *Emir Bucharski*, *Amurets* and *Razyashchi* laid a mine barrage in the Nukko-Worms channel, while *Vsadnik* and *Finn* laid mines in the channel near Odensholm, after which the Division went to Lapvik. After the departure of these last units from Rogekul, Captain 2nd Rank Rogge, together with ten officers and fifteen seamen, began demolishing the base.

While this was going on the German minesweeping work continued in the Kassar Wiek and Irben Straits. In the Moon Sound the sweeping work allowed the heavier German forces to slowly penetrate the Sound and by the afternoon of 19 October *Kolberg* and *Strassburg* were lying off Schildau, and *König* followed on the next day. *Kronprinz* and *Markgraf* remained anchored north of Paternoster and west of Werder respectively.

Arensburg had now become the main German base. Early on the morning of 19 October the steamers *Buenos Aires* and *Coralie Hörlock*, the hospital ship *Titania* and the tug *Wilhelms Cords* entered Arensburg Roads. During the day the steamer *Altenburg* followed them. Escort was provided by the torpedoboats, which preceded the steamers in the 225 metre-broad swept channel through the minefields of the Irben Straits. Navigation for the large steamers in the narrow channel was not easy. The wind was not inconsiderable and variable, and the current was strong, making the passage of the straits a difficult task. The buoylayers *Mellum* and *Wilhelms*, piloted by *Blitz*, laid a number of light buoys to aid navigation. The small harbour at Mento was quickly used as a base for German minesweepers working in the Irben Straits.

At midday a wireless message from the Russian wireless station at Dagerort lighthouse to Kontreadmiral Razvozov was intercepted: 'Please dispatch two torpedoboats immediately'. At about 1345hrs the leader of the II AG, Kontreadmiral Reuter, took the cruisers *Königsberg*, *Nürnberg* and *Danzig* to intercept them. The VI Torpedoboat Flotilla provided an anti-submarine screen, whilst, after point White, the 4th Minesweeper Half Flotilla preceded them on the northerly course with broken out sweeper gear. Three torpedoboats were dispatched over points Gamma, Green and Red to intercept a point on longitude 22° east, to cut off the Russian line of retreat. Towards 1500hrs information arrived that two Russian boats had been dispatched, but towards 1700hrs none had been sighted, so Kontreadmiral von Reuter decided to discontinue the advance. The Germans retired over the same course.

During the course of the afternoon, at about 1600hrs, *Friedrich der Grosse* arrived in Tagga Bay from the Putziger Wiek, with Vizeadmiral Souchon aboard. *Kaiserin* and *König Albert* remained in Putzig. Towards 2010hrs *Friedrich der Grosse* and *Moltke*, with Vizeadmiral Schmidt aboard, put to sea for Arensburg, where they later anchored. In the meantime the defences of Arensburg harbour had been improved. On 18 October the net layer *Eskimo* and the minelayer *Nautilus*, with 120 mines, had arrived there. During the course of 19 October *Eskimo* laid a series of net barriers off Arensburg Bay to secure it from submarines. A Russian net was also found and was redeployed east of Abro Island. The laying of a second net was entrusted to the newly-arrived net layer *Rossal*, freeing *Eskimo* to depart for the Moon Sound the following day.

CHAPTER TEN

20–30 October: Conclusion of the Campaign

After arriving in Lapvik early on 20 October, the commander of the Russian VI Division Torpedoboat-Destroyers, Captain 1st Rank Ekimov, was dispatched to Cape Lekhtma at 1400hrs, with the torpedoboats *Voiskovoi*, *Donskoi Kazak* and *Moskvityanin*, together with guard vessels No 25 and No 27, to evacuate the crew of the Tachkona batteries. As they put to sea, *Moskvityanin* suffered a failed circulation pump and damage to the helm, which also failed. On the horizon, in the southeast quadrant, submarines were observed in two positions (although they were not clearly distinguishable) and Captain 1st Rank Ekimov therefore dispatched *Moskvityanin* and a guard vessel back to Lapvik, whilst he turned towards one of the submarine positions and opened fire, prompting it to dive. The Russian unit then resumed its course towards Dago, which was maintained until 2100hrs, then, when 9.5 nautical miles west-northwest of Odensholm, the division chief decided to return to Lapvik.

The operation had been at the request of the batteries at Tachkona. When the position became hopeless the crew of the batteries were ordered to demolish their guns and evacuate to Worms. The guns of the battery were destroyed but the large magazine and one other remained intact, and were complete with shells and cartridges. During the evening Colonel Veselago reported that he, the majority of the gun crews and many of the 427th Regiment had arrived on Worms.

On the morning of 20 October the German 17th Infantry Regiment had continued their advance across Dago Island in two columns: the III Battalion through Grossenhof towards Kertel, the I Battalion in the same direction through Nemba, and the II Battalion moved forwards to Grossenhof.

The vanguard of the II Cyclist Battalion, the 2nd Company, advanced towards Helterma and after a battle lasting only one hour they captured a group of about 450 Russians at the quay.

While the 17 Regt continued to advance through to Kertel, the II Cyclist Battalion advanced towards the batteries at Cape Tachkona and Lekhtma, on the northern extremity of the island. There they found the two batteries at Cape Tachkona and Cape Simperness, four 12-inch and four 6-inch pieces, destroyed.

The III Battalion, 17 Regt, turned to the west from Kertel and, still on 20 October, reached the Manor estate at Hohenholm without meeting the Russians.

The island of Dago was now totally occupied by the Germans. Only 750 Russians were taken prisoner, but much materiel and supplies were captured, including a clothing factory at Kertel.

At sea, the morning of 20th October saw the netlayer *Eskimo* depart for the Moon Sound. When south of Abro she was attacked by the British submarine C32, under the command of Lieutenant Satow. C32 had been maintaining a guard in the German buoyed channel and in a calm sea launched two torpedoes at *Eskimo* from the starboard side. Both torpedoes passed astern of of the net layer but her two escorting torpedoboats, S176 and V186, immediately took up the hunt for the submarine, which had the misfortune to break surface after launching her torpedoes, a trimming problem which seems to have dogged the English boats. Immediately, Lieutenant Satow took his boat down to 20 metres depth, followed by a hail of depth charges. Now C32 began to suffer damage, the compass failed, the electric lights in the aft boat failed and the conning tower made water. The submarine crept off at 20 metres depth towards Rüno and at 2000hrs surfaced near there. Investigations showed extensive damage which convinced her commander that she was incapable of further employment. He assumed that the Moon Sound, the Riga Gulf and Pernau were in German hands and therefore he decided to scuttle his boat and strike out across country with his crew for Reval. On the morning of 21 October he put C32 aground in Waist Bay but to his great consternation found that Pernau was still in Russian hands. It was pointless to change his plan, however, as both exits from the Riga Gulf were occupied by the Germans and the crippled boat had no chance of escape. Unsurprisingly, when German torpedoboats were sighted off Waist Bay, Lieutenant Satow completed the destruction of C32 with explosives before he and his crew escaped ashore. This latest submarine attack had, however, caused Vizeadmiral Behncke further concern and he dispatched three torpedobootes to the area south of the net barrier in the southern Moon Sound.

The netlayer *Eskimo* continued to Kuiwast Roads and on 21 October, according to plan, laid a net barrier to the northwest of Schildau Island. The barrier was a double, 12 metre-deep net barrier, 3.25km in length. After laying the barrier *Eskimo* returned to Arensburg during the afternoon. The minelayer *Nautilus* was to have blockaded the channel east of Schildau with U-mines, but the water depth was too shallow and therefore the mines were loaded onto motorboats of the II Minesweeper Flotilla and were laid by them. Seventy mines were laid, after which *Nautilus* returned to Arensburg.

The Special Unit had successfully completed, and in some cases overstepped, its operational tasks. On the morning of 20 October the Admiralty Staff proposed a request to dismantle the Special Unit and Vizeadmiral Ehrhard Schmidt fully concurred and immediately answered:

> Dissolve the Special Unit on 25 October. Hand over the remaining lines of communication and escort duty to BdAdO, whose forces shall include the S-Flotilla, the Net Barrier Unit of the Baltic, *Nautilus*, the 7th Torpedoboat Half Flotilla and one *sperrbrecher*, which are considered adequate forces. *Kaiserin* and *König Albert* can immediately be detached from Putzig to the North Sea. The Fleet Train can assist the transports of the II [Transport] Section to transport troops away from Arensburg to Libau. Traffic to Dago available shortly when mine-free channel in Kassar Wiek and Soelo Sound effected.

Vizeadmiral Schmidt had not desired to prolong the operation any longer than necessary, and he fully appreciated the importance of having the most powerful fleet units fully action-ready in the North Sea.

Nevertheless, during the course of the night of 21 October the Army High Command requested the Admiralty Staff to temporarily occupy the island of Kyno and make frequent demonstrations against the Lithuanian coast with its ships. The Admiralty Staff consented and the task was given to the 2nd Admiral of the III Battle Squadron, Kontreadmiral Seiferling, who was allocated *Markgraf, Strassburg,* five torpedoboats, the *sperrbrecher* vessel *Lothar* and the 3rd Minesweeper Half Flotilla. The demonstration was scheduled for 25 and 26 October, whilst a proposed operation to occupy the island of Worms was rejected. At about 1000hrs on 25 October the unit passed through the vessels anchored in Kuiwast Roads and took course south. Off Larina Bank the 3 MSHF took station ahead of the group with their minesweeper gear deployed. Frequent slipping of the gear in the shallow water caused continual delays so that it was only at 1600hrs that *Markgraf* arrived in the proposed bombardment position, 3 nautical miles off Kyno lighthouse. Shortly afterwards *Markgraf* opened fire with her starboard medium-calibre battery at ranges of 4,800 to 5,200 metres. After the bombardment, *Markgraf* continued southwards and, shortly after 1900hrs, anchored 12 nautical miles southwest of Salis. At around the same time, *Strassburg, Lothar* and four torpedoboats, which had been delayed by the *sperrbrecher*'s low speed, anchored 15 nautical miles west of Hainasch.

The following morning, *Markgraf* continued the operation so that at around 0740hrs she was able to bombard Hainasch with seventeen shells from her starboard medium-calibre guns at a range of around 11,000 metres. Then, suddenly, just as *Markgraf* ordered the preceding 3 MSHF to turn onto a westerly course, the sweeper gear of T65 fouled a mine and exploded it. The stern of the minesweeper was rent open but the boat remained afloat for twenty minutes before capsizing, allowing the entire crew to be saved. The minesweeper unit had pushed onto a Russian mine barrier that had been laid after the fall of Riga to protect the seaward flank of their XII Army. The bombardments concluded when *Strassburg* shelled Salismunde at 0800hrs with some fifty-five rounds. After this the German ships retired, again in the wake of the 3 MSHF and took course on Arensburg, at the direction of Vizeadmiral Schmidt. On the morning of 27 October the unit anchored safely inside the net barrier on Arensburg Roads.

The further demonstrations desired by the Army High Command (OHL) were to be conducted by *Markgraf* alone, until she could be replaced by the ships of I Battle Squadron. Therefore the chief of the Special Unit detached *König* and *Kronprinz* to the North Sea. They quit Kuiwast Roads on the morning of 26 October but their journey home was not without incident. The sea was rough and there was a strong southwest wind so that when they were between Windau and Backofen at around 1744hrs, both ships scraped the bottom. In the rising seas it was reckoned that the pitching ships' draughts approached 12 metres and the area was known to have many uncharted rocks. Both ships later required docking for repairs to their double bottoms.

On 28 October, the 1st Division of the I Battle Squadron arrived in Putzig Wiek. On 30 October, the reconnaissance group IV AG, consisting of the cruisers *Regensburg*, *Stralsund* and *Pillau* arrived in Pillau. After replenishing their coal stocks in the Putzig Wiek, *Ostfriesland* and *Thüringen* were expected in Arensburg on 30 October. *Markgraf* was no longer required and Vizeadmiral Schmidt detached her to the North Sea also. At midday on 29 October *Markgraf* quit Arensburg Roadstead, escorted by G89. At 1430hrs *Markgraf* was about 8 nautical miles north-northwest of Michael's light, travelling in the buoyed channel, when suddenly she was rocked by two mine detonations in rapid succession. Three wing passage cells on the starboard side filled with water, for a total of 260 tonnes. Fortunately, there were no personnel losses and the ship was able to hold her course and speed. At first *Markgraf* went to Neufahrwasser, then on to Kiel, where, on 1 November 1917, Kontreadmiral Seiferling disembarked before the battleship continued to Wilhelmshaven. From 6 to 23 November she was repaired in the Imperial Dockyard.

In the buoyed channel, it appeared that a marker buoy had been displaced by the currents and stormy weather, although perhaps some of the mines of barrier 2 had been missed. The BdAdO ordered the 8th

Minesweeper Half Flotilla to examine the mine-free channel that same day, but no further mines were found.

Vizeadmiral Schmidt now took a strong stance against further demonstrations inside the Riga Gulf. The recent storm meant that mines and buoys were continually drifting and there were only a few narrow swept channels for the large ships. The autumn also brought periods of poor visibility which meant it was often impossible to obtain a position fix. The chief of the Special Unit telegraphed his concerns to the Admiralty Staff, pointing out that the gains of further operations were minimal, whilst the risks were great, and recommended that all forces of the High Sea Fleet, including the I Battle Squadron and IV AG, should return to the North Sea. The OHL agreed and corresponding orders were raised on 31 October; after a very successful operation it seemed pointless to risk major losses in mopping up.

Vizeadmiral Schmidt handed over command to Kontreadmiral Hopman and, early on the morning of 2 November, he departed Arensburg Roads with *Moltke*, *Ostfriesland* and *Thüringen* for Putzig Wiek. The unit arrived there on the morning of 3 November whereupon Vizeadmiral Schmidt transferred to his old flagship, *Ostfriesland*, and detached *Moltke* to the North Sea. A telegram from the Admiralty Staff later that day dissolved the Special Unit. Vizeadmiral Ehrhard Schmidt dismissed himself on the following day and conveyed the following message to the forces hitherto under his command:

> On November 3rd the 'Special Unit' was dissolved. I am grateful for the undertaking against the Baltic Islands and now hand over command and retire as 'Chief of the Special Unit'.
> Full recognition and thanks to the leaders and men!
> Honour and glory to those who lost their lives! They are with God our all merciful Warlord and our beloved Fatherland.

In the meantime, a 'Government of the Baltic Islands' was formed, with its seat in Arensburg. Many of the local inhabitants were descended from Germanic people and were not troubled by the appearance of the German army and navy. The first governor was Generalleutnant Freiherr von Seckendorff, who was conveyed from Libau to Arensburg aboard SMS *Strassburg* on 31 October.

General von Kathen and his staff departed Arensburg aboard *Strassburg* the following day. On 3 November, Generalleutnant von Estorff and the staff of the 42nd Infantry Division and 131 Regt followed on two transport steamers, whilst the remainder of the division, 17 Regt, departed on the following day. On 7 November, the last part of the II Transport Section, the steamers *Batavia* and *Chemnitz*, went to Arensburg, where they finished unloading and departed for Libau on 10 November. At the same time the minesweeping work continued incessantly.

After the conclusion of Operation Albion the chance of a clash with the Russian fleet appeared more remote than ever. Although the Naval Forces of the Riga Gulf had fought determinedly and resolutely, the higher Russian command remained reluctant to commit their heavier forces to a confrontation. Both Admirals Bakhirev and Razvozov had committed themselves to action with the German forces, which was characteristic of officers who were veterans of the Russo-Japanese War, but their warlike resolve was not supported by the Russian high command. Once again political ineptitude had overstepped strategic good sense.

All the German hopes and desires for a successful operation to capture the Baltic Islands had come to fruition. However, a further revolution in Russia served to muddy the waters. On 7/8 November the so-called 'October Revolution' (it was still October according to the old Gregorian calendar) began and Lenin's Bolsheviks seized the Winter Palace in St Petersburg, or Petrograd as it was renamed, and formed a new revolutionary government. A civil war soon broke out across Russia between the 'Red' communists and the 'White' monarchists. Nevertheless, the Bolsheviks immediately took steps to get Russia out of the war. On 5 December 1917 a preliminary suspension of hostilities between the Central Powers and Russia was announced and on 22 December armistice discussions began in the town of Brest-Litovsk. Some of the terms were concerned with the rights of Poland and the independence of the Baltic States. Just as in 1856, the question of Finland's autonomy and the independence of the smaller states became a sticking point in negotiations, but, nevertheless, vast quantities of German men and materiel were released to participate in the great offensive on the western front in March 1918.

Captain 2nd Rank Kosinski wrote:

> The Moon Sound operation was successfully concluded by the Germans, and this had enormous significance for the further course of the war. The flank of our land army had been turned and was naked, and of necessity what they had to think about was not holding the enemy, but about their own rescue, with the possible occupation of Reval by the enemy, in our rear. The result of our being forced from Moon Sound was our further retreat and the possible abandonment of Reval.

Indeed. But not only was the gateway to Reval open, but also the gateway to the remainder of the Finnish Gulf, including Helsingfors and St Petersburg. At the beginning of February 1918 the Finnish minister Svinhufvud and his Government requested assistance from the German Government in their fight against the communist 'Reds', who were dominating the country. The German High Sea Fleet once again detached a 'Special Unit' of battleships which successfully landed troops on Aland Island, Hango and finally Helsingfors, the Finnish capital. In this way the Finnish Government was restored, the 'Reds' were crushed, and Finland was liberated and finally gained independence from Russia. Without control of the Baltic Islands this operation would not have been possible. Then, in late 1918, the Allies landed troops at Murmansk, in northern Russia, and began marching on St Petersburg. The German response was to again form a 'Special Unit' in August, which embarked troops and stood ready in Kiel. The bold objective of this force was the occupation of St Petersburg. All was in readiness to begin the operation and German small cruisers were already conducting reconnaissance deep inside the Finnish Gulf near Kronstadt. However, the deteriorating war situation did not allow this operation to be carried out; the troops were disembarked, and the battleships returned to the North Sea. Likewise, this planned operation was only conceivable because of the capture of the Baltic Islands.

Operation Albion, the conquest of the Baltic Islands, had been an unqualified success. The predictions of Grossadmiral Prinz Heinrich had come true and every objective had been achieved and even surpassed. Not only had it been a tactical and strategic success, perhaps greatly influencing the Russian desire to continue the war, but Operation Albion and subsequent operations in Finland proved that the High Sea Fleet and Imperial Navy were not only successful fighting units, but also a decisive political instrument, able to influence the future of nations and the war in accordance with the Government's political objectives.

The Imperial Navies, both Russian and German, could indeed be proud of their respective achievements, but these came at a cost. German losses were seven minesweepers, nine trawlers and smaller boats, and one torpedoboat. The German Imperial Navy lost a total of 156 dead and 60 wounded, whilst the Army lost 54 dead and 141 wounded. The Russians and Allies lost the battleship *Slava* and destroyer *Grom*, the British submarine C32, and numerous steamers. There were 20,130 Russian prisoners and they surrendered 141 guns and 130 machine guns. Whilst cooperation between the Russian Army and Navy had been almost non existent, the Germans could be very satisfied with the cooperation between their Imperial Navy and Army, which stood them in good stead for subsequent operations. The battle for the Baltic Islands represented a particularly high point in the history of the Kaiserliche Marine.

APPENDIX I

Sea Forces of the Special Unit

Chief of the Special Unit:	Vizeadmiral Ehrhard Schmidt
Chief of Staff:	Kapitän zur See von Levetzow
Admiralty Staff (Admiralstab) officers:	Korvettenkapitän Dietrich Meyer
	Kapitänleutnant Tegtmeyer
	Kapitänleutnant Firle
Navigation Officer:	Kapitänleutnant Kiep

Flagship:
Moltke   Kapitän zur See Gygas

Battle Squadrons
III Battle Squadron
Commander:	Vizeadmiral Behncke
2nd Admiral:	Kontreadmiral Seiferling
König	Kapitän zur See Weniger
Bayern	Kapitän zur See Rohardt
Grosser Kurfürst	Kapitän zur See Goette
Kronprinz	Kapitän zur See Rösing
Markgraf	Kapitän zur See Mörsberger

IV Battle Squadron
Commander:	Vizeadmiral Souchon
2nd Admiral:	Kommodore Meurer.
Friedrich der Grosse	Kapitän zur See von Lessel
König Albert	Kapitän zur See Varrentrapp
Kaiserin	Kapitän zur See Grasshoff
Prinzregent Luitpold	Kapitän zur See von Hornhardt
Kaiser	Kapitän zur See Loesch

Reconnaissance (Aufklarungs) Forces
C-in-C of Reconnaissance Forces of   Kontreadmiral Hopman
the Eastern Baltic (BdAdO):

II Reconnaissance Group (II AG)

Commander:	Kontreadmiral von Reuter
Königsberg	Fregattenkapitän Karl Feldmann
Karlsruhe	Fregattenkapitän Tietgens
Nürnberg	Fregattenkapitän Hildebrand
Frankfurt	Fregattenkapitän Seidensticker
Danzig	Korvettenkapitän Adalbert Prinz von Preussen

VI Reconnaissance Group (VI AG)

Commander:	Kontreadmiral Hopman
Kolberg	Fregattenkapitän Kurt Frank
Strassburg	Fregattenkapitän Quaet-Faslem
Augsburg	Fregattenkapitän Lutter
Tender *Blitz*	Korvettenkapitän Hauck
Nautilus	Korvettenkapitän Franz Pfeiffer

Torpedoboats

I Leader of Torpedoboats (I FdT):	Kommodore Heinrich
Emden	Fregattenkapitän Freiherr von Gagern

II Torpedoboat Flotilla

Commander:	Korvettenkapitän Heinecke
B98	

3rd Half Flotilla

Commander:	Kapitänleutnant Hans Kolbe
G101	
V100	
G103	
G104	

4th Half Flotilla

Commander:	Korvettenkapitän Faulborn
B109	
B110	
B111	
B97	
B112	

VI Flotilla

Commander:	Korvettenkapitän Werner Tillessen
V69	

12th Half Flotilla
Commander: Korvettenkapitän Lans
V43
S50
V44
V45
V46

13th Half Flotilla
Commander: Kapitänleutnant Zander
V82
S64
S61
S63
V74

VIII Flotilla
Commander: Korvettenkapitän Nieden
V180

15th Half Flotilla
Commander: Kapitänleutnant Vollheim
V183
V185
V181
V184
V182

16th Half Flotilla
Commander: Kapitänleutnant Stohwasser
S176
S178
G174
S179
V186

X Flotilla
Commander: Korvettenkapitän Hundertmarck
S56

19th Half Flotilla
Commander: Kapitänleutnant Wilhelm Rebensburg
T170

T169
T172
G175
T165

20th Half Flotilla
Commander: Kapitänleutnant Freiherr Röder von
V78   Diersburg
V77
G89
S65
S66

7th Half Flotilla
Commander: Korvettenkapitän Graf von der Recke
T154   Vollmerstein
T158
T157
T151
T160
T145
T143
T140
T139
Hydroglider   Oberleutnant zur See Peytsch

U-Boats
U-Boat Flotilla Kurland
Commander: Kapitänleutnant Schött
UC 56   Kapitänleutnant der Reserve Kiesewetter
UC 57   Kapitänleutnant Wissmann
UC 58   Kapitänleutnant Vesper
UC 59   Kapitänleutnant Lefholz
UC 60   Oberleutnant zur See von Fischer
UC 78   Oberleutnant zur See Kukat

Barrier Breaker Vessels
Sperrbrechergruppe
Commander: Korvettenkapitän der Seewehr Simonsen
Rio Pardo
Lother
Schwaben
Glatz

Minesweepers
II Minesweeper Flotilla
Commander: Kapitänleutnant Doflein
A62

3rd Minesweeper Half Flotilla (3rd MSHF)
T136   Kapitänleutnant Von der Marwitz
M67
M68
M75
M76
M77
T59
T65
T68
T82
T85

4th Minesweeper Half Flotilla (4th MSHF)
T104   Kapitänleutnant Maxim von Zitzewitz
T53
T54
T55
T56
T60
T61
T62
T66
T67
T69

8th Minesweeper Half Flotilla (8th MSHF)
M64   Kapitänleutnant Erich Koellner
M11
M31
M32
M39
A35

3rd S-Half Flotilla*
T141   Korvettenkapitän Goethe
Tender *Primula*
Tender *Fiora*
15 motorboats

Minesweeper Group of Coastal Protection Half Flotilla East
Commander: Oberleutnant zur See der Reserve Rudolf
6 trawlers   Nordmann

I Minesweeper Division (Riga)
Commander: Kapitänleutnant Astheimer
11 motorboats

II Minesweeper Division
Commander: Korvettenkapitän August Altvater
Tender *Ammon*
12 motorboats

III Minesweeper Division
Commander: Kapitänleutnant Weidgen
Tender *Indianola*
12 motorboats

IV Minesweeper Division
Commander: Kapitänleutnant der Reserve N A Kipke
Tender *Hochkamp*
Picket boat O2
10 motorboats

Anti-submarine Service
S-Flotilla of the Baltic*
Commander: Fregattenkapitän von Rosenberg
T144

1st S-Half Flotilla
T142   Kapitänleutnant der Reserve Sach
A32
A28
A30
32 trawlers and drifters

2nd S-Half Flotilla
T130   Kapitänleutnant der Seewehr Wahlen
A31
A27
A29
24 trawlers and drifters

Repair vessel *Donau*
Coalsteamer *Adeline Hugo Stinnes*
3 motorboats
Transport steamer *Castor*
Transport steamer *Coburg*

Net Barrier Unit of the Baltic
Commander: Korvettenkapitän Kaulhausen
Eskimo
Rossal
Net-layer *Burgfried*
6 tugs and several lighters

Fleet Train (Tross)
Commander: Kapitän der Seewehr Sachse
Dispatch boat T132
Hospital ships: *Imperator* , *Kehrwieder* , *Titania, Viola*
3 provisions steamers
Coal steamer
Water vessel
4 ammunition steamers
Oil steamer
Buoy-layers: *Wilhelms, Mellum*
Cable steamer: *Alster*

Recovery group
4 tugs and pump steamers
7 tugs for landing work including *Netter, Falkenstein, Jägersburg, Wilhelm Cords, Stein, Sturm*
10 lighters
8 light vessels
Blockships: *City of Belfast, City of Cadiz*

Transport Fleet
Commander: Fregattenkapitän von Schlick

I Section
Commander: Fregattenkapitän Max Fischer
Chemnitz
Cassel
Batavia
Friedrichsruh

II Section
Commander: Kapitänleutnant Ernst Wather
Oron
Sangara
Coralie Hörlock
Borderland

III Section
Commander: Fregattenkapitän Keller
Scharnhorst
Buenos Aires
Frankfurt

IV Section
Commander: Korvettenkapitän Glüer
Bahia Castillo
Giessen
Schleswig
Badenia
Oswald (Pioneer steamer)
Altenburg (reserve)

With Pioneers
Equity
Corsica

Airships
L30   Oberleutnant zur See Vermehren
L37   Kapitänleutnant Paul Gärtner
LZ113   Kapitänleutnant Zaeschmar
LZ120   Kapitänleutnant von Lossnitzer
SL8   Oberleutnant zur See Gerold Ratz
SL 20   Kapitänleutnant Guido Wolff

Air Service
Commander of Flyers
with Special Unit: Kapitänleutnant Berthold

Aircraft tender *Santa Elena*   Oberleutnant zur See Holzapfel
Airstation Libau   Oberleutnant zur See Hubert Klein
Airstation Windau   Kapitänleutnant Mans.
Airstation Angernsee   Kapitänleutnant der Reserve Pechel

I Torpedo Aircraft Section	Leutnant zur See Stinsky
Jagdstaffel of the 8 Armee	Leutnant Roth.
Naval Land Jagdstaffel (in reserve)	Leutnant der Reserve Wieland

Note

* The S- designation denotes, roughly translated, 'Picket', indicating an anti-submarine role.

Appendix II

Units of the Sea Forces of the Riga Gulf

Commander:	Vice Admiral M K Bakhirev
Staff:	Captain 1st Rank Muromtsev
Flag officer:	Leitenant Sokolov

Battleships

Graschdanin	Captain 1st Rank Rudenski
Slava	Captain 1st Rank Vladimir Antonov

Cruisers

Bayan	Captain 1st Rank Timirev
Admiral Makarov (from 14 Oct)	
Diana (from 16 Oct)	

Destroyer Divisions

Commander:	Rear Admiral G K Stark
Torpedoboat-destroyer *Novik*	

I Division Torpedoboat Destroyers (Novik *class*)

Commander:	Captain 2nd Rank Pilsudski
Pobeditel	
Zabiyaka	
Grom	Leitenant Anatoly Vaksmut

II Division Torpedoboat Destroyers (Novik *class*)

(under direct authority of Rear Admiral Stark)

Desna
Samson
Lieutenant Il'in
Captain Izylmetev (from 17 Oct)

III Division Torpedoboat Destroyers (Novik *class*)
Commander: Captain 1st Rank Shevelev
Izyaslav
Avtroil
Konstantin
Gavriil

IV Division
Commander: Captain 1st Rank Postelnikov
General Kondratenko
Pogranitschnik

V Division
Commander: Captain 1st Rank Zelenov
Vsadnik
Amurets
Finn
Moskvityanin
Emir Bukharski

VI Division
Commander: Captain 1st Rank Ekimov
Stregushchi
Donski Kazak
Zabaikalets
Voiskovoi
Ukraina
Turkmenets Stavropolski (from 14 Oct)
Strashnyi (from 16 October)

Auxiliary Units Attached to Division
Pechora

Transports:
Oka
Libau (Headquarters Division)
Vodoley No 1

Blockships:
Lava (Hospital Ship)
Minelayer No 4

Launches:
Dozornyi
Ilim
Moryak

III Division Guardship Unit
Steam Launches: No 1, No 2, No 3, No 4
Motor Launches: No 2, No 3, No 8, No 9
Tender *Tralshchik No 12*

English Submarines
C26, C27, C32.

Guardship Unit of the Baltic Sea
VIII Division Torpedoboat-Destroyers
Likhoi (from 15th October)

XI Division Torpedoboat-Destroyers
Gromyashchi
Sil'Nyi
Deyatel'Nyi
Del'Nyi
Storozhevoi (from 14th October)
Razyashchi

II Division Guardship Unit Dispatch Unit
Commander: Senior Leitenant Beklemishev
Barsuk
Gornostai
Vydra

III Division Guardship Unit Dispatch Unit
Khorek
Laska

I Division Guardship Launches
SK 1, SK 2, SK 3, SK 4, SK 5, SK 6, SK 7, SK 8, SK 9, SK 11, SK 12
Tender: BK 1

II Division Guardship Launches
Commander: Captain 2nd Rank Kira-Dinzhan.
SK 16, SK 17, SK 18, SK 19

Division of Minesweepers of the Baltic Sea
II Division Torpedoboats
Prytki
Retivyi
Rezvyi

III Division Minesweepers
Minrep
Udarnik

IV Division Minesweepers
Kapsyul'
Gruz
Krambol

V Division Minesweepers
Minesweeper No 3
Minesweeper No 8
Minesweeper No 23

VI Division Minesweepers
Planeta
Minesweeper No 11

I Division Minesweeper-Launches
Motor launches: No 2, No 3, No 5, No 7
Minesweeper Tender No 7

II Division Minesweeper-Launches
Minesweeper Tender No 10

Attached unit for Division: Minesweeper No 4

Minelaying Detachment of the Baltic Sea

Minelayers
Amur
Volga

Shallow-draughted Minelayer Detachment
I Division Shallow Minelayers
Zeya
Bureya   Senior Leitenant Semenov

III Division Shallow Minelayers
Pripyat   Leitenant S I Medvedev.

Gunboats
Chrabry   Senior Leitenant Rennenkampf.
Grozyashchi   Captain 2nd Rank Orlovski-Tanaevski.
Chivinets   Leitenant Afanasev.

Detached Units for Aerial Division
Tug boat *Aviun*

Transport Division of the Baltic Sea
III Detachment Transport
General Zimmerman

VI Detachment Transport
Obsidian
Vassian

Detached transport:
Buki

Coal Transports:
Glagol
On
Pokoj

Refrigerated transport:
Sukhona

Special transport:
Vodolei No 2

Pilot Management and Beacons Baltic Sea
Transports:
Artel'shchik
Samoed

Port unit:
Brigitovka

Ship Comparison

GERMANY

Ship name	Displacement (tonnes)	Main armament	Gun range (metres)
Battleships			
Bayern	32,200	8 x 38cm	23,200
König	28,600	10 x 30.5cm	20,400
Grosser Kurfürst	28,600	10 x 30.5cm	20,400
Markgraf	28,600	10 x 30.5cm	20,400
Krinprinz	28,600	10 x 30.5cm	20,400
Friedrich der Grosse	27,000	10 x 30.5cm	20,400
König Albert	27,000	10 x 30.5cm	20,400
Kaiserin	27,000	10 x 30.5cm	20,400
Prinzregent Luitpold	27,000	10 x 30.5cm	20,400
Kaiser	27,000	10 x 30.5cm	20,400
Battlecruiser			
Moltke	25,400	10 x 28cm	19,100
Small Cruisers			
Königsberg	7,125	8 x 15cm	17,600
Karlsruhe	7,125	8 x 15cm	17,600
Nürnberg	7,125	8 x 15cm	17,600
Emden	7,125	8 x 15cm	17,600
Frankfurt	6,601	8 x 15cm	17,600
Strassburg	5,281	7 x 15cm	17,600
Kolberg	4,915	6 x 15cm	17,600
Augsburg	4,882	8 x 15cm	17,600
Danzig	3,783	10 x 10.5cm	12,200
Torpedoboats			
B98	1,374	4 x 10.5cm 6 x 50cm torpedo	

V69	924	3 x 10.5cm	
		6 x 50cm torpedo	
V180	650	2 x 10.5cm	
		4 x 50cm torpedo	

Russia

Ship name	Displacement (tonnes)	Main armament	Gun range (metres)
Battleships			
Slava	15,800	4 x 30.5cm	21,200
Graschdanin	15,254	4 x 30.5cm	16,100
Armoured Cruisers			
Bayan	7,775	3 x 20.3cm	14,100
Admiral Makarov	7,775	3 x 20.3cm	14,100
Diana	6,657	10 x 15.2cm	12,800
Gunboats			
Chrabry	2,000	5 x 13.0cm	16,400
Grozyashch	1,700	4 x 15.2cm	16,400
Chivinets	1,400	4 x 12.0cm	11,000
Destroyers			
Novik	1,280	4 x 10.2cm	13,200
		8 x 45cm torpedo	
Grom	1,280	4 x 10.2cm	13,200
		8 x 45cm torpedo	
General Kondratenko	750	2 x 10.2cm	13,200
		3 x 45cm torpedo	
Vsadnik	750	2 x 10.2cm	13,200
		3 x 45cm torpedo	
Ukraina	730	2 x 10.2cm	13,200
		2 x 45cm torpedo	
Deyatel'Nyi	382	2 x 7.5cm	13,200
		2 x 45cm torpedo	

Ship Damage and Losses

German Damage and Losses

During preparation work

6 October	T54 struck mine and sunk.
7 October	T31 struck mine and sunk.
8 October	M75 struck mine, damaged and towed in.
	Cladow (minesweeper) struck mine, damaged and towed in.
	T85 struck mine, damaged and towed in.
10 October	Hydroglider lost to either mine or internal explosion.

During Operation Albion

12 October	*Bayern* struck mine and damaged.
	Grosser Kurfürst struck mine and damaged.
	A28 struck on stern by dud shell from Battery No 34.
	Corsica struck mine and beached.
	S25 run aground and damaged.
	V82 grounded and damaged.
14 October	*Altair* (picket boat) struck mine and sank.
	Delphin (picket boat) lost, seemingly on a mine.
	G101 ran aground and towed off.
15 October	B98 struck mine and damaged.
	T56 ran aground and eventually abandoned.
	B110 grounded.
	B112 grounded and detached.
	S63 ran aground but not damaged.
16 October	*Indianola* torpedoed by C27 and beached near Arensburg.
17 October	M77 damaged by shellfire from Russian battleships and shore batteries.
	M67 damaged by shellfire from Russian battleships and shore batteries.
	T53 ran aground briefly but not damaged.
	A35 ran aground briefly but not damaged.

17/18 October	S64 struck mine and sank.
18 October	T66 struck German mine and sank.
	B111 struck mine and damaged.
	Strassburg struck bottom but not damaged.
	Kronprinz struck bottom but not damaged.
20 October	T144 ran aground in Soelo Sound during afternoon.
	B109 ran aground in Soelo Sound during afternoon.
	S36 ran aground in Soelo Sound during afternoon.
	Tug *Stein* ran aground in Soelo Sound during afternoon.
21 October	*Roland* (minesweeper No 12) struck mine and sank.
22 October	*Gutheil* (drifter) struck mine and sank.
	Glückstadt (minesweeper No 14a) struck mine and sank.

After the operation

24 October	F3 (minesweeper) struck mine and sank.
	A32 stranded, towed away, and then sank.
26 October	*Sangara* ran aground and towed away.
	T65 mined in sweeper gear and sank.
	König and *Kronprinz* both struck bottom in heavy seas.
29 October	M68 struck mine, beached and written off.
	Markgraf struck mine and damaged.
	Tarasp (minesweeper boat) capsizes whilst under tow by her tender.
30 October	*Biene* (minesweeper motorboat) sunk by a direct hit.
	Kehrwieder (picket boat) stranded and sank.

Russian Losses

14 October	*Grom*
16 October	*Esti*
17 October	*Slava*
	Glagol
	Pokoj
	Artel'shchik sunk as blockship.
	General Zimmerman sunk as blockship.
19 October	*Pregrada*
	Tor grounded.
	Toledo

APPENDIX V

Russian Batteries on the Baltic Islands

Battery No	Calibre and Number of Guns	Traverse Angle	Range	Location of Battery
30	4 x 6"/45	130°	14,100m	Worms Island
31	2 x 75mm AA	–	–	Rogekul
32	4 x 6"/45	140°	16,500m	On Moon near Woi
32a	2 x 75mm AA	–	–	On Moon near Woi
33	4 x 6"/45	130°	14,100m	Werder
33a	3 x 75mm AA	–	–	Werder
34	4 x 120mm/50	140°	12,800m	On Dago, near Serro
36	4 x 10"/45	140°	14,700m	On Moon near Woi
37	4 x 6"/50	140°	14,600m	Cape Dirhamn
38	4 x 6"/50	140°	14.600m	Cape Simpernas, Dago
39	4 x 12"/50	140°	25,600m	Cape Tachkona
39a	3 x 57mm AA	–	–	Cape Tachkona
40	4 x 120mm/50	140°	12,800m	Swobe Peninsula, near Karust
40a	3 x 75mm AA	–	–	Swobe Peninsula, near Karust
41	4 x 130mm/50	180°	17,000m	Swobe Peninsula, near Karust
41a	3 x 75mm AA	–	–	Swobe Peninsula, near Karust
43	4 x 12"/50	160°	27,800m	Cape Zerel
43a	3 x 75mm AA	–	–	Cape Zerel
43b	3 x 75mm AA	–	–	Cape Zerel
43v	3 x 75mm AA	–	–	Cape Zerel
43g	4 x 47mm AA	–	–	Cape Zerel
45	4 x 6"/45	100°	16,500m	Cape Hundsort, Tagga Bay
46	4 x 6"/45	100°	14,100m	Cape Ninnast, Tagga Bay
47	4 x 6"/45	140°	16,500m	Dago, near Hermuste
48	3 x 75mm AA	–	–	Lodde, at Arensburg
50	4 x 75mm AA	–	–	Kielkond
51	4 x 75mm AA	–	–	Kielkond

Bibliography

Listed below are the chief sources used in the preparation of this book, including all those from which direct quotations have been made in the main text.

Arndt, Peter, *Deutsche Sperrbrecher* (Stuttgart, 1979).

Bakhirev, M K, *Report* (St Petersburg, 1998).

Bartinev, N, *Battle of the Zerel Battery* (St Petersburg, 2000).

Breyer, Siegfried, *Battleships and Battlecruisers 1905–1970* (Munich, 1970).

Busch, Fritz Otto, *Drei Kleine Kreuzer* (Berlin, 1936).

Busch, Fritz Otto, *Unter der alten Flagge 1914–1918* (Berlin, 1935).

Graf, Harald K, *On Novik* (reprinted St Petersburg, 1997).

Greger, Rene, *The Russian Fleet 1914–1917* (London, 1972).

Groner, Erich, *Die deutschen Kriegsschiffe 1815–1945* (Munich, 1982).

Hildebrand, H, H Rohr and A Steinmetz, *Die deutschen Kriegsschiffe* (Herford, 1979).

Hopman, Albert, *Das Kriegstagebuch eines deutschen Seeoffizier* (Berlin, 1925).

Kosinski, A M, *Moon Sound Operations of the Baltic Fleet in 1917* (Leningrad, 1928).

Makela, Matti, *Das Geheimnis der Magdeburg* (Koblenz, 1984).

Von Mantey, Eberhard, *Auf See unbeseigt, Band 1 and 2* (Munich, 1922).

Von Mantey, Eberhard, *Unsere Marine im Weltkrieg 1914–1918* (Berlin,1927).

Von Mantey, Eberhard, *Der Krieg in der Ostsee Band 3* (Berlin, 1964).

Nekrasov, George M, *Expendable Glory* (New York, 2004).

Ruge, Friedrich, *S.M. Torpedoboate B110* (Windsor, 1972).

Ruge, Friedrich, *In vier Marine* (Munich, 1979).

Staff, Gary, *German Battlecruisers 1914–1918* (Oxford, 2006).

Timirev, *Recollections of a Naval Officer.*

Von Tschischwitz, Erich, *Blaujacken und Feldgraue gegen Oesel* (Berlin, 1934).

Wilson, Michael, *Baltic Assignment* (London, 1985).

Witthoft, Hans-Jurgen, *Lexikon zur deutschen Marinegeschichte* (Herford, 1977).

Index

German Forces:

A27, 123, 156

A28, 23, 27, 123, 156, 169

A29, 84, 85, 123, 156

A30, 156

A31, 85, 156

A32, 86, 123, 156, 170

A35, 119, 155, 169

A62, 102, 119, 131, 133, 155

Adalbert, Prinz von Preussen, 152

Adeline Hugo Stinnes, 157

Ahlefeld, Kapitänleutnant, 86

air arm units:

  I Torpedo Flugzeug Staffel, 12, 13, 159

    Aircraft 1372, 12

  Aircraft 1374, 12

  Aircraft 1376, 12

  Aircraft 1377, 12

  Aircraft 1378, 12

  Airstation Angernsee, 158

  Airstation Libau, 158

  Airstation Windau, 12, 158

  Jagdstaffel of the 8 Armee, 158

  Naval Land Jagdstaffel (in reserve), 158

Alster, 157

Altair, 69

Altenburg, 140, 158

Altvater, Korvettenkapitän, 156

Ammon, 17, 156

Army units:

  I Cyclist Battalion, 16, 31-2, 41

  I Pioneers, 17

  II Cyclist Battalion, 16, 31-2, 41, 47, 62, 65-6, 91, 128, 134, 137, 143

  II Infantry Cyclist Brigade

  II Pioneers, 17

  III Pioneers, 17

  IV Cyclist Battalion, 62, 65-6, 97

  V Cyclist Battalion, 62, 66, 91-2, 124, 130

  VI Cyclist Battalion, 67

  1st Cyclist Company, 32, 45, 61

  2nd Cyclist Company, 32, 45, 47, 61-2

3rd Cyclist Company, 32, 45, 61

4th Cyclist Company, 45, 47, 61

5th Cyclist Company, 45, 61-2

6th Cyclist Company, 45, 61-2

42nd Infantry Division, 62, 64, 66, 91, 147

65th Infantry Brigade, 15, 38-9, 62, 64-6, 87, 92, 123

17th Infantry Regiment, 15, 31-2, 38-9, 41, 62, 65-7, 91-2, 95, 135, 143-4, 147

131st Infantry Regiment, 15, 23, 25, 31-2, 38-9, 64, 67, 70-1, 78, 80, 88-9, 91, 94, 147

138th Infantry Regiment, 15, 20, 24, 25, 31, 38-9, 41, 66-7, 91-2, 95, 123-5, 130-1

255th Reserve Infantry Regiment, 15, 31-2, 38-9, 66-7, 87, 91-2, 124, 130

Sturmkompanie 18 (Winterfeld), 16, 31-2, 41, 44, 47, 53, 59, 61-2, 64, 66, 84, 91-2, 95, 98, 123-5

Landing Korps Ahlefeld, 86, 93, 120

Astheimer, Kapitänleutnant, 156

Augsburg, 4, 60, 102-3, 152

B97, 25, 152

B98, 24, 36, 57, 85, 87, 98, 152, 169

B109, 25, 152, 170

B110, 25, 85, 152, 170

B111, 25, 128, 152, 170

B112, 25, 85, 152, 169

Badenia, 158

Bahia Castillo, 27, 158

Batavia, 147, 157

battleship squadrons:

  I Battle Squadron, 4, 146-7

  III Battle Squadron, 3, 17, 20-1, 25, 27, 32, 78, 89, 110, 123, 132, 145, 151

  IV Battle Squadron, 14, 17-8, 20-1, 23, 27, 32, 67, 70, 80-1, 88, 125, 138, 151

Bayern, 3, 20-2, 27-8, 32-3, 151, 169

Behncke, Vizeadmiral, 3, 21, 32, 78, 81, 87, 102-5, 107, 110, 112, 118, 122, 132-3, 149, 151

Berring, Oberst, 15, 38, 66, 92
Berthold, Kapitänleutant, 158
Biene, 170
Blitz, 4, 20, 24, 78, 140, 152
Borderland, 120, 158
Buenos Aires, 140, 158
Burgfried, 158

Cassel, 157
Castor, 157
Caurus, 85
Chemnitz, 147, 157
City of Belfast, 157
City of Cadiz, 157
Cladow, 17, 169
Coburg, 93, 157
Coralie Hörlock, 140, 158
Corsica, 20, 27, 158, 169

Danzig, 4, 149, 152
Delphin, 169
Diersburg, Kapitänleutnant Freiherr von, 154
Dietze, Oberleutnant zur See, 86
Doflein, Kapitänleutnant, 17, 102, 105, 107, 112, 131, 133, 155
Donau, 157
Dormagen, Oberluetnant, 89
Emden, 4, 17, 20-4, 28, 31, 35-7, 52-3, 57, 84, 86-7, 93, 99, 128, 152
Equity, 20, 24, 158
Eskimo, 27, 141, 144, 157
Essen, Leutnant der Reserve, 12
Estorff, General, 3, 64-7, 91, 95, 147

F3, 157
Falck, Major, 39
Falkenstein, 157
Faulborn, Korvettenkapitän, 36, 152
Feldmann, Fregattenkapitän, 152
Fiora, 155
Firle, Kapitänleutnant, 151
Fischer, Oberleutnant, 15, 67, 69, 80, 89, 94
Fischer Oberleutnant zur See, 100, 154
Fischer, Fregattenkapitän, 157
Fleet Train, 157
Frank, Fregattenkapitän, 103, 105, 152
Frankfurt, 4, 152
Frankfurt, (transport) 158
Friedrich der Grosse, 4, 23, 67, 70-2, 81, 94, 140, 151
Friedrichsruh, 157
Frizen, Major von, 62

G89, 146, 154
G101, 55, 59, 152, 169
G103, 55, 57, 59, 152
G104, 57, 152
G174, 153
G175, 154
Gagern, Fregattenkapitän Freiherr von, 67, 152
Gärtner, Kapitänleutnant, 100,131, 158
Giessen, 158
Glatz, 4, 154
Glückstadt (minesweeper No 14a), 170
Glüer, Korvettenkapitän, 154
Goethe, Korvettenkapitän, 155
Goette, Kapitän zur See, 151
Grasshoff, Kapitän zur See, 151
Grosser Kurfürst, 3, 21, 32, 151, 169
Gutheil, 170
Gygas, Kapitän zur See, 151

Hauck, Fregattenkapitän, 152
Heinecke, Korvettenkapitän, 152
Heinrich, Grossadmiral Prinz, 1, 5, 149
Heinrich, Kommodore (I FdT), 4, 21, 24, 28, 29, 31, 36-7, 55, 57-9, 67, 84-5, 96, 98-100, 117, 119-21, 123, 127-8, 152
Hildebrand, Fregattenkapitän, 152
Hochkamp, 156
Holzapfel, Oberleutnant, 158
Hopman, Kontreadmiral (BdAdO), 4, 50, 60-1, 70, 77-8, 81, 84, 101-2, 104, 107, 112, 118-9, 131-2, 145-7, 151-2
Hornhardt, Kapitän zur See von, 151
Hundertmarck, Korvettenkapitän, 153
hydroglider, 13, 154, 169

Imperator, 157
Indianola, 60, 103-5, 156, 169

Jägersburg, 158
Joachim, Prinz von Preussen, 91

Kaiser, 4, 20, 52-3, 55, 93, 120, 151
Kaiserin, 4, 20, 67, 70-2, 81, 140, 145, 151
Karlsruhe, 4, 152
Kathen, Generale der Infanterie, 17, 67, 91, 94, 124, 147
Kaulhausen, Korvettenkapitän, 27, 152
Kaweczynski, Oberst, 65, 67, 135
Kehrwieder, 157, 170
Keller, Fregattenkapitän, 158
Kelm, Oberleutnant zur See, 119
Kiep, Kapitänleutnant, 151
Kiesewetter, Kapitänleutnant der Reserve, 154

Kipke, Kapitänleutant der Reserve, 156
Klein, Oberluetnant, 158
Koellner, Kapitänleutant, 110, 155
Kolbe, Kapitänleutant, 152
Kolberg, 4, 60, 102-3, 119, 132, 140, 146, 152
König, 3, 18, 50, 78, 102, 104-5, 107-10, 112-15, 118, 133, 140, 151, 170
König Albert, 4, 23, 67, 70-2, 81, 140, 145, 151
Königsberg, 4, 27, 140, 152
Kronprinz, 3, 33, 50, 78, 102-3, 110, 112-14, 125, 133, 140, 146, 151, 170
Kukat, Oberluetnant zur See, 154

L30, 13, 100, 158
L37, 13, 100, 158
Laebell, Stabsingenieur, 22
Lans, Korvettnekapitän, 153
Lefholz, Kapitänleutant, 154
Lessel, Kapitän zur See, 151
Lindemann, Leutnant zur See, 22
Levetzow, Kapitän zur See, 3, 151
Loesch, Kapitän zur See, 151
Lorenz, Oberleutnant (I) der Reserve, 21
Lossnitzer, Kapitänleutant, 13, 100, 158
Lother, 4, 145, 154
Lutter, Fregattenkapitän, 152
LZ113, 13, 100, 158
LZ120, 13, 100, 158

M11, 155
M31, 17, 155
M32, 155
M39, 155
M64, 155
M67, 112, 135, 169
M68, 155, 170
M75, 17, 155, 169
M76, 155
M77, 103, 112, 155, 169
Mans, Kapitänleutant, 12, 158
Markgraf, 3, 32, 132, 140, 145-6, 151, 170
Marwitz, Kapitänleutant, 110, 132, 155
Matthiass, Oberst, 15, 24, 43, 66, 95, 123
Mellum, 102, 140, 157
Meurer, Kommodore, 20, 151
Meusel, Kapitänleutant, 113
Meyer, Offizierstellvertreten, 64
Meyer, Korvettnekapitän, 151
Minesweeper Forces:
  I Minesweeper Division (Riga), 156
  II Minesweeper Division, 17, 24, 81, 109, 120, 125, 155

II Minesweeper Flotilla, 4, 17-18, 20, 27, 50, 98, 102, 105, 144, 155
III Minesweeper Division, 60-1, 102-3, 107, 110, 112, 118, 131, 156
IV Minesweeper Division, 60-1, 81, 102-3, 156
3rd Minesweeper Half Flotilla, 4, 81, 101-3, 107-8, 110, 112, 115, 118-9, 132-3, 145-6, 155
4th Minesweeper Half Flotilla, 4, 27, 125, 140, 155
8th Minesweeper Half Flotilla, 4, 17, 27, 78, 102, 107-10, 118, 131-2, 147, 155
Minesweeper Gruppe of Coastal Protection Half Flotilla East, 156
Moltke, 3, 17, 20-2, 87, 140, 147, 151
Mörsberger, Kapitän zur See, 151

Nautilus, 4, 141, 144, 145, 152
Net Barrier Unit of the Baltic, 4, 27, 145, 157
Netter, 157
Nieden, Korvettnekapitän, 153
Nordmann, Oberluetnant zur See der Reserve, 156
Nürnberg, 4, 27, 140, 152

O2, 156
Oppen, Oberluetnant der Reserve von, 69-70, 89
Oron, 158
Ostfriesland, 146, 147
Oswald, 120, 158

Pechel, Kapitänleutant der Reserve, 158
Peytsch, Oberluetnant zur See, 13, 154
Pfeiffer, Korvettnekapitän, 152
picket (anti-submarine) forces:
  1st S-Half Flotilla, 27, 156
  2nd S-Half Flotilla, 28, 156
  3rd S-Half Flotilla, 61, 77, 102-3, 155
  Picket Flotilla of the Baltic, 4, 18, 103, 123, 156
Pillau, 146
Primula, 60, 155
Prinzregent Luitpold, 4, 20, 151

Quaet-Faslem, Fregattenkapitän, 152

Ratz, Oberleutnant zur See, 100, 158
Rebensburg, Kapitänleutant, 153
Recke-Vollmerstein, Korvettnekapitän Graf von der, 154

Redern, Hauptmann von, 66
Regensburg, 146
Reconnaissance Forces:
  II Reconnaissance Group (II AG) 4, 17,
    125, 140, 152
  IV Reconnaissance Group (IV AG), 146-7
  VI Reconnaissance Group (VI AG), 4,
    77, 152,
Reuter, Kontreadmiral, 4, 27, 140, 152
Rio Pardo, 4, 154
Rohardt, Kapitän zur See, 22, 151
Roland, 170
Rosenberg, Fregattenkapitän von, 18, 22,
    29, 31, 35-6, 59, 62, 66, 84-7, 123, 128, 156
Rösing, Kapitän zur See, 131
Rossal, 27, 140, 157
Roth, Leutnant, 159
Rowehl Leutnant zur See der Reserve, 12
Ruge Leutnant zur See, 25, 117

S25, 169
S36, 170
S50, 53, 55, 84-5, 121-2, 128, 153
S56, 153
S61, 28, 37, 122-3, 153
S63, 28, 85, 121, 153, 169
S64, 23, 122-3, 153, 170
S65, 154
S66, 154
S176, 144, 153
S178, 153
S179, 153
Sach, Kapitänleutnant der Reserve, 156
Sachse, Kapitänleutnant der Seewehr, 157
Sangara, 120, 158, 170
Santa Elena, 87, 158
Scharnhorst, 158
Schmidt, Vizeadmiral, 3-4, 12, 17-18, 20, 27,
    32-3, 81, 96, 99, 102, 123, 125, 127-8, 140,
    145-7, 151
Schleswig, 158
Schlick, Fregattenkapitän, 93, 157
Schött, Kapitänleutnant, 154
Schurer, Leutnant zur See der Reserve, 12
Schwaben, 4, 154
Seckendorff, Generalleutnant Freiherr
    von, 147
Seidensticker, Fregattenkapitän, 152
Seiferling, Kontreadmiral, 145-6, 151
Simonsen, Korvettenkapitän der Seewehr,
    154
SL8, 158
SL20, 100, 158

Sluyter, Major, 41
Souchon, Vizeadmiral, 4, 23, 67, 80-1, 88,
    140, 151
Sperrbrechergruppe, 50, 154
Stein, 157, 170
Stinsky, Leutnant zur See,12, 159
Stohwasser, Kapitänleutnant, 153
Stralsund, 146
Strassburg, 4, 60, 102-3, 119, 132-3, 140,
    145-7, 152, 170
Sturm, 157

T31, 169 T53, 119, 155, 169
T54, 17, 169
T55, 55, 155
T56, 155, 169
T59, 155
T60, 155
T61, 155
T62, 55, 155
T65, 146, 155, 170
T66, 132, 155, 170
T67, 155
T68, 155
T69, 155
T82, 155
T85, 17, 155, 169
T104, 155
T130, 28, 156
T132, 157
T136, 155
T139, 120, 154
T140, 154
T141, 86, 155
T142, 156
T143, 154
T144, 29, 52, 59, 84, 99, 123, 128, 156, 170
T145, 154
T151, 154
T154, 154
T157, 154
T158, 154
T160, 99, 154
T165, 154
T169, 70, 71, 154
T170, 70, 71, 154
T172, 154
Tarasp, 170
Tegtmeyer, Kapitänleutnant, 151
Thüringen, 146, 147
Tietgens, Fregattenkapitän, 152
Tillessen, Korvettenkapitän, 152
Titania, 140, 157

Tornau, Leutnant zur See, 12
Torpedoboat Forces:
  II Torpedoboat Flotilla 4, 17, 20, 24, 55,
    57, 59, 84-5, 99, 120, 152
  VI Torpedoboat Flotilla, 4, 67, 125, 140,
    152
  VIII Torpedoboat Flotilla, 4, 78, 103,
    152
  X Torpedoboat Flotilla, 4, 152
  3rd Torpedoboat Half Flotilla, 24, 27,
    32, 152
  4th Torpedoboat Half Flotilla, 24, 31,
    36, 96, 152
  7th Torpedoboat Half Flotilla, 145, 154
  12th Torpedoboat Half Flotilla, 152
  13th Torpedoboat Half Flotilla, 23, 29-
    30, 36, 59, 84, 96, 99, 120-1, 125, 153
  15th Torpedoboat Half Flotilla, 23, 32,
    50, 153
  16th Torpedoboat Half Flotilla, 60,
    153
  19th Torpedoboat Half Flotilla, 125,
    153
  20th Torpedoboat Half Flotilla, 103,
    154
Transport Units:
  I Transport Section, 27, 157
  II Transport Section, 27, 102, 134, 145,
    147, 158
  III Transport Section, 158
  IV Transport Section, 158
Tschischwitz, Oberst von, 39, 47, 86, 94,
  131

U-Boat Flotilla Kurland, 154
UC56, 154
UC57, 52, 84, 154
UC58, 100, 101, 154
UC59, 154
UC60, 100, 101, 154
UC78, 52, 81, 154

V43, 153
V44, 120, 153
V45, 120, 153
V46, 53, 55, 84, 153
V69, 152
V74, 23, 85, 122-3, 153
V77, 154
V78, 154
V82, 23, 37, 153, 169
V100, 25, 56, 85, 99, 120-2, 127, 152
V180, 78, 132-3, 153

V181, 153
V182, 153
V183, 153
V184, 132-33, 153
V185, 153
V186, 144, 153
Varrentrapp, Kapitän zur See, 151
Vermehren, Kapitänleutnant, 13, 100,   158
Vesper, Kapitänleutnant, 101
Viola, 98, 123, 157
Vollheim, Kapitänleutnant, 153
Vollmerstein, Korvettenkapitän Graf von
  der Recke, 154

Wahlen, Kapitänleutnant der Seewehr, 156
Wather, Kapitänleutnant, 158
Weidgen Kapitänleutnant, 107, 156
Weniger Kapitän zur See, 151
Wieland, Leutnant der Reserve, 159
Wilhelm Cords, 140, 157
Wilhelms, 101, 140, 157
Winterfeld, Hauptmann von, 16, 24, 31,
  45, 47, 59, 81, 124
Wissmann, Kapitänleutnant, 84, 154
Wolff, Kapitänleutnant, 158

Zaeschmar, Kapitänleutnant, 100, 158
Zander, Kapitänleutnant, 23-4, 29-30,
  36-7, 121-2, 153
Zitzewitz, Kapitänleutnant, 155

Russian Forces:
1 Battleship Brigade, 9, 138
2 Battleship Brigade, 138
1 Cruiser Brigade, 9
2 Cruiser Brigade, 138

AdmiralMakarov, 8, 67, 77, 85, 96-7, 99,
  101, 127, 139, 161
Afanasev, Leitenant, 58, 165
Aktiv, 67
Amur, 8, 27, 139, 164
Amurets. 37, 58-9, 77, 82-4, 117, 140, 162
Andrei Pervozvannyi, 9
Antonov, Capitan 1st Rank, 114, 116-7,
  161
Army units:
  107 Infantry Division, 25, 44, 47, 49, 92,
    95
  1 Estonian Regiment, 131
    173 Infantry Regiment, 33
  425 Infantry Regiment (Kargopol), 5, 39,
    69, 70, 89, 94

426 Infantry Regiment (Povenets), 5, 21, 41, 92
427 Infantry Regiment (Pudozh), 120, 137, 143
470 Infantry Regiment (Dankov), 131
471 Infantry Regiment. (Kozel), 131
472 Infantry Regiment (Massalski), 5, 89, 92
Death Battalion, 33, 45, 58, 65, 91, 123, 125, 130-1
Artel'shchik, 133, 165, 170
Aviun, 165
Avtroil, 35, 51, 77, 98, 130, 162

Bakhirev, Vice Admiral, 8-10, 16, 24, 28-30, 33-8, 49, 51-2, 56, 70, 74-5, 77, 79, 81, 94-6, 101, 108-9, 112-3, 115-6, 121, 125, 127, 130-2, 134, 138, 148, 161
Barsuk, 163
Bartinev, Leitenant, 11, 60, 70-4, 79, 80, 93-4
batteries:
Battery No 32, 6, 95, 118
Battery No 33, 6, 118
Battery No 34, 5, 20-1, 23, 28
Battery No 36, 6, 45, 48,118
Battery No 37, 5
Battery No 38, 5, 120, 137
Battery No 39, 5, 120, 130, 135, 137.
Battery No 40, 6, 78, 80
Battery No 41, 6, 78
Battery No 43, 6, 11, 15, 23, 49, 60, 69-72, 74, 78-9, 81, 93
Battery No 44, 49, 79
Battery No 45, 5, 20
Battery No 46, 5, 20, 21, 25, 47, 48
Battery No 47, 120
Bayan, 8, 49, 52, 77, 108, 110, 113, 115, 116, 121, 127, 139, 161
Beklemishev, Starchi Leitenant, 163,
BK 1, 163
Black Sea Nr 2, 37
Bogatyr, 52, 101
Borsakowski, Col, 69
Brigitovka, 165
Bubnov, Kontre Admiral, 138
Buki, 65, 165
Bureya, 101, 121, 122, 164

C26, 8, 103, 118, 119, 163
C27, 8, 103, 104, 118, 163, 169
C32, 8, 51, 103, 104, 144, 149, 163
Capitanain Izylmetev, 161

Cheremisov, General, 138
Chernomorski 2, 116
Chetverakhin, Capitan 2nd Rank, 95, 130, 131
Chivinetz, 8, 33-6, 51, 58, 85, 96, 127, 131-3, 139, 165
Chrabry. 8, 33-5, 51, 53, 55-8, 85, 96, 101, 121, 139, 165
Cromie, Capitan, 103

Del'Nyi, 67, 95, 101, 108, 113, 163
Desna, 29, 30, 52, 85, 96, 139, 161
destroyer units:
I Division Torpedoboat Destroyers, 5, 8, 37, 51, 53, 55, 57, 58, 101, 127, 139,161
II Division Torpedoboat Destroyers, 8, 85, 101, 127, 161
III Division Torpedoboat Destroyers, 8, 28, 30, 51, 52, 96, 98, 101, 121, 127, 130, 162
IV Division Torpedoboat Destroyers, 8, 29, 30, 95, 96, 101, 127, 162
V Division Torpedoboat Destroyers, 8, 49, 58, 84, 85, 95, 101, 116, 127, 139, 162
VI Division Torpedoboat Destroyers, 8, 58, 77, 95, 96, 101, 115, 117, 121, 127, 143, 162
VIII Division Torpedoboat Destroyers, 8, 163
XI Division Torpedoboat Destroyers, 8, 108, 115, 163
Deyatel'Nyi, 95, 101, 108, 113, 139, 163
Diana, 8, 101, 108, 139, 161
Donski Kazak, 84, 113, 116-7, 139, 143,162
Downie, Leitenant, 103, 118-9
Dozornyi, 163

E1, 17, 18
Ekimov, Capitan 1st Rank, 58, 77, 117, 143, 162
Elachich, Starchi Leitenant, 128, 137
Elba, 61, 135
Emir Bukharski, 101, 140, 162
Essen, Admiral, 5
Esti, 101, 170

Finn, 52, 58-9, 140, 162
Fok, Starchi Leitenant, 10

Galler, Starchi Leitenant, 114
Gavriil, 33, 51, 98, 130, 139, 162
Gedle, Michman, 117

General Kondratenko, 28, 52, 130, 133, 139, 162
General Zimmerman, 11, 84, 133, 165, 170
Glagol, 108, 118, 165, 170
Goncharev, Michman, 72
Gornostai, 163
Graf, H K, 56
Graschdanin (*Tsarevitch*), 8, 35, 51, 77, 79-84, 93, 101, 108, 110, 112-6, 121, 127, 139, 161
Grigorev, Leitenant, 11
Grom, 30-1, 35-6, 53, 55-7, 85, 98, 105, 107, 118, 149, 161, 170
Gromyashchi, 51, 163
Grozyashchi, 8, 28-30, 58, 85, 96, 99, 127, 139, 165
Gruz, 95, 131, 164
guardship units of the Baltic Sea.
 I Division Guardship Launches, 163
 II Division Guardship Launches, 163
 II Division Guardship Unit Dispatch Unit, 163
 III Division Guardship Unit Dispatch Unit, 163
 III Division Guardship Unit, 163

Ilim, 163
Imperator Pavel I, 9
Izyaslav, 30, 35-7, 51, 77, 98, 130, 162
Ivanov, General, 44, 92, 95
Izhe, 67, 139

Kapsyul, 95, 131, 164
Khorek, 163
Kira-Dinzhan, Capitan 2nd Rank, 12, 163
Kleisti, Michman, 34, 45, 47
Knüpfer, Capitan 1st Rank, 10-11, 16, 70, 73, 79, 80, 93
Konstantin, 35-7, 51, 53, 55, 57-8, 121, 139, 162
Kosinski, Capitan 2nd Rank, 30, 59, 82, 148
Kovshov, Michman, 117
Krambol, 95, 164

Larosh, Michman, 93
Laska, 116, 163
Latvia, 34, 37
Lava, 162
Lesgaft, WO, 23
Libau, 9, 95, 162
Lieutenant Il'in, 34, 52, 84, 96, 139, 161
Likhoi, 127, 139, 163.

Lindeberg, Leitenant, 74
Loman, Capitan 2nd Rank, 11

Maksutin, Leitenant, 11
Manikhin, 11
Martynov, General, 125, 131
Mazurenko, Engineer, 114, 117
Medvedev, Leitenant, 37-8, 121, 165
Mine Forces:
 I Division Minesweeper – Launches, 95, 130, 164
 I Division Shallow Minelayers, 164
 II Division Minesweeper – Launches, 127, 164
 III Division Minesweepers, 127, 163
 III Division Shallow Minelayers, 165
 IV Division Minesweepers, 127, 164
 V Division Minesweepers, 127, 164
 VI Division Minesweepers, 164
 Minelaying Detachment of the Baltic Sea, 164
 Minesweeper No 3, 164
 Minesweeper No 4, 162, 164
 Minesweeper No 8, 164
 Minesweeper No 11, 164
 Minesweeper No 23, 164
 Minesweeper Tender No 7, 164
 Minesweeper Tender No 10, 164
 Shallow Draughted Minelayer Detachment, 164
Minrep, 131, 164
Moryak, 163
Moskito, 116
Moskvityanin, 58, 59, 84, 96, 117, 139, 143, 162
Muromtsev, Capitan 2nd Rank, 8, 10, 11, 108, 161

Novik, 8, 30, 34, 35, 36, 37, 58, 108, 121, 139, 161

Obsidian, 165
Ogilvi, 83
Oka, 162
Okhotnik, 10
Oleg, 52
Olga, 139
On, 135, 165
Orlovski-Tanaevski, Capitan 2nd Rank, 29, 30, 58, 165

Panferov, Leitenant, 10
Pechora, 162

Penelope, 13
Pilkin, Kontre Admiral, 9
Pilsudski, Capitan 2nd Rank, 51, 53, 55, 57-8, 161
Planeta, 164
Pobeditel, 35, 37, 51, 53, 55-8, 139, 161
Pogranitschnik, 28, 52, 130, 133, 139, 162
Pokoj, 108, 118, 165, 170
Polikarpov, Leitenant, 11
Popov, Colonel, 64
Popov, Yakov, 44.
Postelnikov, Capitan 1st Rank, 28, 30, 96, 162
Pregrada, 135, 170
Prestin, Starchi Leitenant, 61, 66

Pripyat, 8, 34, 37-8, 51, 53, 55, 59, 98, 101, 120-1, 128, 130, 165
Prytki, 64

Razdenov, Ensign, 11
Rayovzov, Kontre Admiral, 9, 33, 52, 58, 82, 95, 101, 121, 127, 130, 134-5, 137-8, 140, 148
Razyashchi, 29, 35, 36, 37, 84, 127, 139, 163
Rennenkampf, Starchi Leitenant, 53, 56-7, 165
Respublika, 9
Retivyi, 164
Rezvyi, 164
Rogge, Capitan 2nd Rank, 140
Rudenski, Capitan 1st Rank, 81, 116, 161
Rurik, 9
Rybaltovski, Starchi Leitenant, 110, 117

Safonov, Leitenant, 24, 100
Samoed, 165
Samson, 35, 37, 58, 84, 96, 139, 161
Satow, Leitenant, 103-4, 144
Savkin, Miner, 72-3
Sealy, Leitenant, 103-4
Semenov, Leitenant, 121, 164
Severski, Michman, 24
Shevelev, Capitan 1st Rank, 30, 52, 58, 98, 131, 162
Shishko, Capitan 2nd Rank, 33, 65, 123, 131
Shternberg, Leitenant, 34
Shteven, Leitenant, 100

Sil'Nyi. 113, 116, 132, 139, 163
Slava. 8, 75, 77, 85, 96, 99, 101, 108, 110, 112, 113, 114, 115, 116, 117, 121, 122, 132, 148, 161, 170.
Sokolov, Leitenant, 108, 161.
Stark, Kontre Admiral, 8, 29, 30-1, 34-8, 49, 51-2, 58, 95, 102, 108, 116, 121, 161
Storozhevoi, 67, 113, 116-7, 139, 163
Stankevich, Leitenant, 58
Stepanov, Leitenant, 10
Strashnyi, 101, 162
Stregushchi, 77-8, 84, 96, 139, 162
Sukhona, 165
Sveshnikov, Kontre Admiral, 16, 33, 49

Tikhanovich, Ensign, 80
Timirev, Capitan 1st Rank, 108, 115-6, 161
Timofeev, Leitenant, 11
Toledo, 135, 170
Tor, 135, 170
Tovarishch, 127
Tralshchik No 12, 163
Tsarevitch (Graschdanin), 112, 125
Turkmenets Stavropolski, 67, 77-8, 84, 113, 121, 139, 162

Udarnik, 131, 164
Ukraina, 51, 70, 79, 113, 139, 162

Vaksmut, Leitenant, 56, 161
Vassian, 65, 165
Vavilov, Leitenant, 24
Ver, Ensign, 47
Verderski, Vice Admiral, 9
Veselago, Colonel, 128, 130, 135, 137, 143
Vodolei No 2, 165
Vodoley No 1, 162
Voiskovoi, 51, 70, 79, 113, 116, 132, 139, 143, 162
Volga, 8, 101, 127, 139, 164
Vsadnik, 49, 58-9, 84, 96, 98, 140, 162
Vydra, 163

Zabaikalets, 49, 52, 58, 118, 132, 139, 162
Zabiyaka, 30-1, 35, 37, 51, 53, 55, 57-8, 139, 161
Zelenov, Capitan 1st Rank, 49, 162
Zeya, 101, 164